# URUGUAY

*Portrait of a Democracy*

# URUGUAY

*Portrait of a*

# DEMOCRACY

By RUSSELL H. FITZGIBBON

*NEW YORK*

RUSSELL & RUSSELL

1966

# A los Uruguayos,

BUENOS VECINOS TANTO PERSONAL
COMO RETÓRICAMENTE

# Foreword

It is both Uruguay's fortune and her misfortune to be sandwiched in between Brazil and Argentina, each enormously larger in terms of both area and population as well as possessed of more of the world's attention.

"Uruguay by Absent Treatment," "Interlude in Uruguay," and "A Day in Montevideo" are some of the actual chapter heads or subheads used by writers who quickly sail or fly from Buenos Aires to Rio de Janeiro (or the reverse) and give Uruguay a seemingly casual glance out of the corner of an eye as they pass by or over. All of which is a cause for no little irritation. It is an irritation understandably felt by many Uruguayans but also shared by those *norteamericanos* who, taking the time and trouble to get acquainted with the country, have come to know and love it. It can be categorically stated that the vast majority of people in the United States know far too little about this small South American republic, which is one of the world's friendliest, most progressive, and most democratic countries. This volume has been written as a modest contribution toward remedying that deficiency of acquaintance.

It was the privilege of the writer and his family to spend almost all of 1951 in Uruguay. It was possible during that time not only to see Montevideo and its people and activity at firsthand but also to visit for shorter intervals a majority of the departments and most of the other important cities of the country.

We felt as had W. H. Hudson many decades ago when he wrote in *The Purple Land*, his half autobiographical classic, that "The simple spontaneous kindness with which these people treated me had a flavour about it, the like of which I have seldom experienced elsewhere. It was not the common hospitality usually shown to a stranger, but a natural, unstrained kindness, such as they might be expected to show to a beloved brother or son who had gone out from them in the morning and was now returned."

A book is, of course, a wholly inadequate introduction to a country. There is no substitute for going and seeing. If this volume whets any appetites, however, to make that long but rewarding trip it will have well served its purpose.

Uruguay, staunch little democratic output between its two giant neighbors, is a corner of South America that we need to know a great deal better. "Broad and alien is the world," more and more citizens of these United States are finding; and Latin America, although it shares with us the same hemisphere, often seems just as alien as any other area. This is particularly unfortunate. In the cosmic clash of political ideologies and forces that seems destined indefinitely to be our lot, it is important that we know how to win governments and influence nations.

The average Uruguayan should strike a responsive chord for *norteamericanos*. Get him to talking about his country and you will find he is immensely proud of it. He realizes it cannot throw weight around in the international scales to match that of its great immediate neighbors, much less that of the United States, the Soviet Union, and other powers. But he feels that there are things of the mind and heart and soul which compensate for the lack of millions of square miles and tens of millions of people, for the lack of great ore beds, heavy industry, and a completely gadgeted civilization.

He will tell you that his country doesn't have a spectacular history in the conventional sense but that it has found itself. He will admit, quite without apology, that his country's army is small and its navy practically nonexistent but will tell you with quiet pride (and entire truth) that its government is one of the most democratic to be found anywhere, that the educational system is perhaps Latin America's best, that its health and welfare services are duplicated in but few other places on the globe.

These, then, are the Uruguayans—immensely worth knowing.

It is always a pleasant obligation in such an undertaking to acknowledge assistance received. The writer is indebted to many persons either for reading and criticizing various portions of the manuscript or for providing information directly contributing to its preparation. Among them may be mentioned these persons in Montevideo: Dr. Alfredo Bals, Sra. Enrique Caroselli; Dr. and Mrs. Philip Conard and Miss Marian Derby of the Instituto Crandon; Sr. Walter Espiga of the Comisión Nacional del Turismo; Dr. and Sra. Adolfo Halty, Dr. George P. Howard; Dr. Adolfo Morales of the Ministerio de Salud Pública; Srta. Selma Trinkle; and Dr. Daniel D. Vidart of the Ministerio de Ganadería y Agricultura. Several members of the United States Embassy staff were of considerable and varied assistance: the Hon. Christian N. Ravndal (the then Ambassador), Miss Margaret Hall (director of the Biblioteca Artigas-Wáshington), and Messrs. Thomas G. Allen, Dale E. Farringer, Francis W. Herron, Robert W. Ross, and Eugene S. Staples. Mr. Warren A. Nyberg and Dr. H. Jackson Davis, both formerly of Montevideo but now again resident in the United States, were of much help.

Several colleagues at the University of California at Los Angeles assisted materially: Dr. John A. Crow, Dean Robert W. Hodgson, Drs. Donald S. MacKinnon, Kenneth D. Naden, Roy J. Smith, and Flaud C. Wooton. Members of the U.C.L.A. Library staff were of unfailing courtesy and helpfulness; if it be not invidious to limit that acknowledgment, two in particular should be mentioned: Mrs. Esther Euler and Miss Hilda M. Gray.

I have also to thank the Honorable José A. Mora, Uruguayan Ambassador to the United States, and Dr. George Wythe of the United States Department of Commerce.

For permission to reprint, sometimes in slightly modified form, certain chapters which originally appeared as periodical articles, the writer is indebted to the editors of *Church History*, *Economic Geography*, the *History of Education Journal*,

*Inter-American Economic Affairs*, the *Journalism Quarterly*, and *Social Science*.

Grateful acknowledgment is made to the Doherty Foundation and to the Social Science Research Council, both of New York City, for generous fellowships which made possible the year in Uruguay. For a like reason the writer is indebted to officials and agencies of the University of California.

For provision of pictures used in the volume the writer is obligated to the Comisión Nacional del Turismo, the Ministerio de Instrucción Pública y Previsión Social, the Pan American World Airways, and the Pan American Union.

Perhaps his greatest obligation is to his wife, Irene C. Fitzgibbon, his son, Alan, and his daughter, Katherine. They fully shared his liking for and admiration of Uruguay. They consistently proved sympathetic and constructive critics and colleagues. It would be little distortion to list them, particularly the first of those mentioned, as coauthors.

Russell H. Fitzgibbon

Pacific Palisades, California
October, 1953

# Contents

# Illustrations

# URUGUAY

*Portrait of a Democracy*

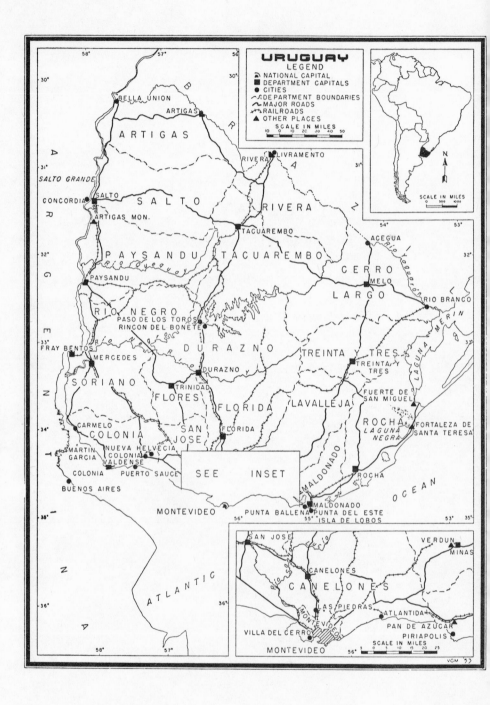

# 1

# Pawn of Empires

God, gold, and glory, those three incentives which played so great a part in the expansion by the Spaniards through seemingly endless millions of square miles in the New World, had little to do with the building of Uruguay. The drama of Spanish empire building records Uruguay merely as an interlude, an entr'acte. The role of the players in three centuries of Spanish colonial domain is little more than the traditional "voice without."

And yet, out of such humble, almost insignificant beginnings has come what is perhaps the most advanced state of all Latin America. Probably nowhere in the Western Hemisphere has Fate been more surprisingly and gratifyingly unpredictable than in shaping the destiny of South America's smallest country.

The pattern of Uruguay of those early years was not cut from a cloth which interested imperial Spain. Indeed, the undulating plains on the east bank of the Uruguay River were a paltry area over which Spain could scarcely be bothered—especially as there was nothing to attract the attention of a Pizarro or a Cortés.

The year 1516 marked both the beginning for Uruguay and the end for Ferdinand of Aragon, architect of an empire the like of which the world had not yet seen. For more than forty years Ferdinand had ruled Aragon and—with Isabella, the regal wife of a regal husband—the larger Spain. They had included some of the most momentous years in all of Spain's history. The climax had come in 1492.

In 1492, not because a strong-willed and persevering Genoese navigator had made a venturesome voyage west across the ocean sea, but because, on January 2 of that year, the might of Spain had finally, after long centuries, conquered the last remaining Moorish stronghold in Granada. It was the end of the Reconquest. For almost 800 years Christian had fought Mohammedan. Back and forth across the face of Spain battle had been waged or armistice had uneasily prevailed. Like Alexander, Ferdinand and Isabella could now bemoan their fate: no more worlds to conquer.

Then, in that same fateful year, Columbus gave them a new world. The sweep of empire went forward. From the small stage of central Spain it spread to the vast New World. Mile by eager mile the Spanish spread down the coasts, up the rivers, through the valleys, across the mountains. The standards of Spain moved on unabated until the year of Ferdinand's death in 1516. Isabella had been dead for a dozen years and Columbus for a decade.

Balboa "upon a peak in Darién" had proved in 1513 that the lands Columbus had found were not the Cathay and Cipango and Spice Islands he had thought them to be. The problem then came to be that of getting through the land mass so that the East might still be gained by sailing west. Down the South American coast one navigator after another pushed the "farthest south."

Juan Díaz de Solís, a pilot major of Spain and a trusted conquistador, was one of the intrepid sailors. By early in 1516 he had got farther south than any predecessor. The land began curving away to the west, and Solís was hopeful that at last he had found the end of the continent or at least a strait which would lead him through it. He could not immediately know that he was sailing into the mouth of a great "river," but he did soon learn that the water was becoming less salty, more muddy.

Solís' landfall, the first ever made by a European in what is now Uruguay, was about seventy miles east of the present site of Montevideo. (By only a short distance Solís missed being the first foreign tourist to land at Punta del Este!) Almost immediately after Solís and his party had landed they were attacked by a band of savage Indians, the Charrúas, whose descendants for more than 300 years would be a plague to Spanish settlers. Solís and all the men in the landing party except the cabin boy were killed. That the Indians were not cannibals, as the Spanish feared, was proved by the rescue, eleven years later, of the cabin boy by Sebastián Gaboto (Cabot). Solís' senior lieutenant, who had remained on board in command of the small vessel, was disheartened by the holocaust and ordered a return to Spain.

Solís, impressed by the lessened saltiness of the estuary up which he had been sailing, proposed to give it the name of Mar Dulce—Sweet Sea. For a brief time, however, it was known as the Río Solís. Another name given early favor was Santa María. The name which prevailed, however, illogical though it was, was the Río de la Plata, the Silver River. The name testified, not to quantities of the precious metal found on its shores, for there was none, but to the elusive though persistent hope that the riches of a Peru or a New Spain (both yet undiscovered in 1516) might be found in the region of the Plata. Despite the ironic lack of precious metal the maps will permanently carry the name of the River of Silver, the Río de la Plata.[1]

Four years after Solís' fatal voyage the Plata again saw a Spanish expedition. This time it was a much more renowned navigator who led it. He was the Portuguese captain, Fernando Magelhaes—the Spanish called him Magallanes and the English Magellan. He sailed under the banner of the boy emperor Charles V, and from the Plata he inched down the Argentine coast until in the far south he came to the strait to which a grateful world would later give his own name. Sailing through its dangerous miles he came to the great South Sea and crossed it, only to lose his life in the Philippines as Solís had in Uruguay. His men returned to Spain, however, and thus completed the first circumnavigation of the globe.

As legend has it, a lookout of Magellan's saw, while his

[1] The name, incidentally, should never be rendered in English as "the La Plata"; that is equivalent, of course, to doubling the article if the name is translated. The Briticism "Plate River" has nothing to commend it.

ships were proceeding up the Plata some miles off the southern
coast of Uruguay, a blur on the horizon which he at first took
to be a low-lying dun-colored cloud. The blur gradually took
form, however, and the lookout suddenly called down, *"Monte
vide eu"*—"I see a mountain." It is what the folklore of history
recounts as the incident which gave Uruguay's later capital its
name.

The "mountain" seen by this unsung lookout on the horizon
may be called that only out of courtesy. Actually, Montevideo's
Cerro is less than 500 feet in elevation, but in the flatness of the
surrounding landscape it must have assumed mountainous proportions to the lookout. The name underwent various changes:
Some historians quote the original phase as *"monte vi eu."* An
early transformation was to Santo Vidio. Some early maps
labeled the headland Monte Seredo and others Monte Seride.
Later, some referred to it as San Ovidio or Monte Vidio. By
the time the city was founded, a little more than two centuries
after Magellan's voyage, the name Montevideo was natural, almost inevitable.[2]

The long centuries between Magellan and independence
were, in reality, a short tale soon told. A leading Uruguayan
historian says, indeed, that his country had no history until the
days of Popham, *i.e.*, about 1805. This is too broad a statement, but it is true that the centuries until the nineteenth provide few events of high relief, virtually nothing of the tissue of
battles, gold and silver and pearls, viceregal pomp, and the
drama of Jesuit and Black and Gray Friars that make up the
pages of history in many of the Spanish colonies.

Action there was, and in plenty, but it was the action of detail, and unspectacular detail, that goes unchronicled. The far-
reaching Sebastian Cabot built a fort some miles up the Uruguay River on its eastern shore. Half a century later, near its
ruins, the town of Salvador was founded, the first "permanent"
settlement in Uruguay—but it does not now exist. The first
systematic attention was thus given to that "eastern shore" or
Banda Oriental which long gave the country its name.

---

[2] This romantic account of the capital city's naming is now frowned
upon by sober historians. It is more prosaic, but probably more historically
accurate, to explain the name as an attempt to pronounce certain abbrevia-
tions which appeared in old manuscripts describing the region.

Extensive settlement was discouraged, well-nigh precluded, because the region was occupied by the savage Charrúa Indians. The lack of precious metals and stones reduced the incentive for conquering them, and successive expeditions sent by the Spanish from Buenos Aires across the broad river failed flatly in their purpose. Finally, what the captain and the conquistador could not accomplish the padre and the friar succeeded in doing. The Indians, never numerous, were reduced to a more tractable group.[3]

During the long generations of the colonial period the gently rolling, well-watered plains of Uruguay were really home for only two kinds of inhabitants: The wild cattle which overran the whole area of the Plata within a few years after their release by the early Spaniards, and the equally wild gauchos. Personification of independence, even of anarchy, the gaucho was spiritual kinsman to the Brazilian vaquero, the Venezuelan llanero, and even the early cowpoke of our own western plains.

A passionate love of freedom, freedom from all trammels, was graved deep in the gaucho's character. Courage was the cornerstone of his being, and his vigorous life in the open made a rude sort of epic poetry that resounded long and vibrantly in the Uruguayan story. The roughhewn harmony of the gaucho has been frozen in enduring bronze by the great sculptor Zorrilla de San Martín in the monumental statue which stands where Calle Constituyente opens into Dieciocho de Julio in central Montevideo.

"Don't Fence Me In" might well have been the gauchoan leitmotif. As long as he could ride over the rolling countryside as freely as did W. H. Hudson's semiautobiographical hero even as late as the latter half of the nineteenth century, just so long could his spirit soar and his imprint be left on both soil

[3] The Charrúas and their fellows left names on the land—such un-Spanish designations as Yi and Hum, Yaro and Cuareim, Ituzaingó and Cuñapirú—but contributed nothing to the bloodstream of the nascent Uruguayan nation. The last of the Charrúas, four in number, were captured in 1832 and taken to Paris for exhibition and anthropological study. The Guaranís, a much more far-flung aboriginal family, and those on whom the Jesuits imposed their famous system of reductions or missions, were located to the north and northwest. Other and lesser groups of aborigines in Uruguay included the Yaros, the Chanás (the name is now borne by a favored Uruguayan brand of coffee!), and the Bohanes.

and character. Just so long, as one writer of the Plata neatly put it, was the age of the gaucho the "age of leather." Clothing, furniture, even housing, he improvised from the ever available cattle hides and bones.

But as early as the beginning of the nineteenth century the surveyor, the fence builder, the lawyer with his land titles, began to fan out from Montevideo, and before their insidiously peaceful advance the gaucho could only wilt. Tying him down to a fenced and surveyed ranch was in most cases to sign his institutional death warrant. Those who resisted the confinement and refused to conform to the alien and advancing civilization sometimes became *matreros*—criminals or outlaws—and were hunted down at times almost like wild beasts.

The gaucho was a cultural prototype whose influence was tremendous in Uruguay. His feuds and knife fights were not the stuff of which conventional history is written, however.

For long years the soil of Uruguay was a battleground over which the tide of empire flowed in the continuing struggle between Spain and Portugal, more narrowly between the Spanish Platine center at Buenos Aires and the giant Portuguese colony of Brazil. The uneasy union of the two Hispanic powers and their empires from 1580 to 1640—the "Babylonian captivity" of Portugal—by no means welded their respective national policies. Once Portugal was again free, rivalry was resumed, even intensified. The buffer territory of the Banda Oriental was a natural scene of conflict.

After the founding, abandonment, and refounding of Buenos Aires, the Portuguese countered, an even century after the second colonization of the Spanish settlement, by establishing directly across the Plata from it the town of Nova Colonia do Sacramento. Spanish forces from Buenos Aires promptly attacked and seized Colonia but, on orders from Spain, soon surrendered it to Portuguese authority. Again the Spanish occupied Colonia in 1705 but again, a decade later, they surrendered it.

Patently the Portuguese would attempt to consolidate a hold on the north bank of the Plata. Actually they pushed on to the site of Montevideo, but the Spanish, much closer to a base of operations, expelled them. Zabala, the governor at Buenos Aires, finally accomplished in 1726 the founding of San

Felipe de Montevideo with seven families from the larger settlement across the river. The settlement's nucleus was the Fuerte de San José, hard by the present *aduana* or customs house and across the bay from that "mountain" which Magellan's lookout had seen two-hundred-odd years before.

Settlers were not easy to attract to this frontier post where Portuguese wrath (not to mention that of the Charrúas) might be visited upon them at any time. A few were induced to come from as far away as the Canary Islands and Galicia, but the inducements had to include such rewards as a grant of the rank of hidalgo—which made the colonist, etymologically, a "son of someone" (*hijo de algo*), a minor title of nobility—payment of transportation, a gift of 200 cattle and 100 sheep to each person, etc. Even after a quarter of a century the settlement, eventually destined to push the million mark, could count fewer than 1,000 inhabitants.

It was neither colonial fortitude nor chance, however, which called the turns for the Banda Oriental; high politics played that role. Hidalgo and padre and capitán might propose, but it seemed that it was courts and chancelleries, kings and premiers in Europe which disposed. A treaty of 1750 gave Portuguese Colonia to Spain in return for some of the famous Jesuit reductions in Paraguay. When, after a decade, Portugal had not delivered, Charles III of Spain had a convenient excuse in 1761 for annulling the treaty. The following year Spanish forces again seized Colonia and with it the not inconsiderable prize of twenty-seven English merchant vessels anchored there. Not only Colonia and the rest of modern Uruguay fell to Spanish troops but also much of Rio Grande do Sul, Brazil's present most southern state. But again, high politics! By treaty of 1763 not only Rio Grande do Sul but also Colonia went back to Portugal.

One of the most skillful practitioners of high politics at the time was Portugal's Marquis of Pombal, prime minister for a quarter of a century. Back of Pombal and back of Portugal stood Britain, ally and protector of the small peninsular state for long centuries. In secrecy Pombal directed officials at Colonia to seize nearby desirable Spanish lands. On Spanish protest he then denied or belittled such actions but continued to harbor aggressive designs and to send re-enforcements.

Spain, outraged, sent an expedition of 9,000 men in 1776 to southern South America. Colonia, that perennial football, was again captured in 1777, and the major Spanish army might have followed by again conquering Rio Grande do Sul. Hostilities were suspended in that year, however, and a new treaty finally and permanently gave Colonia to Spain.

Back of the puppets on the small stage of Uruguay vast imperial forces moved the figures. Portugal's steps were often the bolder because of the might of England behind her. Albion was usually ready to exact her toll and even as early as the eighteenth century English eyes were turning toward the area of the Plata. But the 1770's saw England preoccupied with the revolt of her own North American colonies. Simultaneously, France's Vergennes took his country into the American Revolution in an effort to promote the further disruption of Britain's empire. Hence, England could neither extend further aid to Portugal nor present a bill for the aid she did give. But for such circumstances it is a fair guess whether Uruguay would not have become other than "the Purple Land that England *lost*," as W. H. Hudson nostalgically called it many years later.

It was in the American natal year of 1776 that Spain, largely because of the increasing military and political tension in the area of the Plata, separated vast areas of her southern colonies from the distant control of the viceroy at Lima and established them as the new viceroyalty of La Plata. Buenos Aires was inevitably its viceregal seat and hence Montevideo and the Banda Oriental were further confirmed in that psychological subordination to the transplatine metropolis which so long characterized them.

The early years of the nineteenth century saw empire contending with empire more grandly than had ever occurred before. The fate of Spanish and Portuguese dominions now became inextricably intertwined with the destinies of the even more powerful British and French domains. France was, for practical purposes, Napoleon, and Britain for long years engaged in a titanic struggle with him.

The Spanish empire was disintegrating. The Spanish Bourbons—who had never forgotten anything because they had never learned anything!—saw their hold over their colonies relentlessly relaxing. But they stubbornly refused to take even the elementary steps which might have preserved the empire to them for at least additional decades or generations.

Colonies, the world over, were rapidly changing hands. It was a bewildering time of imperial flux. The British who, a quarter of a century before, had lost valuable colonies along the North American seaboard, had now, early in the nineteenth century, consolidated a foothold in the southernmost part of Africa. It was a foothold which the redoubtable Rhodes almost a century later would help to spread in a majestic sweep to the north.

For the time being the forces commanded by the British admiral, Sir Home Riggs Popham, were free. Partially seemingly on his own initiative he sailed for the mouth of the Plata River. The British in recent years had been given a briefing on Spanish possessions in South America. The man responsible was Francisco de Miranda, Venezuelan precursor of Spanish-American independence, who, in a long career of propaganda in foreign parts, tried to interest the British, among others, in aiding the involuntary disintegration of the Spanish empire. Popham capitalized on the possibility.

Aided by General Beresford's force of 1,650 men Popham easily took the important Spanish center of Buenos Aires; the viceroy, incompetent and cowardly, had previously sent most of his forces to Montevideo and himself fled to Córdoba at the British approach. The royal funds at Buenos Aires were dispatched to London and there received with carnival gaiety.

But never was Popham more wrong than in assuming that the inhabitants would not fight or that seizing and holding the river ports would be a simple matter. Santiago de Liniers, a Frenchman who in 1805 was rounding out three decades in Spanish service, and at that time commanded Spanish naval forces in the Plata River, established contact with creoles in Buenos Aires, obtained 1,150 soldiers from the governor of Montevideo, and forced Beresford's surrender. The viceroyalty was Liniers' reward.

The recapture of Buenos Aires was, of course, a humiliation for His Imperial British Majesty's government. It must be avenged. Late in 1806, the British sent a force of 10,000 men under the incompetent Whitelock. He captured Montevideo early in 1807, but when he moved against Buenos Aires in July of that year he was badly defeated by *porteño* forces, with a loss of 3,000 men. That settled the issue: the English then evacuated the entire region. For seven months Montevideo and other coastal points had been occupied by British forces. Several hundred English merchants followed in the wake of the troops. The invaders began publication of *La Estrella del Sur*, and the southern star, intended as a medium of propaganda against Spain, profoundly influenced creole thought in that previously isolated colonial town. The leaven of separation was stirring. Montevideo and Buenos Aires had made common cause against the British, but perhaps it would be better now for the *orientales* to throw off *porteño* domination as well.

In 1808 Liniers ruled as viceroy at Buenos Aires. At Montevideo Javier Elío served as military commander. Spain lay under the yoke of invading French forces, and the puppet king, Joseph, enthroned by his imperial brother, Napoleon, ruled a sullen Spain. A central junta of resistance, later assisted by British forces under Wellesley (soon to be Lord Wellington), organized the opposition to the French. After a time Elío succeeded in persuading the Spanish central junta to accept his control at Montevideo as independent of Buenos Aires. The seeds of revolution against Spain were sprouting at Buenos Aires. Montevideo, for the time, remained the more loyal to the Spanish crown, in part because it was primarily a military post.

When fighting broke out in 1810, Upper Peru (which later became Bolivia), Córdoba, Asunción, and Montevideo, all at least nominally subject to control from Buenos Aires, refused to recognize the authority of the patriotic junta at that city and continued a superficial allegiance to the Spanish regency. Elío in 1811 prepared to take the offensive against Buenos Aires. But the revolutionary spirit burned brighter in other parts of the Banda than at the garrison town of Montevideo. Hence, when Elío made ready to move against Buenos Aires, the hinterland of the Banda flamed into counteraction under a man destined to become "the father of Uruguay." He was José Gervasio Artigas.

# 2

~~~~~~~~~~
~~~~~~~~~~

# Uruguay Comes of Age

Uruguay is peculiarly fortunate in its patriot-hero Artigas. The country is small in area and population and perhaps it is fate that it should have a father of independence less renowned than the greatest heroes of the South American revolutions. Less famous than Bolívar or San Martín, perhaps less than O'Higgins or Sucre, he still was cut to heroic pattern. San Martín and Bolívar won their greatest victories outside their native Argentina and Venezuela; hence, they are shared with other countries. Not Artigas, who is Uruguay's alone. Sucre's luster is somewhat dimmed by the shadow of Bolívar. Francia of Paraguay, Páez of Venezuela, and others had aberrations of character or career which marred their full acceptability as *patres patriarum*. Not Artigas. Bold, resourceful, devoted, persistent, he had few if any of the flaws which would later tip a literary or historic halo awry. He was *muy hombre*, his compatriots would say of him. Uruguay may well take pride in him. Artigas must share the patriotic regard of Uruguayans with the Thirty-Three. But he was one and they were a third of a hundred, and it is easier to concentrate esteem on a single person than on almost three dozen.

Artigas had for many years been a captain in the Spanish forces assigned to keep order in the interior. He had helped resist the British invasion. Now he offered his services to the junta at Buenos Aires, recruited troops from among the gauchos and half bandits of the Uruguayan hinterland, won a notable victory at Las Piedras which opened the way to Montevideo, and then besieged the capital city itself during the winter of 1811, from May to October. Elío saved Montevideo only by inviting the Portuguese forces from Brazil. He was asking the camel to put its nose inside the tent. Alien troops from the north poured into Uruguay and by July, 1811, dominated a large part of the country. Even Elío became alarmed. In October he concluded a treaty with Buenos Aires which provided that the siege of Montevideo be lifted and that all troops, including those of Artigas, of Portugal, and of Spain, be withdrawn from the country. Not until 1812, however, were the reluctant Portuguese actually persuaded to leave. Until then, the people of the Banda were left largely at the mercy of the Portuguese and Spanish forces.

Artigas faced that situation by beginning an evacuation so planned as to traverse the entire area and to remove all civilians who wished to accompany him. This was the famous "exodus to Ayuí" on the west bank of the Uruguay River, a renowned episode in the annals of the Uruguayan independence movement. In all, some 13,000 men, women, and children, in addition to about 3,000 troops, were guided to the little town on the Argentine side of the Uruguay a few miles above Salto. When the Portuguese commander entered Paysandú, now a city of 50,000, some seventy-five miles south of Salto, he found it occupied only by two aged Indians. Some elderly people and children died of the incredible hardships encountered in the exodus but the great majority survived. For some months these thousands lived in a temporary camp, oxcarts and trees their only shelter. Uruguay's population at the time probably did not exceed 60,000: Montevideo had perhaps 13,000 inhabitants. The exodus included, then, about a fourth of the people of the whole country. In heroic proportions it resembled the later Boer treks in South Africa.

The treaty of 1811 was soon broken and the siege of Montevideo resumed. Artigas by that time had emerged as the champion of federalism against the unitarism of Buenos Aires.[1]

[1] Federalists were those who, unlike the protagonists of identical name in the young United States, favored a weak central government for the

Serious friction consequently arose in a constitutional assembly which met at Buenos Aires in 1813. For the guidance of representatives from the Banda Oriental Artigas authored the famous "Instructions of the Year XIII" which became the banner of the federalist element in the whole region of the Plata. The influence of the United States was evident, both of its Constitution and of its earlier Articles of Confederation. (It was Artigas, indeed, who once said of a volume of United States history: "A copy of this should be in the hands of every Oriental [*i.e.*, Uruguayan] child."). On technical grounds the delegates from the Banda were denied seats in the assembly across the river. There followed several months of strained relations between Artigas and the authorities at Buenos Aires.

Artigas lifted his siege of Montevideo at the beginning of 1814, but there ensued several months of confused triangular warfare among the Uruguayans, Spanish, and *porteños*. In June of the same year Montevideo was surrendered by the Spanish to a *porteño* general, thus permanently ending Spanish dominion in the Banda Oriental. But the civil war continued. Artigas, thorough gaucho *caudillo* [2] though he was, formed and led a confederation of Uruguay and the upriver Platine provinces. In the orotund phrase of the time he was "Chief of the Orientals and Protector of Free Peoples." The next year or so saw Artigas at his zenith, ruling over, roughly, a third of a million square miles. Had the skein of history been woven but slightly differently, he might have become master of the whole of the Plata basin. As it was, he was enabled to defeat the forces of Buenos Aires early in 1815 and force them from Uruguayan soil.

The seeds of his political philosophy proved his own undoing. He preached and fought consistently against the centralism of Buenos Aires' rule. By the same token, his hold over Entre Ríos, Santa Fe, Corrientes, and Córdoba, in addition to Uruguay itself, could not consistently be solidified. No form of

---

whole area of the Platine provinces, or, by the same token, more autonomy for the provinces themselves. Unitarists (or unitarians or centralists) would strengthen the central government at the expense of the outlying areas.

[2] A caudillo was a (usually) military chieftain whose hold over his men was based largely on his personal magnetism, bravery, and dashing qualities, and the consequent blind, adoring allegiance of his followers. He was a man on horseback.

government was established: Artigas' control was merely that of force or influence. The essence of the confederation was decentralization and it had no readily exploitable economic resources.

Capitalizing on the disorder, a Portuguese army of 10,000 men again invaded the Banda from Brazil in 1816. Montevideo fell in January of 1817, with Artigas bitterly contesting every inch of the way. The war continued for more than four years, however, and at one stage Artigas even invaded Brazil. Further, he commissioned privateers to harass Portuguese shipping even off the port of Lisbon itself. But the unequal struggle was an impossible one. His forces suffered a bad defeat in January, 1820. Artigas and 300 of his men escaped; the field of battle was left with 800 dead and *fifteen* wounded.

For some months Artigas continued, from an Argentine base, the struggle against the unitarists of Buenos Aires. In September, 1820, he was forced to take refuge in Paraguay where Dictator Francia imprisoned him for a few months but then released him to enjoy (if the word be not a travesty) a small farm and an inadequate pension. There he died on September 23, 1850, thirty years to the day from his entering Paraguay. Exiled for long years from his homeland, even as were O'Higgins and San Martín, he must often have meditated upon the ingratitude of republics. The proper honoring of his memory was left for the later generations of the Uruguayans he strove to free.

The fall of Artigas ended effective resistance to the Portuguese. A subservient Uruguayan congress in 1821 declared the Banda annexed to Portuguese Brazil as the Cisplatine Province. Brazil's independence from the mother country the following year simply meant, for Uruguay, an exchange of a Portuguese master for a Brazilian. Some Uruguayan chronicler might well have written, like Tom Paine half a century earlier, that they were times that tried men's souls.

In December, 1824, patriot forces won the last great victory over Spain in the battle of Ayacucho in Peru. Its echoes resounded throughout South America. They reverberated with particular importance among the group of Uruguayan exiles in Buenos Aires. Under the inspired leadership of Juan Antonio Lavalleja a band of them perfected plans to free their fatherland from the Brazilian yoke. How many were they who slipped across the Uruguay River at night, carefully muffling the sounds of their boats, lest the patrolling Brazilian vessels intercept them? *Thirty-three.* These were the immortal Thirty-Three, who in their pitiful and heroic, their impossible and inspired way set out to free their country of Brazil's best armies, totaling thousands of men. It was Leonidas and his men against the Persian hordes, replayed on an Uruguayan stage.

The standard of revolt having been raised in Uruguay, the strong arm of Fructuoso Rivera, a former lieutenant of Artigas, was quickly added to hold it high. The sheer impossibility of the odds attracted a prairie fire of support in Uruguay. The patriots soon controlled enough territory to justify the convening of an assembly. This body voted union with Argentina —and the fat was in the fire. War promptly followed between Brazil and Argentina, and again, as in the bloody years when Portugal and Spain had fought each other, Uruguay was the battleground. Argentine forces won most of the battles, but both sides were soon exhausted, and the war was continued only because popular pressure in both countries demanded it. The memory of colonial rivalry died hard.

Finally, Britain, fully conscious of the injury to commerce inherent in a prolonged struggle, sent her Lord Ponsonby to try to negotiate a peace. He was successful, and a grateful Montevideo has named a broad avenue in his memory. Hostilities ended in 1828, and both Argentina and Brazil recognized Uruguayan independence. Uruguay was now free, at least in the eyes of international law and of her own constitutional prescription. But not for long years would she be free from the covetous interest of her larger South American neighbors, or, indeed, from that of Europe's two greatest powers. Nor, worse, had she yet won her freedom from that internal rivalry, strife, and bloodshed which for decades prevented her from becoming the enlightened and progressive country she is today.

The author of a popularly written travel book about the east coast of South America wrote that "The history of Uruguay is . . . the dullest that any nation of South America can present. . . ." That verdict, ungracious at best, could probably only refer to the last seven decades of the nineteenth century. Uruguay had no great wars, with their chances for der-

ring-do and glory—if any wars have glory. She had few great
heroes of peace in the nineteenth century. She was even lacking
in notable *caudillos*—a Juan Manuel Rosas of Argentina, a
Guzmán Blanco of Venezuela, or a García Moreno of Ecuador.

Uruguay was in a sorry state in the years just after the
eviction of the Brazilians and Argentines. Charles Darwin
visited there briefly on his famous scientific expedition around
the world which he recounted in his *Voyage of the Beagle*. Residents of Colonia, he reported, were proud of their representatives in congress because all were sufficiently literate to sign
their names. Darwin met a rural mail carrier whose route included several of the republic's most important towns but whose
pack carried only *two* letters. The Uruguay of that day probably counted fewer than 70,000 inhabitants, a fifth of whom
lived in Montevideo. Even the population in cattle had suffered
grievously from the wars. The country's only exports were
small quantities of hides and jerked beef.

The first important task of independence was to build a
constitutional flooring under the structure of the state. That
was accomplished in 1830 and resulted in a document destined
to remain the fundamental law for more than four score years,
Latin America's third longest in life. Elections in 1830 put
General Rivera in the presidency. The sequence was simple:
Rivera controlled the army; the army dominated congress;
congress elected the president; ergo—Lavalleja (of the Thirty-
Three), his opponent, soon revolted.

The two in 1835 agreed on Manuel Oribe, another of the
Thirty-Three, for president, but again fighting broke out in
1836. It was in that latter year that Rivera's forces began
using the color red to distinguish themselves, and the Lavalleja-
Oribe adherents white. Thus were born the Colorados and the
Blancos who still, more than a century later, dominate the
Uruguayan political scene. It was only in chromatic selection
that the two groups resembled the Lancastrians and Yorkists
of an earlier England, but their distinctness of coloration
seemed to give an enduring division to Uruguayan politics.

The history of Argentina in the 1830's and 1840's was the
biography of Juan Manuel de Rosas. He was the *enfant terrible*
of Platine politics for many years and the chief cause—or excuse—for British and French intervention in the affairs of that

area. His evil genius led him not only to hold his own country prostrate but to interfere in Uruguayan affairs as well. If we can give Rosas credit for any sort of political philosophy or consistency at all it was because, though primarily a power-mad opportunist, he wanted to weld Argentina into a tightly knit state and even to expand its territory by cavalierly taking over neighboring regions.

Civil war continued to be the order of the day in the troubled little republic across the river from Argentina. Rosas began his meddling in Uruguayan affairs as early as 1836. That country suffered from its geographical closeness to Buenos Aires; Paraguay, which also fired Rosas' acquisitive temperament, was fortunate in being more distant. Rosas promptly began to give aid and comfort to Oribe and the Blancos—support when they were in the ascendancy and asylum when their fortunes were low. On the other hand, those northern Argentine provinces which chafed under the iron restraint which Rosas applied to them were happy to ally themselves politically with the Uruguayan Colorados.

A further complication of those murky years was the involvement of the leading European powers. The highhanded treatment meted out by the Argentine stormy petrel to some French nationals brought retaliation by France in the form of a naval blockade of Buenos Aires. The French also extended aid to the Uruguayan enemies of Rosas and enabled them to regain control in Montevideo. Rivera, who became president of Uruguay in 1839, declared war on Rosas as "the tyrant of the immortal people of South America," and, allied with the Argentine province of Corrientes and with the help of 1,000 French troops, was able to drive Rosas' forces from Uruguayan soil.

In 1840, however, the French reached an understanding with Rosas and withdrew their ships and men from the region of the Plata. Rosas could now resume the offensive against his enemies, Argentine and Uruguayan. Oribe took command of combined Blanco and Argentine forces which invaded Uruguay and made serious headway. What the Uruguayans call the Great War began in February, 1843, and revolved particularly around the eight-year siege of Montevideo, which thereby earned the epithet of "the New Troy."

Rivera's support came not only from his own Colorado followers but also from three dissident Argentine provinces. Wearing the Colorado red during a part of the following years was a soon to be famous son of Italy, Giuseppe Garibaldi. A considerable part of Montevideo's population at that time was of direct European extraction—Spanish, Italian, and French—because of relatively large-scale immigration in the half dozen years just preceding the siege. These elements rallied vigorously to the protection of Montevideo. Garibaldi's command consisted of a contingent of Italians who, with 3,000 French Basques, played a notable role in the capital's defense.

France, and also Britain, returned to the scene in 1845 because of resentment against Rosas' designs on Uruguay and his treatment of their own nationals. For four years Anglo-French squadrons intermittently blockaded Buenos Aires and at the same time protected Montevideo's free access to the sea. During the period, indeed, the Uruguayan capital became the commercial center of the Plata region and its merchants profited correspondingly. The allied domination of the Plata also discouraged Argentine land campaigns against Uruguay.

Montevideo suffered relatively little from the years of the wars and the siege. Social life went on apace, theaters remained open, trade boomed. It was the hinterland which paid the price of war. The contest became in reality not one between Rivera and Oribe (Rivera was actually removed from command and exiled in 1846 for failure to press attacks against the interior) or one simply between Colorados and Blancos. It was also a struggle, deeper than merely political and military, between the capital and the *campo*, between the Montevideanos and the people of the country districts. The latter suffered seriously. The cattle industry perforce suffered from military operations and bandit depredations. The river blockade prevented the export of products from the considerable areas controlled by Oribe's Blancos.

The capital appeared to have lost the contest when in 1849 the British and French forces, having tired of their unsuccessful efforts to bring Rosas to book, brought pressure to bear on Montevideo to agree to an armistice which amounted virtually to a surrender. Before it could be completely carried out, however, an Argentine provincial governor had revolted against

Rosas. Brazil intervened in that conflict, most of Oribe's troops deserted after Argentine forces friendly to the Colorados invaded Uruguay, and a compromise political settlement between Blancos and Colorados followed. A small Uruguayan force joined the revolting Argentine elements which finally overthrew Rosas early in 1852. Venancio Flores, a Colorado and the last of the classic *caudillos* of Uruguay, was later to request and receive Brazilian aid against the Blancos. An advance payment on account had to be made in 1851, when Brazil extracted a favorable boundary treaty which whittled away thousands of square miles Uruguay had claimed in the north.

The decade and more of war, domestic and international, left a miserable bequest to Uruguay. Education and public works went virtually unsupported for long years. The legacy included predominance of military leaders—the dismal Latin American *caudillismo*—internal strife and hatreds, governmental weakness.

Political turmoil and party dissension continued to be the lot of unhappy Uruguay. Dom Pedro II, emperor of Brazil, sent 4,000 troops into Uruguay in 1854, at Flores' request, but stability failed to be restored in spite of—some would say because of—their presence. They were withdrawn after two years. Blancos continued in national power for several years after Flores' overthrow and ouster in 1855. In 1863, however, Flores and other Colorados invaded Uruguay with support from both Argentina and Brazil. There now entered the wings of the Uruguayan stage one of the most flamboyantly curious of all Latin American *caudillos*.

Francisco Solano López, dictator of Paraguay from 1862 to 1870, was perhaps the megalomaniac *par excellence* in all Latin-American political history. Brilliant, but unstable, cruel, vain, and unprincipled, he wanted to ape the imperialistic career of Napoleon I, whose life and legend he had studied at close range while Paraguayan diplomatic representative in France. He appears to have planned to include at least two Argentine provinces and perhaps also Uruguay as part of a greater Paraguay which would have made a respectably sized empire on the map. He was also suspicious of the designs and intrigue of Brazil and Argentina, even after Rosas was overthrown in the latter country. Those countries on their part were aroused by the militaristic preparations and ambitions of López.

The currently dominant Blancos in Uruguay were having diplomatic difficulties with Brazil because of alleged mistreatment of Brazilian subjects resident in Uruguay. One Brazilian method of getting satisfaction was to intervene at that stage in support of Flores and his fellow Colorados, who had already been receiving secret assistance from Argentina. Dictator López claimed to have appeals for aid from the Blanco government in Uruguay, and on that basis he demanded, but failed to get, explanations from Brazil and Argentina of their attitudes and intentions toward the government in Montevideo. In August of 1864, López protested against an ultimatum the Brazilian government had sent to the Blanco regime and declared that Brazilian occupation of Uruguayan territory would upset the balance of power in the region of the Plata.

Brazil ignored López' protest and sent her troops across the Uruguayan border. López then took warlike steps against Brazil, without a formal declaration of war, and, in order to attack Brazil from the south, he requested Argentina's permission to send Paraguayan troops across the former's territory. When the Argentine president refused, a López-dominated Paraguayan congress declared war on Argentina.

In the meantime, political control had changed in Uruguay. The Colorados under Flores had again returned to power in Montevideo. Hence, on May 1, 1865, the Argentine, Brazilian, and Uruguayan governments negotiated a secret offensive and defensive alliance against López. The war, which continued for five dreary years, found Uruguay distinctly a junior partner. Her chief suffering was not from the war itself but from the continuation of her own internal plots, counterplots, mutinies, and revolutions. These tended to be lessened, though not ended, when Flores, who escaped Paraguayan bullets, was assassinated in 1868 in Montevideo's streets. That event was held by some historians to have marked the end of Uruguay's era of anarchy and turbulence, but the change which occurred in the next three decades was at best only one of degree.

A peace of sorts came to Uruguay through Argentine mediation in 1872. The dominant Colorados contracted to give the Blancos control of the police in four of Uruguay's territorial departments, plus the neat sum of 500,000 pesos in cash. The precedent was thus set for a series of later agreements by which offices and money for the Blanco minority provided insurance against revolution. The great Blanco landowners were often satisfied to control their own districts, and the device of bribery, to give it a blunt name, was a less costly solution for party rivalry than was civil war.

The social and economic face of Uruguay was meanwhile changing. The picturesque and sometimes picaresque gaucho was disappearing before the inexorable advance of a modernized cattle industry. A hungry Europe, demanding more and better meat, provided the capital which opened a large plant for processing preserved meats and meat extracts at Fray Bentos on the Uruguay River in the early 1860's. *Estancieros* were forced by economic circumstance to abandon to some extent the old casual and careless methods of stock raising in favor of practices which would produce the better grades of beef demanded by the new processing techniques. The same decade of the 1860's saw Uruguay's first railway built.

A gradual change was being made, too, in the character of the Uruguayan population. In the half decade or so before the beginning of the siege of Montevideo considerable European immigration had taken place. This stopped almost completely during the Great War. Indeed, it was estimated that during the dozen years of war and political strife between 1840 and 1852, the country's population declined from 200,000 to 132,000. After that it again began growing rapidly and by 1872 was estimated to have reached 420,000. Much of the gain was due to increased immigration. The number of immigrants between 1861 and 1874 was reported to be 170,000; it is impossible to determine the net gain from that source inasmuch as no statistics were kept on the number of Europeans returning to their homes after a longer or shorter stay in Uruguay.

The new migrants did not inherit the traditional political quarrels of Uruguay. Many of them settled in Montevideo and went into business. In such an occupation they had little patience with the disorder and virtual anarchy which had so long been practically endemic in Uruguay. The new trend in stock raising made *estancieros*, too, less tolerant of civil strife. The financial "accommodation" worked out between the two major parties also tended to make revolution less profitable. The stronger administrations which ruled in Uruguay for the next decade or so gave less play to a free press and free political process but, at the same time, more opportunity for development of order, of business, of intellectual activity.

The *caudillo*, as one Uruguayan historian puts it, was giving way to the professional soldier. The army as an organized force came into its own because of improved techniques and weapons but while militarism in Uruguay never reached the spectacular heights—or depths—that it did in some other Latin American countries, a succession of professional soldiers did dominate Uruguayan affairs for two decades or so.

The first of these, Colonel Lorenzo Latorre, came into power in 1875. A year later, when the president of the country attempted to demonstrate some degree of independence of Latorre (then his war minister), the latter ousted him and established himself openly as a dictator. For more than three years he ruled by a minor reign of terror during which important opponents were in some cases assassinated, or again simply disappeared. Nevertheless, it was during Latorre's dictatorship that the remarkable educational work of José Pedro Varela came to fruition, and other intellectual activity increased notably. Latorre's suppression of normal political expression permitted energies to be diverted into other channels.

But a nascent political consciousness, to say nothing of an inherited political turbulence, could not be stilled. A disillusioned Latorre resigned in 1880, saying in his valedictory manifesto: "On retiring from public life, I am dejected to the point of thinking that our country is an ungovernable country. With such a conviction, I do not have the civic courage to confront for a longer time the rough mission imposed on me by vote of the National Congress."

Colonel Máximo Santos, the then minister of war, inherited control of the government but did not manipulate his elevation to the presidency until 1882. The harsh dictatorship continued and gave rise not only to incipient revolutions within the country but also to diplomatic involvements with foreign powers. Santos was succeeded in 1886 by General Máximo Tajes who, in the now increasingly familiar pattern, stepped into the presidency from the ministry of war. Tajes found it necessary to placate previously dissident elements in both political parties, which both Latorre and Santos had refused to do. He also disbanded some of the more turbulent and unreliable army regiments.

Tactics of the sort gradually lessened the political influence of the army and paved the way for a restoration of civilism as a basis for government. Civilian presidents came into office beginning in 1890, but one of them, Juan Idiarte Borda, a dictator, was assassinated in 1897 while reviewing troops in Montevideo. Political feeling at that time was more inflamed because of armed conflict of several months' duration, the so-called "Nationalistic Revolution," which had broken out between the two parties. Aparicio Saravia, a Blanco *caudillo* of the interior, led the revolt, but again the malcontents were bought off with a large sum of money.

The chief of state elected in 1903, fourth of a series of civilians to hold the presidency since 1890, was José Batlle y Ordóñez, son of a former president, and himself a man who was to leave an impression on Uruguay unequaled by any other man. Batlle served two terms, 1903–07 and 1911–15, and his influence continued through his life and afterward. His first term saw, in 1904, Uruguay's last revolution or civil war. The improvement of political and electoral conditions thereafter offered less incentive to revolt.

Batlle's conviction that presidential dominance was a basic political evil for Uruguay led to the drafting of a new constitution in 1917 in which his idea of a collegiate executive was partially adopted. This bifurcated arrangement—a president and an independent national council of administration—operated during the 1920's. President Gabriel Terra, elected in 1931, deemed the system inoperable and at the end of March of 1933 engineered a *coup d'état* by which he set himself up as a dictator pending the writing of Uruguay's third constitution, in 1933–34. Under this constitution, which abolished the divided executive and re-established a more normal presidency, Terra served as constitutional president from 1934 to 1938.

The coming of World War II involved Uruguay in an early incident of high dramatic quality. It was the battle of the Graf Spee in Plata waters in December, 1939. Uruguayans sometimes claim rather wryly that it is the only thing about their history that *norteamericanos* know! The German pocket battle-ship, fighting bravely but hopelessly against a strong British naval force, put into Montevideo harbor in a badly damaged condition. When the Uruguayan government, in accordance with international law, required it to leave within a three-day period the ship was scuttled just outside the harbor to avoid a British *coup de grâce*.

Early the following year the government uncovered a Nazi plot to engineer a revolt in Uruguay by which that country would have been converted into a German agricultural colony. The dispatch to Montevideo of two United States cruisers helped allay Uruguayan fears.

For four hundred and thirty-odd years the north shore of the Plata and the eastern shore of the Uruguay have been known to Europeans and their descendants. For two centuries and a quarter Montevideo has been a name on the map. It is one of the youngest of Latin America's capitals. High adventure passed Uruguay largely by. The triplex lure of God, gold, and glory, which drew so many Spaniards over such vast areas, was represented in Uruguay only by the desire to serve the Deity. Of gold there was none and of glory little. The cruel facts of political geography made it Uruguay's fate to become a buffer battleground for imperial forces greater by far than her own.

In the revolutionary epoch the courageous tenacity of Artigas and the sheer daring of the Thirty-Three relieved an otherwise relatively prosaic development whose foci were outside Uruguay itself. Following independence came weary decades of internal disorder sometimes akin to anarchy. Only with the turn of the nineteenth century, with the coming of tens of thousands of new Europeans who had no part in the inherited political quarrels, with the growing economic importance and social consciousness of the population did Uruguay develop into the staunch and mature, the intelligently democratic land that it is today.

Uruguay has won her battles and campaigns and wars. They have been battles against political disorder and insta-bility, campaigns against illiteracy and ignorance, wars against a blightingly low standard of living. Who can call that a dull history?

# 3

*All Roads Lead to Montevideo*

Latin American cities have the personalities of women. Buenos Aires aspires to be a Parisienne sophisticate. Rio is a gay and carefree dancer. Lima is a duenna with an air of colonial aristocracy. But Montevideo, Uruguay's capital, is a neatly dressed, intelligent, and unspectacular wife with whom you can spend a long and happy life.

The city is friendly, it is clean, it deserves its title of the City of Roses. And, furthermore, in terms of city planning and services rendered its inhabitants, it is one of the most progressive cities of the world. One should not assume that city planning means that Montevideo is laid out according to some architect's neat pattern on a drawing board. It is not a Canberra, Australia, a Goiânia, Brazil, or even a Washington, D. C., in terms of design. Like most other cities it "just growed."

In reality, Montevideo is three cities. The "Old City" dates from 1726 and was less than half a square mile in area. It occupied only the small peninsula extending west from the present Plaza Independencia. The peninsula forms a protecting arm for the large bay of Montevideo. It is recorded that by a year after its founding the settlement had two houses of wood and forty made of hides. About the middle of the past century the Old City began to burst at the seams. It spread out, east and north, to include what is called the "New City," which has an area several times as large as the original portion. The boundary was, roughly, the Bulevar Artigas which runs north from Punta Carreta and then makes a right-angled turn to reach approximately to the northern extremity of the bay.

By early in the present century another big wave of growth was under way. This spread Montevideo out east, north, and west to form the "Newest City," as some call it. It, again, has several times the area of the Old and the New City combined. Planners foresee that in another generation Montevideo will double its present area. They anticipate that long "fingers" of settled areas will reach out for miles to the boundaries of the Department of Montevideo.

Probably nowhere else in the world does a city so dominate a country as Montevideo dominates Uruguay. The city is not only the political capital but also the financial, commercial, industrial, social, cultural, educational, and religious center of the country. No other Uruguayan city has more than about one-seventeenth of Montevideo's population.

It is Montevideo's port, as much as any factor, which has "made" the city. Through it pass more than three-fourths of all Uruguay's imports and exports. Through it have come the thousands of Italians, Spaniards, Basques, and others who make up a good part of Montevideo's 850,000 population. Walk along the docks and you find a typically busy transportation scene. Great quantities of merchandise are piled up on the pavement. Electric cranes move back and forth along the water front. The enormous *aduana* or customs house dominates the whole area. Yet big as it is, the *aduana* hasn't always been able to cope with the mountains of goods moving through the port.

The *aduana* typifies the Old City, for that section is largely devoted to shipping, finance, and business. Though relatively few of its buildings date back to the colonial period, the Old City conveys the colonial atmosphere. Perhaps that impression is given primarily by the narrow streets. Modern traffic being what it is, almost all streets in the Old City have been made one-way arteries. The Plaza Constitución is the heart of the older section. Fronting the plaza are the dignified old Cathedral, the Foreign Ministry occupying the old *cabildo* or municipal building, one of the government-owned banks, two large hotels, and many business houses. Along one side of the plaza, on all but the really rainy days, is to be found a selection of Montevideo's "shine boys." Some of them are "boys" of sixty or more years but the shine is equally good, the attitude equally courteous. The benches along the neatly trimmed lawns are a favorite spot for those who want to watch and feed the plaza's pigeons.

The eastern end of the peninsula, which is to say the eastern side of the Old City, was marked at the end of the colonial period and during the wars for independence by sturdy walls. It was those walls that the British breached in 1806 to capture and occupy briefly the Uruguayan capital. The present-day Anglican church is located on the site of the British breakthrough.

A convenient dividing point between the old and new cities is Montevideo's main square, the Plaza Independencia. Here centers much of the life of the city. Here is the great equestrian statue of Artigas, father of his country, and here is the Executive Palace.

Fronting on the Plaza Independencia, too, is Montevideo's newest and one of South America's finest hotels. On another side is one of the curious sights of the city, its skyscraping architectural monstrosity, the Palacio Salvo. The apartment dwellers in the upper floors are fortunate indeed in the magnificent views they have.

The writer once mailed back a picture postcard of the Palacio Salvo to a friend in the United States, describing it on the reverse side as once South America's tallest and still probably its ugliest building. A week or so later, when he again stopped in the same neighborhood branch post office, the friendly proprietress chuckled and said, "*¿El Palacio Salvo es muy feo, eh?*" ("The Palacio Salvo is very ugly, is it?")

Puzzled for a moment, the writer finally saw the light, laughed, and replied, "Oh, you read English, do you?" No, she didn't, but her daughter did, it seemed!

The professional occupants of the Plaza Independencia itself are not bootblacks but photographers and maté carvers. The photographers, for a small charge, will take your picture against the Artigas statue as a backdrop. Many a tourist invests in that friendly and authentic souvenir of Montevideo.

The carvers ply their trade on the plaza's benches on all sunny days. "Maté," or Paraguayan tea, is not only the national beverage of Uruguay, so to speak, but it is also the small gourd out of which the liquid is drunk through the silver "straw" or *bombilla*. You can buy a plain gourd in any neighborhood store for a few centésimos but many Montevideanos, and tourists, prefer more elaborate ones. These are what the artisans on the Plaza Independencia benches carve, sometimes to order. Pastoral scenes, often of the gaucho, are among the favorite motifs the men cut through the dark surface of the maté to the whiter wood beneath. They always have an appreciative audience—and often a buyer.

A North American asked an Uruguayan friend how many people in his country drank maté. The friend countered by asking, "How many in your country drink 'cokes'?" "Oh, practically everybody." "Well, that is the number here who drink maté."

It is by no means just the rural dwellers who make a daylong habit of sipping maté. Grizzled old residents of Montevideo, and many younger ones, too, can be seen strolling along the streets or sitting in the parks or in front of their homes or shops, the inevitable maté with its *bombilla* cupped in one hand. On the beaches during "the season" (December to February) one of the essential services is provided by the temporary cabaña which advertises *agua caliente* for replenishing thermos bottles which in turn refill the matés carried by the bathers lolling on the beach. Making the maté, the drink, is almost a rite.[1] Uruguay will lose a precious bit of local color if the maté "habit" disappears.

Running west from the Plaza Independencia is Montevideo's "Main Street," the Avenida 18 de Julio, on which are located many of the big department and other stores, moving-picture theaters, and public buildings. The "Eighteenth of July" commemorates the birth date of Uruguay's first constitution in 1830. At the upper end of the avenue, close to the famous Batlle Park, is the beautiful obelisk designed by Zorrilla de San Martín to commemorate those who wrote that first constitution. "Dieciocho," as the avenue is familiarly called, is much wider,

[1] *Cf.* "The Purple Land of Uruguay," by Luis Marden, *National Geographic Magazine,* November, 1948.

as befits its role as the backbone of the New City, than its extension, Calle Sarandí, on the westerly side of the Plaza Independencia.

Thirteen blocks away from the plaza which marks its beginning, the avenue forks, the northern branch extending on to the Batlle Park and the southern (under a different name) running on to the coast in the suburb of Pocitos. It is at the fork in the avenue that the magnificent statue of the gaucho stands, mounted and roweled, spear aloft, holding historic communion with the equestrian Artigas in the Plaza Independencia about a mile away. Close by the Gaucho, on his left, rears the twelve-story height of the Intendencia or municipal building. An annex is still under construction (Montevideanos just shake their heads when asked when it will be completed), but the main building contains busy city offices and is a model of design and construction.

Fronting the Intendencia and filling a considerable open space between it and Dieciocho, one of the principal *ferias* or open-air markets of Montevideo is held two mornings a week. On those mornings the whole paved area teems with the little stalls of the vendors of fruit, flowers, vegetables, meat, cheeses, and almost any other edible the housewife may wish. For all the hours of the morning the buying and selling goes on vigorously. By noon it tapers off and by early afternoon the last traces of carrot tops, wilted cabbage leaves, and other litter are being swept up. An hour or so later the area is as immaculate as ever.

Eventually, if or when Montevideo's imaginative city planners see their dreams realized, the area surrounding the Intendencia will become a great civic center with other public buildings appropriately placed in parklike surroundings. That must wait, however, until politics can temper the resistance of private ownership of property, much of which would have to be sacrificed to make the change.

The *feria* is a Montevideo institution of recent growth. The biggest of the markets is a permanent undercover installation near the Plaza Independencia. Most of them are small neighborhood affairs, operated only a particular half day each week. A portion of a street will be blocked off or a vacant lot occupied and for several hours the wives and servants of the neighbor-

hood look over the wares for food and flowers for the well-sup-
plied Montevidean tables. Bargains abound in these neighborhood markets. The hucksters don't have the overhead charges
of rent and other items which confront the permanent shopkeeper. Indeed, the municipal government at times follows a
deliberate policy of opening a new *feria* here or there in Montevideo as a means of controlling neighborhood prices in the
fixed establishments and keeping food costs down for the consumer.

One of the surprising aspects of the small local market, at
least for those who have seen them in other Latin American
countries, is the very general practice of housewives doing their
own shopping and carrying the purchases home themselves. In
many Latin American cities this would mean an instant loss
of caste, but democratic Uruguay has broken down the traditional mores. Anything serves for carrying home all sorts of
groceries. The favorite device is the plastic-net shopping bag.
It may allow an occasional small potato to slip through its
large mesh but it is light and generally serviceable. Also used
are oversized purses, small, home-manufactured, wheeled carts,
baby buggies, and even more curious devices. The explanation
Uruguayans give for the willingness of housewives to do their
own marketing goes back to conditions during World War II.
At that time the frequent unavailability of servants and the
general scarcity of some commodities led housewives to begin
doing much of their own marketing, and they have since continued it. The trend is an interesting one. On Tristan Narvaja
Street each Sunday morning a length of five or six blocks is
reserved for one of the larger periodic *ferias*. Seemingly everything, including the most attractive and diminutive puppies,
birds, fish, and other pets, is offered for sale.

The weekly markets are doubtless disliked to the point of
resentment by the many small shopkeepers who, for half a day,
see their patronage drop away to a trickle. Their number is
the proverbial legion. In the residential districts almost every
block will have one or more small shops offering an amazing
variety of foods and other articles. Some of the shops are
merely converted single-car household garages. The stock of
a particular item is often necessarily small. But, for that matter, the buying habits of the average Montevidean household

are similarly small scale. There is competition, too, from the street vendors. The drivers of the small, brilliantly colored, horse-drawn wagons selling bread or fruits or vegetables or flowers may ring the same housewife's doorbell a dozen times a day in their leisurely rounds of a particular section of the city.

If we go back to Dieciocho to continue our casual progress out its length, we soon pass the Plaza of the Thirty-Three, named to commemorate that brave band of patriots. Many Montevideanos might look momentarily puzzled by the use of that name for the plaza. They universally call it the Plaza de los Bomberos (firemen) because it is there that the city's central fire station is located. The familiar fire siren of United States cities is a far less common sound in Montevideo. Building construction is in many cases almost completely fireproof. One may live for months in a residential section without seeing firetrucks on their noisy way to a conflagration.

A few blocks farther out Dieciocho one passes the University of Montevideo or, officially, the University of the Republic. Actually, the imposing building houses only the Faculty (or College) of Law and that of Economic Sciences. The hundred-and-thirty-odd-year-old national library is also housed in this structure pending completion of its own edifice nearby. The national university will probably never have its own centralized campus as several of the Latin American national universities now do. The Faculties of Engineering and Architecture, for example, have new and well-equipped buildings in widely separated parts of the city. Other faculties are also physically far removed from one another.

At the end of Dieciocho, beyond the obelisk, one enters a lovely, tree-shaded parkway forming the approach to Batlle Park. On opposite sides stand the residences of the United States and British ambassadors, and there are other imposing homes in the neighborhood. The Batlle Park, or Parque José Batlle y Ordóñez, commemorates Uruguay's greatest citizen, its two-term president. The park's major feature is the great Centenary Stadium opened in 1925 to celebrate the country's hundredth birthday. Here the rabid Uruguayan *fútbol* fans gather by the scores of thousands to see the national championships and other big games. *Fútbol* means soccer to the Uruguayans.

"Of course, you will see the Covered Wagon," is a bit of "must" advice every Uruguay-bound tourist receives. The reference is to José Belloni's world-famous statue of the *carreta* and its oxen and mounted gaucho guide. The beautiful bronze group, close by the stadium in Batlle Park, evokes the past as much as the great *fútbol* bowl and its teeming thousands of fans do the present.

Montevideo's zoological garden is not many blocks from the Batlle Park. It was the gift of a public-spirited citizen many years ago. The quarters are now cramped and there are plans for moving the garden to more extensive grounds in the western part of the city. In the meantime, the "zoo" is one of the popular attractions of Montevideo. Children frequent it and, of course, as with circuses in the United States, parents often have to go along "just to take the children."

Another of the great arteries of Montevideo is the Avenida Agraciada, which branches off diagonally to the north from Dieciocho near the Plaza Independencia. Agraciada, viewed from Dieciocho, points directly toward the Legislative Palace a little more than a mile away. This avenue is one of Montevideo's widest, and the long approach to Uruguay's largest public building, the home of its congress, affords the city's most notable street vista. Agraciada has been improved greatly and is lined with many highly attractive modern office buildings. One of them houses the United States embassy offices; another, across the street, one of the government-owned banks.

The Legislative Palace is an imposing granite and marble structure, far more impressive than the modest Executive Palace on the Plaza Independencia. One explanation of the disparity is that the congress of democratic Uruguay wanted it thus to be known that it was more important than the executive branch of the government. The total cost of the great structure was more than $12,000,000. Its interior provides a practical display of Uruguay's wealth in building stone: forty-five varieties of marble from the hinterland of the country are used. Fine carpets, beautiful woods, stained-glass windows, and stirring historic paintings help to make it a memorable structure for both tourist and Uruguayan alike. The Legislative Palace has enough open space around it to set it off properly. Ultimate plans call for an even more spacious treatment of the surroundings. This unfortunately has not yet been done for all public buildings of large proportions, notably the Bank of the Republic in the Old City.

Curving around the bay to the north and northwest is a nineteenth-century section of the city containing many fine old family residences, veritable mansions in some cases.

About a mile north of the bay is located the Prado, the largest and oldest of Montevideo's parks. It is an unofficial monument to one of Montevideo's many public-spirited citizens of the past, José Buschental. Don José was a European financier, intimate friend of some of the royal houses of Europe, and married to a niece of the Brazilian emperor, Dom Pedro II. Wealthy Montevidean families of the time (about the middle of the past century) had their palatial estates in the vicinity of the Miguelete River, then in the country but now entirely surrounded by Montevideo. It was there that Don José settled. The summer heat found the important families retiring to their villas and quintas to stroll under the trees, fan away the flies, and drink well water. They had a prejudice against use of ice, which was suspected of causing "spasms." Buschental bought and developed an estate of some 175 acres, centering around a Renaissance manor house. The grounds were laid out in wonderfully attractive gardens, parks, and woods. He dredged and beautified the Miguelete River, spanned it with arched bridges, built artificial lakes and fountains, and imported exotic fish from India and Japan to fill them.

An Uruguayan writer of many years ago thus described Don José's creative fancy: "The parks were planted with the rarest species of trees from the five parts of the world; the greenhouses were filled with tropical plants; hairy cacti, with fantastic orchids, felty begonias, and giant ferns. Rare plants from Madagascar, India, Borneo, Malacca, and even from the remotest countries were brought. In the patio of the grange . . . the exotic fancy of Buschental created a miniature zoo with the smaller wild animals, such as frisky and mischievous monkeys, long-snouted anteaters, birds of multicolored feathers, cobras and pythons from the Brazilian forests."

The estate became a fantastic Alcazar of the Plata River, but Don José's affairs did not prosper and he had to return to Europe. The grounds passed to the government, were ultimately doubled in size by the purchase of neighboring villas, and have become the lovely Prado Park. The Prado's most renowned feature is its famous rose garden containing more than 800 varieties. When they are in full bloom in November they make a spectacular riot of color and fully justify Montevideo's nickname of the City of Roses.

Other fine parks, large and small, are scattered over the area of Montevideo. One of the largest, and the capital's most popular park, is that honoring the memory of Uruguay's outstanding literary giant, José Enrique Rodó. Rodó Park, too, has its elaborate gardens thick with roses. Serving as a backdrop for them are ombú, palm, paradise, and eucalyptus trees. One of the park's best-known features is its large artificial lake with its gondolas and small boats. Hard by the lake in Rodó Park is the miniature castle which serves as a combination administration building and children's library. Nearby, too, is the National Museum of Fine Arts. The park's most notable statue is, quite appropriately, the group dedicated to Rodó. One of Montevideo's fine beaches adjoins the Rodó Park and close by, still as part of the water-front park plan, are the summer theater and the attractive new building of the University's Faculty of Engineering. Immediately to the south and extending down to Punta Carreta, Montevideo's southernmost point, is the extensive course of the Uruguayan Golf Club.

Several miles out to the east, beyond the city proper and close to the excellent new airport, is the huge and recently developed Franklin D. Roosevelt National Park. Its plantings of trees and the excellent care given it bid fair to make it one of the well-known national parks of the continent.

When Montevideo began its third wave of growth early in the present century, much of the expansion was to the east. It was then, both as cause and effect, that the city became aware of one of its greatest treasures—its magnificent beaches. A long string of white sand, crescent-shaped beaches extends like pearls on a necklace, for miles along the shores of the Plata. These playas or beaches—Ramírez, Pocitos, Buceo, Malvín, Carrasco, and smaller ones—are now the pride and joy of all true Montevideanos, and rightfully so. A particular beach may be only a hundred yards or so in length or, on the other hand, a mile or more. Separating them are usually short, rocky spits extending out into the water, some the location of a small light-house, others of a flagpole or a fishing pier. The winds and river currents which have piled the clean, white sands on the northern banks of the Plata have indeed been generous to Montevideo and Uruguay, just as they have been harsh in their treatment of the Argentine coast across the river.

The city fathers in Montevideo have capitalized on the fortune Nature has given them. Only Rio and a few other cities can match the magnificent water-front development the Uruguayan capital has achieved. For miles from the downtown section the Rambla winds along the shore of the Plata. Its various sections are named for foreign countries or their great men. Two of them commemorate United States presidents, Wilson and Franklin Roosevelt. Almost no private or commercial building is permitted between the Rambla and the water. The river side of the broad avenue is buttressed, in most of its length, by a low granite wall, with stone benches at intervals. Between the low parapet and the water lies only the dazzling sand of the beaches or the picturesque rocks of the occasional spits between them.

Until the present century the settlements along the shore of the Plata, oceanward from Montevideo proper, were but isolated and undistinguished villages. Pocitos, for example, was only a small fishing village. Then, when Montevideo "discovered" its beaches and simultaneously began a new wave of growth, the coastal settlements were swallowed one by one. Pocitos, Buceo, Malvín, and Carrasco were all engulfed within the growing metropolis. Now those formerly humble beach suburbs possess some of the city's most fashionable areas and its most lavish tourist hotels.

One of the biggest problems of a rapidly growing city such as Montevideo is transportation. Half a century and more ago, horse-drawn cars served. Later the streetcars were electrified and Dobbin was retired. Still later, the more convenient and adaptable bus became the bulwark of Montevideo's transportation system. Now the trackless trolley is beginning to replace the autobus. The chief impression one gets of the buses is that they are crowded. Many of them carry signs saying that there is room for forty persons seated, ten standing, and seven on the rear platform. That is a model of understatement. (The signs,

Montevideanos tell you, came with the buses.) The number of seated persons remains fixed but those standing in the aisle and on the platform can be multiplied by two or three times beyond the posted number. At rush hours—noontime and in the evenings—the daring young man in Montevideo is not to be found on the flying trapeze but hanging on the rear step of the sardine-packed bus, half a shoe sole keeping a precarious place on the step and one hand grimly clutching the most convenient handrail. But everyone stays happy.

The midday congestion of transportation is caused by the Montevidean custom of the siesta. Because of the latitude, which is about that of Los Angeles in the northern hemisphere, the siesta is not as climatically necessary as in the tropics, but large numbers of the people are devoted to it. Many offices and small shops close for two or three hours in the middle of the day.

Thousands of those who must go downtown drive their own cars, of course. Many of them are, for a variety of reasons, small makes of European automobiles. In recent years more foreign exchange has usually been available to buy European cars than those imported from the United States. The smaller European makes are cheaper to buy and also much more economical in operation. Gasoline is high-priced in Montevideo; about half its retail price is taxes. Bicycles are very common on the Montevideo streets. Many are light, strong English and continental makes. Only the bus and the automobile have enabled Montevidean suburbs to leapfrog along the coast of the Plata as they have done in late decades. The long fingers of settled areas that extend out from the older part in many directions would be impossible without such transportation. When the occasional bus strikes occur, the city is indeed hard hit. More bicycles are pressed into service, friendly neighbors "give a lift" with their automobiles, and trucks with makeshift seats spring into service, as if by magic, to duplicate many of the bus routes.

Montevideanos are talking *subterraneo* or subway in recent years. It would be an expensive business for the city and many of the soberer heads doubt that it would be a wise venture. There may be a little envy of Buenos Aires' excellent metro or subway system across the river. It is perhaps one of the very

few ways in which Montevideo shows an unhappy wish to "keep
up with the Joneses."

Farthest out to the east of the suburbs is Carrasco, almost
at the limits of the Department of Montevideo. Its wonderful
tree-shaded streets, neatly trimmed lawns, and new, brick,
stone-trimmed, tile-roofed houses make it perhaps the most
attractive residential section of the whole great city. It is a
veritable garden city in itself. Carrasco has houses entirely
surrounded by lawn. The large part of Montevideo is made up
of residences and business buildings immediately adjoining one
another in the traditional Latin American style.

The city planners have perhaps a more intelligent view of
residence arrangement than those of almost any other city of
South America. There is not much they can do about gaining
open space at the sides of the houses, especially when many
lots are so narrow. But the law has required since 1916 that
new house construction be set back from the street and space
provided in front for a strip of lawn. It is a policy both sensible
and esthetic. All properties, even vacant lots, fronting on paved
streets must be fenced. It is difficult to perform a face-lifting
operation on a city except by long, slow evolution. Montevideo's urban authorities and experts are guiding not only the
city's growth, however, but also its appearance. The design
and setting of Montevideo's newer homes are as attractive as
can be found anywhere in South America.

So rapidly is Montevideo growing that residence, business,
and industrial construction goes on continually all over the
city. Much of the work on smaller buildings is, despite Montevideo's modernity, quite primitive. Bricks, tile, and buckets of
cement are passed or tossed up from workman to workman in a
human chain linking the ground and the second or third or even
fourth floor where work is currently going on. Many such
processes are done by hand in spite of the relatively high cost
of labor. It all adds to the high cost of homes in Montevideo.
A common accompaniment of the crew of workmen on a small
construction job is the makeshift grill which is built so that,
fed with a fire of chips or small sticks, the noonday meat can be
barbecued. This is the ever-present *asado*.

There are other great traffic arteries. Avenida General
Flores, named for that early military and political figure, runs

to the north from the Legislative Palace. On the way it passes the large Faculty of Medicine, one of the most heavily attended medical schools in the hemisphere, with more than 1,600 students. Avenida Italia reaches out to the distant suburb of Carrasco. The avenue's beginning is at the charming little *plazuela de Italia.* At least it is called that on the maps, but to all Montevideanos it is the *plazuela del lobo.* Its central feature is the bronze of the Roman wolf suckling the infant Romulus and Remus. The statue was a gift of the city of Rome to Montevideo.

Just east of Batlle Park, which Avenida Italia bounds on the north, is located the giant Hospital de Clínicas, Uruguay's newest and largest hospital structure. It is the latest addition to the splendid system of medical services the little South American republic provides its population. Not far away are the privately operated Italian and British hospitals.

Calle Rivera strikes off to the east from Dieciocho de Julio and extends to the city's main cemeteries in Buceo, the section just to the east of Pocitos. These cemeteries, one of them so heavily wooded that it resembles a park almost as much as a *campo santo,* are the scene of most of Montevideo's burials. Here, at almost any time, can be seen the fantastically ornate hearses. Their elaborately carved black ornamentation is one of the curious sights of Uruguay's capital.

It is on Montevideo's streets, of course, that the visitor sees much of the life of the city. They are crowded at almost any hour, except, perhaps, early in the morning of a holiday. The crowds may be the men and women of Montevideo going about their daily tasks. They may be the noisy, happy groups of uniformed school children entering or leaving the many school structures scattered throughout the city. The crowds may be those leaving one of the numerous and modern moving picture theaters in the New City. Or they may be the tens of thousands streaming home from the huge stadium in Batlle Park after a championship soccer game. They may be the dozen or more people gathered around one of the myriad newspaper and magazine kiosks which dot the central section. At night, until a late hour, the crowds will be just those who stroll up and down the streets for the pleasure of seeing some thousands of their Montevidean neighbors.

Large numbers of people will be found, day or night, in the indoor and the sidewalk cafés and *confiterías*. The leisurely drinking of coffee and eating of light between-meals snacks give a distinctly Parisian flavor to Montevidean life. Café conversation is apt to be vigorous, and endless. Montevideanos are a friendly and gregarious people and would be in a bad way indeed if forbidden any discussion with their fellows. By and large, most of these people are well dressed. Many people on the streets, workmen included, wear the Basque-inspired beret of dark blue felt. The people dress well because Montevideo is a prosperous city of middle-class population, middle-class homes, middle-class wealth. Many of the women (and men, too, for that matter) are living proof that Uruguay is by no means a land of starvation. Don't look around on the Montevideo streets for the swarthy complexions and high cheekbones to be found in the Andean countries. The features are European. The hair is blond or brunette or red—it is all a matter of the individual. People are short and often slight of build.

There are sections, of course, where the appearance of the people, the buildings, and the streets is less attractive. Around the bay to the northwest, for example, lies the Cerro. It is not to be labeled a slum section but it is one of much more humble homes and businesses. The streets are very regularly, and rectangularly, laid out; there is none of that delightful informality and irregularity that characterizes most of Montevideo's pattern of streets. Most of the streets in the Cerro are named for foreign countries, a few for cities. There is a Calle Estados Unidos and also a Norte América. It is ironically appropriate that one of the Communist party sectional headquarters is on a corner of the Calle Rusia. The Cerro proper is the parklike low hill which, according to legend, gave the city its name more than four centuries ago.

To the east and south of the Cerro are some of the large industrial establishments of the city. Montevideo is not a highly industrialized center, however. Here, north and west of the bay, are located the Frigorífico Nacional (or national meat-packing plant), the packing plant of a North American firm with its private golf course for its employees, and the refining and processing plant of Ancap. That interestingly coined word is formed from the initials of Administración Nacional de Combustibles, Alcohol, y Portland (*i.e.*, cement). The Montevideanos like that business of making up names from the initial letters or syllables of words. Onda, an efficient and courteous bus company, is not a "wave," as the Spanish dictionary would suggest; rather it is the Organización Nacional de Autobuses. Conaprole, the dominant milk and dairy products agency, is the Cooperativa Nacional de Productores de Leche. The Sodre, a government sponsored musical and cultural agency, is the Servicio Oficial de Difusión Radio-Eléctrica. Causa, an aviation company, is the Compañía de Aviación Uruguaya, S. A. Those letters "S. A." make a convenient terminal, or sometimes beginning, syllable for such words. They don't stand for "South America," as the uninitiated sometimes assume, but for "Sociedad Anónima," or corporation.

Another "depressed area" in Montevideo is the Peñarol section far up to the northwest. Peñarol was originally the location of extensive railroad yards and industrial developments, but it no longer means railroads or factories or slums to the average Montevideano. "Peñarol" means soccer. The name is that of one of Montevideo's two great football clubs; the other is Nacional. *Fútbol* and politics, Uruguayans will tell you in their lighter moments, are the only real topics of conversation in Montevideo!

When a city thinks in terms of those matters rather than about such topics as hunger and pestilence and crime, it is a sign that it is living the good life. Montevideo is that kind of city. Its people take a great and proper pride in their city, their way of life, and their country.

# 4

~~~~~~~~~
~~~~~~~~~

# The Purple Land of Uruguay

No catalog has ever been made of the persons who have described Uruguay as having "a gently rolling landscape." Or, to vary it slightly, "undulating plains." Their number is the proverbial legion. But another legion will come along with the passing years and describe the country in exactly the same terms—because that is about the only way in which it can be described.

Uruguay has not the majestic mountains of Peru and Ecuador. It lacks the lovely lakes of southern Chile. There are no magnificent waterfalls like those at Iguassú, no entrancing bay such as Rio's, no spectacular fireworks like those Nature provided at Paricutín in Mexico. The highest point in the country is only 1,644 feet above sea level, less than 200 feet higher than the Empire State building. The area is 72,153 square miles, the smallest of all the South American countries and just slightly larger than North Dakota or Oklahoma. Not big, as countries go. Or scenically flamboyant or spectacular.

Yet the Middle Westerner driving through the Uruguayan countryside is apt to exclaim, "Why, how like an Indiana landscape those fields look!" Or another *norteamericano*, going through the Department of Rocha, will say, "Look at those palms, it's just like a southern California scene!" Someone else will be reminded of a Pennsylvania pastoral view. These are the scenes one wears like an old, familiar garment—and loves. They aren't the dress-up, show-off scenery which Latin America has in plenty; they are the southern continent's equivalent of Grandma Moses with a little touch of Grant Wood thrown in for good measure.

The geologist writes learnedly of granitic schists, Permian beds, and Triassic basalts, but we are more concerned with what is above the surface than below. Uruguay is a knowable country; practically no acre of it is inaccessible. Hence, the very large part of the land is usable, and used. Arbitrarily assuming a national population of 2,500,000, this means a density of about thirty-five per square mile. So great is the concentration of population in Montevideo, however, that many of the square miles fall very far short of their average.

Uruguay has the advantage of being relatively more nearly surrounded by water than any other Latin American republic except, of course, Cuba. Lake Merim, the Atlantic, and the Plata on the east and south, the Uruguay River along the entire western side, the Río Cuareim and a small tributary, the Río Yaguarón, and a few miles of the Arroyo San Luis on parts of the northern side mean that the literal land boundary is confined to but four short stretches in the north totaling only about 150 to 175 miles in length out of a complete boundary mileage of 1,147. Thus, Uruguay becomes almost an island and doesn't have to worry too much about arguing with its neighbors over how far its territory extends.

If all roads lead to Montevideo it follows, as a matter of exact logic, that if one turns around, all roads must also lead *from* Montevideo. Uruguay's best road is that from the capital to Colonia, the small river port directly across from Buenos Aires. The distance is only about 110 miles and the highway is Uruguay's "show road." Because it forms a part of the Pan American Highway, connecting most directly with Buenos Aires, the road has become an important artery of international travel. Near Montevideo the land is cropped, but one does not have to get far away before the landscape reflects the typical rural economy of pasturing livestock.

The best developed departments are, for obvious reasons, those in the south. The ones with a littoral on the Plata River, for example, rank one, two, three, four, and five in density of population.[1] Nevertheless, the overwhelmingly rural character of Uruguay, outside of Montevideo, is unmistakably revealed even on the way to Colonia.

Eucalyptus trees and different kinds of shrubbery lend variety to the rolling pastures. Telephone poles and fence posts are likely to be adorned with oven birds' nests. These substantial examples of avian architecture are solidly built of mud and straw. Partitions inside divide the nest into two or more "rooms." Normally the nest is not more than about a foot or sixteen inches in any dimension but skyscrapers of half a dozen stories have been found. The owner comes down from the upper levels and exits through the main door on the "ground floor" —which is as it should be. The *hornero* or oven bird and his cheerful warble are a treasured bit of the countryside in many parts of Uruguay. He is chairman of many a rural welcoming committee.

[1] Some of the basic data on Uruguayan departments are shown in the following table:

| Department | Capital (if a different name) | Area (in sq. mi.) | Rank in area | Population | Rank in population | Pop. density (per sq. mi.) | Rank in pop. dens. |
|---|---|---|---|---|---|---|---|
| Artigas | | 4,392 | 8 | 57,854 | 17 | 13+ | 19 |
| Canelones | | 1,834 | 16 | 202,872 | 2 | 111− | 2 |
| Cerro Largo | Melo | 5,763 | 2 | 99,123 | 8 | 17+ | 14 |
| Colonia | | 2,193 | 15 | 132,554 | 3 | 60+ | 3 |
| Durazno | | 5,526 | 3 | 97,140 | 10 | 18− | 13 |
| Flores | Trinidad | 1,744 | 17 | 36,766 | 19 | 21.1− | 10 |
| Florida | | 4,674 | 7 | 107,872 | 6 | 23+ | 8 |
| Lavalleja | Minas | 4,819 | 6 | 117,328 | 4 | 24+ | 7 |
| Maldonado | | 1,586 | 18 | 68,070 | 16 | 43− | 4 |
| Montevideo | | 256 | 19 | 850,000 | 1 | 3,320+ | 1 |
| Paysandú | | 5,115 | 4 | 80,258 | 13 | 16− | 16 |
| Río Negro | Fray Bentos | 3,270 | 13 | 48,814 | 18 | 15− | 17 |
| Rivera | | 3,794 | 10 | 77,407 | 14 | 20+ | 11 |
| Rocha | | 4,280 | 9 | 84,206 | 12 | 20− | 12 |
| Salto | | 4,865 | 5 | 102,987 | 7 | 21.1+ | 9 |
| San José | | 2,688 | 14 | 98,627 | 9 | 36+ | 5 |
| Soriano | Mercedes | 3,560 | 12 | 95,527 | 11 | 27− | 6 |
| Tacuarembó | | 8,112 | 1 | 110,986 | 5 | 14− | 18 |
| Treinta y Tres | | 3,682 | 11 | 70,343 | 15 | 17− | 15 |
| Uruguay | | 72,153 | | 2,538,734 | | 35+ | |

Populations as given in Pan American Union publication (1949), *Uruguay*, p. 11; "latest official estimates, covering up to December 31, 1944."

46

As well harmonized with the landscape as the *horneros'* nests are the many thatched huts to be seen here and there in the countryside. The thatch-roofed house is not as typical of the rural scene in Uruguay as it is in the Indian areas of the Andean countries but, even so, it is frequently seen. There is the difference that in Uruguay the thatch is almost always neatly trimmed around the lower edges, and it makes for an unbelievably better appearance.

Somewhat farther on toward the southwest corner of Uruguay are found the "foreign" settlements of Colonia Valdense, Nueva Helvecia, and Colonia Suiza. Their names betray their background. The Waldensian colony goes well back into the nineteenth century and its residents are the typically sturdy, thrifty members of that European Protestant group. The Swiss settlements—"fine meats, fruits, vegetables, cheeses," so the guidebooks' identification of them runs—are in some measure chalets and more modest dwellings seemingly moved from the Alps themselves.

At the highway's jumping-off-point lies Colonia, one of the oldest settlements in all Uruguay, antedating Montevideo by almost half a century. It is difficult to say what "makes" Colonia: local trade? history? tourism? a way point to and from Buenos Aires? All these contribute but, essentially, Colonia's day was in the past. Even the former inducement of the bull ring is now but a memory because of the outlawing of that sport many years ago. As ports go, Colonia is a typical, placid, small-scale river harbor, smaller, even, than most.

The great Plata River is still about thirty miles wide here, but it is only a few miles from its "source." Push around the vaguely defined southwest corner of Uruguay and you soon reach Carmelo, passing not far away from the town's granite quarries and its old colonial Jesuit orphanage, still of interest because of the design of its brick façade. In the river, a few miles below Carmelo, is the Argentine prison island of Martín García. At Carmelo the Plata ends and the Río Uruguay begins; and across from the town lies the vast delta of the Paraná.

Uruguay's southern exposure is obviously her "house front." By that same architectural projection, the western part of the country, along the Uruguay River, is just as patently the most important "side" of the house. It is here that

Paysandú and Salto, the country's next two cities after Montevideo, are found; here is Fray Bentos with its important meat processing interests; here are the citrus and, potentially, the sugar areas of Uruguay.

On the way up the Río Uruguay the broad lower reach is for more than fifty miles a sort of fluvial lake with a width of up to eight miles. Then at Fray Bentos, capital of the Department of Río Negro, the great river bends sharply to the east for some fifteen miles and narrows considerably. Above that point, for many miles, the course of the stream is filled with islands, some of considerable size. Fray Bentos is one of Uruguay's better river ports. If it were in the United States, it probably would be called Packertown; meat makes it. The dubious distinction of a slaughterhouse odor is not Fray Bentos', however; its aroma is more that of rich beef soup.

Some miles southeast of Fray Bentos the town of Mercedes dominates the lower stretches of the Río Negro. This river, largest internal waterway in the country, really rises in Brazil, flows southwest, cutting Uruguay into two roughly equal parts, and empties into the Uruguay River below Fray Bentos. Mercedes is, for practical purposes, its "head of navigation."

In the back country east of the Uruguay River appear some of the dozens of *cuchillas* which dot the map of Uruguay. Now, the dictionary says the *cuchilla* is a knife (at least that is the principal meaning), and the map says it is a mountain ridge. Most of the *cuchillas* on the Uruguayan landscape fall far short of being topographic knives. At most they are usually low ranges of hills.

Pushing on up the course of the Uruguay River one soon comes, some seventy miles north of Fray Bentos, to Paysandú, the country's second city in size. (If you ask the salteños, it is the *third* city; their own city of Salto ranks second.) The trip by river takes the traveler past the scores of islands, many of them vegetation formed, above Fray Bentos. The now more usual trip by highway reveals more of the fascinating western part of the country. Paysandú was supposedly named for an eighteenth-century missionary, Father Sandú, but the religious spirit is not now so evident as that of commerce and small-scale manufacturing. The life of the town is bustling, but both it and Salto fall so far behind Montevideo in all respects that comparisons are impossible. It used to be that the shipping of ox tongues, by the tens and tens of thousands, was the be-all of Paysandú's activity. Now, however, it has a more varied commerce.

North of Paysandú the Uruguay River is narrower and its navigation more difficult. The east and west banks assume different characteristics. The Río Queguay is an important tributary of the Uruguay, emptying into the bigger river a few miles above Paysandú. Near its mouth are the spectacular cascades which are a scenic feature of western Uruguay and which, if developed hydroelectrically, as has been proposed, will produce some 70,000,000 kilowatt hours of electricity annually. The development will ultimately come but lack of capital may delay it for years.

The next important jump, accessible by river, highway, or rail, is Salto, about seventy miles above Paysandú. On the way, visible from any of the arteries of transportation, is the odd monument to General Artigas. The father of his country once had a fortified camp on the tablelands overlooking the Uruguay River and a grateful people built this colossal monument. It has a pyramidal base surmounted by a column and that by a bust of the hero. The boldly conceived monument on the highest point of the *meseta* is a conspicuous landmark for miles around.

Salto has a "twin" city, Concordia, on the Argentine side of the river. The two cities represent the effective head of navigation on the lower river. The vicinity of Salto possesses amethyst and topaz mines, but the more unusual stones are the curious "water-stones" still occasionally found. Some stones are opaque, others translucent; in the latter, the enclosed liquid can be seen at every movement of the stone. Any small boy, or an adult boy, for that matter, can pick up along the river bank or in the graveled walks of the plazas many a translucent bit of agate or quartz which would delight an amateur geologist's heart.

Both Salto and Paysandú have effectively developed their river fronts. Here are no shacks and slums, no railroad yards or warehouse areas, but, on the other hand, pleasingly designed park zones and amphitheaters which make of the river a distinct civic asset. Salto, like Paysandú, has a thriving local

Ministerio de Instrucción Pública

*José Batlle y Ordóñez (1856–1929), whose democratic vision and
courage molded Uruguayan thinking for half a century. He was
twice elected President of the Republic.*

Ministerio de Instrucción

*José Pedro Varela (1845–1879), Uruguay's leading educator of the 1870's, laid down liberal principles which have become the warp and woof of the national education system.*

trade and a small-scale industry. Many Italians have settled there.

A few miles above the city of Salto lies the Salto Grande. This "great falls" is that only by courtesy: it is not more than two or three meters in height at most points. The volume of water pouring over the jagged rocks makes it impressive, however. A more utilitarian consideration is that the falls blocks navigation. For years the two adjoining countries have discussed a dam, both for power development and to permit canalization, and some day it will be built. In the meantime a boat is able to ply the upper river or the lower river but not both, unfortunately.

A road of sorts—they get less good toward the far corners of the country—runs on north about ninety miles to Bella Unión in the very northwestern corner of Uruguay. Grapes, oranges, and sugar cane may be found here. Ninety miles to the east of Bella Unión lies the small town of Artigas, capital of the northernmost department, of the same name. This corner of the country is the least settled part of Uruguay. The sparseness of population makes for a relative wildness of rural appearance such as W. H. Hudson many decades ago could ascribe to parts farther south; Charles Darwin at a still earlier date could describe even those sections close to the Plata in similar terms.

Returning to Montevideo again as a starting point, the next logical trip is almost due north to the border town of Rivera which, if one plans to go by rail to Brazil, is probably the route that will be taken. A straight line from Montevideo to Rivera divides Uruguay into two almost equal sections. For many miles of the distance going north through the center of the country the highway and the railroad parallel each other very closely. The plan had its advantages as long as the railways were largely British controlled, but now that the Uruguayan government has taken over the complete rail system of the country, the two state-operated transportation services are competing with each other.

North of the departmental capital of Florida (department and town have the same name), the road and railway slowly climb the Cuchilla Grande del Centro, one of the bigger "knives" of the country. They then descend toward the valley

of the Río Yi. On the way, the route passes close by the scene
of the Battle of Sarandí, one of the memorable engagements
(in 1825) of the Uruguayan wars for independence.

In the picturesque valley of the Yi the traveler is fully in
the heart of W. H. Hudson's beloved Purple Land. The valley
of the Yi can perhaps be called as typically Uruguayan as any
part of the country. The Yi is the major tributary of the Río
Negro, but its importance is more historical than economic.
The road and railway cross the Yi at Durazno, capital of the
department of the same name. Had General Fructuoso Rivera
of the famed Thirty-Three had his way, Durazno would have
become the capital of Uruguay. Now it is but a small, quiet,
interior town, dependent, as so many similar towns are, on the
cattle industry.

Some forty miles north of Durazno the route leads to
Paso de los Toros on the Río Negro. This Pass of the Bulls is
not a big or important town as Uruguayan towns go, but it is
only a few miles from one of the biggest and most important
developments in the country, the great hydroelectric project
at Rincón del Bonete. It is Uruguay's TVA.

Originally it was German money, machinery, and know-how
that went into the development of the power project on the
Río Negro. That was in 1937. Then, several years later, the
Germans became involved elsewhere and the Rione development
(that coinage is another instance of the Uruguayan fondness
for telescoping words) fell by the wayside. It was later resumed
under Uruguayan governmental direction with technical and financial assistance from the United States. The dam and the
early phases of the power project were completed a few years
later.

Central Uruguay, in consequence, now has the largest artificial lake in South America, one of some 440 square miles in
area. The lake serves multiple purposes. Primarily, it provides
the source of the hydroelectric power at the dam. When fully
in operation the power capacity will be upwards of half a billion kilowatt hours annually. For some years two high-tension
lines have carried about three-fourths of the ultimate potential
to Montevideo. No longer does Uruguay have to produce its
electricity from the more expensive imported petroleum and
coal. The opening of the huge plant was the government's ex-

cuse for splurging during carnival season a few years ago; it
spent about $100,000 on electric-light displays for Monte-
video's carnival, but some of that expense could doubtless be
charged off to advertising.

Then, too, the Rione project increases the navigable mileage of Uruguay's greatest internal river to about 370 miles.
Railroad flatcars carry small boats around the dam, and
planned locks will further increase navigability. The government has plans for development of a fishing industry in the
lake. A fourth utility is the potential addition to Uruguay's
thriving industry of *turismo*.

The Rione development may quite possibly change the
social as well as the physical map of Uruguay. Ironically
enough, it was a feature of United States supported Uruguayan planning which Nazi propagandists were unable to attack in their disruptive campaigns, because it was Germans
themselves who had begun the project.

Lying north of the Río Negro lake is the sprawling, roughly
triangular department of Tacuarembó. It is Uruguay's largest
in area but next to the last in density of population. In this
part of north central Uruguay the relief becomes somewhat
wilder, rock outcroppings are more common, tablelands more
in evidence. The little town of Tambores ("drums") on the department's western border does not, for example, stem from
any exotic early Indian rites; it simply signifies that here the
configuration of the surface led some person of lively imagination to think of "drums." More rock and less soil do not preclude a reasonably varied agriculture, however; corn, flax,
cotton, wheat, tobacco, sunflower, and peanuts provide a mix-
ture of temperate and subtropical crops.

About seventy miles to the north, and slightly east, of the
town of Tacuarembó is the border town and departmental
capital of Rivera. Both of these north central departments
subtly reveal the increasing distance from Montevideo, the
growing closeness to Brazil. The gaucho costume—loosely
wound scarf about the neck, loose jacket, sash, baggy *bomba-
chas* or trousers gathered at the ankles, light boots—is more
in evidence. So, too, are Negroes. A single street separates the
Uruguayan town of Rivera from its Brazilian twin of Livra-
mento. The two towns live together as congenially as any pair

of urban twins straddling the Canadian–United States border. The tourist, if he takes a little time in the neighborhood of Rivera, likes it for one reason because he can find all sorts of beautiful stones in the vicinity; some are of semi-gem varieties.

If we start again from Montevideo, this time in a northeasterly direction, it is possible to follow the route of the Pan American Highway to Brazil. Some years ago Herbert Lanks wrote very feelingly of his terrific bouts with bad roads in northeastern Uruguay and Southern Brazil.[2] He tackled them, however, during the rainy season and, it must be admitted, that even yet those that are miles away from the capital leave much to be desired.

About seventy-five miles northeast of Montevideo, lies the attractive town of Minas, capital of the Department of Lavalleja. The central plaza appropriately has a statue, not of the almost invariably honored Artigas, but of Lavalleja, leader of the intrepid Thirty-Three. It was in Minas that he was born. The town's name, too, is appropriate: it is in this department that much of the finest stone—marbles, slate, granite, etc.—is quarried. A large proportion of the small and poor deposits of other minerals, coal, and ores, may be found here, too. Uruguayans are not very mineral conscious, however. Some years ago a workman on an *estancia* in the neighborhood found an outcropping of what appeared to be a valuable ore. He dug out a substantial amount and took it to the owner, reporting that the ore was there in exploitable amounts.

"Fill up the hole and say nothing about this to anyone," was the *estanciero's* surprising instruction. What he feared was the prospect of an upset in the traditional rural economy, the coming in of miners who would destroy fences and ruin pasturage, the intervention of a regulatory government, and so on. It was better to forego the illusory prospect of mineral wealth and maintain a placid, pastoral status quo.

Not far from Minas is the lovely "Cascade of the Waters of the Penitent," well worth the somewhat strenuous trip to see it. It is near Minas, too, that the natural springs of the Fuente Salús are found. The famous mineral water is bottled and sold all over Uruguay; it is also used in the brewing of the

[2] Herbert C. Lanks, *By Pan American Highway through South America* (New York, 1942), pp. 179–84.

country's excellent beer. As much of a national shrine as Uruguay possesses is located atop the Cerro del Verdún near Minas. The statue is that of the Miraculous Virgin of Verdún; it is the scene of frequent popular excursions.

From Minas to Treinta y Tres is a distance of about ninety miles. The countryside is prominently occupied—what parts of Uruguay are not!—by those two sterling inhabitants: cattle and sheep. The gaucho is likewise prominent here. Consumption of the bitter maté is traditional and the nostalgic practice of playing the guitar by an evening campfire can still be found. Here, too, are examples of what is to be seen in many parts of Uruguay: the practice of building a secondary road or trail by the side of the improved highway, the unpaved trail being required by law for the driving of livestock so as to protect the improved road.

Both the town and the department of Treinta y Tres commemorate the patriot band. This department and its northern neighbor of Cerro Largo share the slightly wilder topography characteristic of southern Brazil and hence offer more opportunities to the hunter. The fauna are not greatly varied, however; most of the wild animals have long since disappeared from Uruguay. Foxes, deer, and the *carpincho* or water hog are still found in not too large numbers. In the north the small armadillo or *mulita* is the only living representative of the giants whose fossils are found here and there through Uruguay.

Melo, the capital of Cerro Largo, about seventy miles north of Treinta y Tres, has closer ties in some ways with nearby Brazil than it does with southernmost Uruguay. From Melo roads lead to the Brazilian border both at Aceguá to the north and Río Branco to the east. Either may eventually be the main highway outlet to Brazil. At Río Branco, the Uruguayan town named for the great Brazilian foreign minister of some decades ago, a magnificent international bridge across the Yaguarón River stands as a symbol of the long amity between Uruguay and its giant neighbor to the north.

If we start again from Montevideo on the fourth and final —and the shortest—trip through the hinterland our route would take us to the east and northeast along the curving coast to the Brazilian border at Chuy. For many miles, at least

ninety, going east along the shore of the Plata River, southern
Uruguay is dedicated to playland. The highway does not actually run along the coast. It is a few miles inland but it serves
a primary purpose of giving access to the beaches. Ultimately,
the Rambla, Montevideo's magnificent water-front drive, will
be extended eastward at least as far as Atlántida, thirty-five
miles from the capital.

Some seventy-five miles east of Montevideo the road passes
Uruguay's highest elevation, the Sierra de las Animas, 1,644
feet above sea level. A little farther on is the Pan de Azúcar.
Uruguay's Sugar Loaf is far less famous than that at Rio but
its summit is crowned by a great concrete cross of more than
100 feet in height.

To the south, on the coast, is Piriápolis, the country's
classic example of the enterprise of the real-estate promoter.
More than half a century ago Francisco Piria, whose spirit
must now be the *genius tutelae* of all Uruguayan realtors, decided he would develop a resort. His raw material was little
more than a horseshoe bay backed by sand dunes and serrated
hills, but the genius—and the millions—of the promoter made
out of the "City of Piria" one of the major watering places of
modern Uruguay.

Beyond Piriápolis lie Maldonado and, a few miles to the
south, Punta del Este. This Point of the East should really be
Punta del Sur: it is Uruguay's southernmost point, missing the
thirty-fifth parallel by only about two latitudinal minutes, and
lying about four miles farther south than Montevideo. The
latter city is, of course—somewhat to the surprise of most
North Americans—about twenty-two miles farther south than
Buenos Aires and hence the southernmost national capital of
the hemisphere. Punta del Este is truly "the maximum expression of the Uruguayan shore," as a government publicity release restrainedly describes it.

Off the shore from Punta del Este, on the Isla de Lobos, is
one of the two most important fur-seal colonies south of the
equator. For years Uruguayans maintained a lucrative, even
though prodigal, sealing industry. In a few nonconsecutive
years, mostly in the 1880's and 1890's, more than 20,000 skins
were taken annually from several islands near the coast. The
government later gave the rookeries better protection, and they

are now more notable as a tourist attraction than as a source of fur.

Between Punta del Este and Piriápolis another synthetic development has been undertaken, but one falling short of Piriápolis in exploitive value. This is Punta Ballena, so named after Señor de la Ballén, the original owner. The development may be credited to Antonio Lussich, a progressive entrepreneur who, about the turn of the century, bought the property, planted thousands of trees, imported and released rare specimens of birds, and in many other ways laid the basis for a remarkable resort. In the last few years his daughter, Señora Milka Lussich de Vidal, has furthered the planned community with the assistance of a capable young Spanish emigré architect, Antonio Bonet.

About fifty-five miles to the northeast of Maldonado lies Rocha, capital of the identically named department. Rocha and Maldonado are the Atlantic departments—Punta del Este is generally credited with being an arbitrary boundary point between the ocean and the Plata River. On these shores sand dunes proved a very real problem. They were finally anchored, first by grasses, then shrubs, then trees. Hundreds of thousands of pines, palms, and eucalyptus have been artificially planted to halt the creeping dunes.

It is the palms of Rocha that give the department its most picturesque appearance. Seen first in isolated instances, then in small clumps, and a little farther on in almost solid forests, they dot the landscape by the tens of thousands. The Uruguayan palm is a long-lived tree, but it may be doomed. Free-grazing cattle eat the young shoots and effectively prevent it from reproducing. The hazard is increased by the occasional illegal felling of a palm by a rural dweller for the purpose of making palm honey.

The palm is by no means an Uruguayan national tree. That distinction would more likely be held by the full-bodied ombú, the eucalyptus, or the poplar. Even yet, in countless cases, the bottomlands of many streams are pleasantly shaded by trees just as when W. H. Hudson's semiautobiographical hero rode league after league across the Uruguayan plains.

On the ground in this corner of Uruguay (and in many other parts of the country as well) can be seen the small, sober burrowing owl. The ornithologist can often see the *carancho* wheeling about overhead. This curious bird kills small animals for food, but it is also a carrion eater. The most distinctive, though no longer common, example of bird life, however, is the ostrich. To the Uruguayan he is the *ñandú* or *avestruz*. This rhea is smaller than the South African ostrich and his feathers are less valuable. Indeed, they are usually reduced to the ignominy of serving as feather dusters in Montevideo homes. The ostrich, a lot of bird, certainly, serves little economic purpose in Uruguay, though the people of the countryside use the eggs for omelettes. One egg makes a lot of omelette, strongly flavored but edible.

Almost 200 miles around the coast from the capital lies the Laguna Negra, the country's largest natural lake. This Black Lake—or Lake of the Dead, to use its more macabre label—is truly well named. The water falls considerably short of being as dark as ink, but it does have a murky appearance which is startling. The more enthusiastic (or imaginative) Uruguayans insist that the coloration is due to oil seepages beneath the surface of the water; the more likely explanation is subsurface vegetation.

Near the lake is the Santa Teresa National Park of more than 8,000 acres in area. Its central feature is the Fortaleza Santa Teresa, now perhaps the country's most interesting national monument but once the chief defense bastion against Portuguese invasion from Brazil. The fortress dates back to the 1760's and was built after the manner of Vauban, the great French military engineer. After serving its original purpose, the fortress was long left to decay and used only as a "quarry" by people in the vicinity who wanted building stones. It has now been intelligently restored by a historically minded government, and its chapel, museum, barracks, powder magazines, guard rooms, and other features are a constant source of interest to the tourist.

The Santa Teresa Park also includes a zoological collection, a botanical garden, wonderful beaches, colorful ravines, and other points which would justify a long visit.

A few miles north of Santa Teresa and directly on the border is the twin national monument of the Fuerte San Miguel. This fort is smaller than Santa Teresa, but together Saint

Michael and Saint Therese stood guard over the vaguely defined and unrespected frontier for long years in the latter part of the eighteenth century.

Only about four miles to the east of the Fuerte San Miguel is the border town of Chuy. Again, as at Rivera, only the width of a street separates Uruguay from Brazil. Most of the bargains in store purchases are to be obtained on the Brazilian side; either the peso or the cruzeiro is equally acceptable on the one side or the other and people walk across the street just as they would across Main Street in any Stateside town, totally unconcerned with the fact that they have crossed an international boundary.

This, then, is the Purple Land of Uruguay. It is unspectacular as landscapes and countrysides go, but always interesting and always friendly.

# 5

# Playland

A popular magazine published three or four years ago a quite favorably written article about Uruguay. It was illustrated with a picture, among others, of "a Uruguayan debutante," a lovely young lady in bathing suit on the rocky promontory adjoining Punta del Este's beaches. It developed that, ironically but entirely unintentionally, the photographic agency had supplied a picture of an Argentine instead of an Uruguayan beauty. It was not for this reason alone, however, that Uruguayans were slightly irked by the article, excellent publicity though it was.

The article was entitled "Gayest Spot South of the Border," and that, Uruguayans averred, made it sound as if their country were nothing but one big night club.

Uruguay does have night clubs, but it has much more. There are the incomparable beaches, well over 200 miles of them. There are *fútbol* and tennis and golf, racing and yachting and fishing. There is *carnaval*, short of Rio's in size and reputation but fully as colorful. There is the *asado*, beside which the words "picnic" and "barbecue" are but colorless third cousins. But there is still more. It is intangible. It is an attitude of mind.

The Uruguayan, far more than most *latinos*, has come to believe that recreation belongs to him. It is not something for the rich and the wellborn alone, not the exclusive prerogative of the leisured classes, not the foolish hobby of the unpredictable foreigner. It belongs to Juan José Uruguayo, and he is going to make use of it or know why.

Now, that is not to say that he goes at it with all the grim intensity of the farmer who is given a ticket to a Wagner opera and insists on sweating it out. The Uruguayan *enjoys* his sports and recreation, and he wants you to enjoy them, too.

Indeed, enjoyment of life is one of the great characteristics of this great, little nation. It is compounded in part of the ability, all too rare in dignity-ridden Latin America, to laugh at oneself as well as other men and things. There is the "Republic of the Parvenses," for example, undoubtedly the wackiest of Uruguay's multitude of social clubs. This one specializes in deflating stuffed shirts, their own, their guests, just anyone's, for that matter. Practical jokes, buffoonery, and ribbing are carried on as a fine art.[1]

The Uruguayan's enjoyment of sports means, for one thing, that he likes participation sports in addition to spectator sports to a much greater extent than people in many Latin American countries. Bullfighting isn't for Uruguay; it has been legally banned for forty years or more. It is significant, too, that the aristocratic and expensive polo is considerably more the vogue across the river in Buenos Aires.

Walk around the Montevideo streets in a residential section and what is just about the commonest sight? A bunch of boys—aged six to twenty—will be out in the street playing with a ball. Now this ball may be of any reasonable size, almost any shape (you just *thought* balls had to be spherical), and of just about any composition. Lacking anything better, a tied-up bundle of rags will serve the purpose. What happens to the ball? It gets kicked, kneed, batted with head or body, but never passed with the hands. Even the smallest of small fry do it with incredible dexterity. Yes, it's soccer, *fútbol* to the Uruguayans.

What happens to the boys? If the "sandlotters" are good enough, if they diligently practice their homework—or should one say streetwork?—if they have the will and intelligence and guts, they may grow up to become Big Leaguers. In Uruguayan

[1] *Cf.* Michael Scully, "There's Merit in Their Madness," *Reader's Digest*, May, 1948, pp. 90–92.

parlance that means they may play on Peñarol or Nacional, than which there is almost no higher accolade Uruguayans can think of.

Probably the first thing one should do in exploring playland in his playtime is to visit the beaches, which it must be remembered were not "discovered" by the Uruguayans till well after the beginning of this century. For long, long years Uruguayans simply didn't realize what an incomparable asset they had. They do now, however, and *turismo*, of which the beaches are the backbone, has become the third industry of the country. Even yet, however, the wonderful string of beads stretching from Montevideo to the Brazilian border, and to the west of Montevideo, is not as renowned as it should be.

Even if the Argentines can no longer come over in such large numbers, as formerly, all Uruguayans, or so it seems, still go swimming. The national university has no summer session; all of the potential students are at the beaches. Government offices during most of the year operate on a half-day basis, being closed in the mornings. In the summer they reverse that schedule: working in the mornings and leaving the afternoons free for the beaches. Does the family want an outing? Well, the beach is only a few minutes' walk, or a short car or bus ride away.

There are beaches and beaches—the budget type (*económicos*, the Uruguayans might call them, but don't) and then those like Carrasco and Punta del Este. If it is one of the more popular beaches, Ramírez or Pocitos, for example, both reasonably close to the heart of Montevideo, the gleaming, white sand is likely to be crowded with its tens of thousands of people on weekends or holidays. The more fashionable beach, Carrasco, will probably be less crowded (it is about nine miles from the center of the city), and it has as a backdrop two of the capital's swankiest hotels, the Miramar and the Carrasco, both of them resort hostelries.

The showpiece of all Uruguayan resorts, however, is Punta del Este. About a hundred miles east of Montevideo, it occupies a short peninsula which really marks the dividing line, if you can find one, between the Plata River and the Atlantic Ocean. The western side of the peninsula is more protected; it, therefore, is the Playa Mansa, the tranquil beach. On the eastern or Atlantic side there is the Playa Brava, the rough beach, for the more venturesome. By the time the river gets as far as Punta del Este the half-fresh, often reddish waters one finds off Montevideo have given way to the salt, clear water that makes the beaches at Punta del Este true ocean strands.

Beyond Punta del Este? Almost 200 more miles of unparalleled beaches, uncrowded, many with a sort of Robinson Crusoeish atmosphere, all awaiting development. The ad man's most extravagant rhetoric will be needed to describe them adequately.

When Montevideanos made the great discovery a few years ago of their own beaches, the river-front suburbs began leapfrogging out to the east: Pocitos and Malvín and Carrasco and others. All of them were by, of, and for the beaches. From the time when the archbishop formally blesses the waters in a colorful ceremony on December 8, the Day of the Beaches, the season is "officially" open. Hardy souls, of course, will have been braving the briny almost the whole year round, but with early December all Montevideans, it seems, become bronzed beachcombers enjoying life at its most enjoyable.

Cabañas are put up by the score. Little portable pavilions advertise hot water for the maté sipped from the gourd through the *bombilla* or silver straw. Only the sand is more a part of the summer beach than is the maté. The ubiquitous hot dog stand just isn't there. But across the great river-front boulevard, the miles-long Rambla, are many *confiterías*. There you can get sandwiches, cocktails, *helados* (ice cream), or what you will.

And, by the way, if you want to practice your Spanish, don't start by asking what a Spanish word for "sandwich" is. They will have to stop to think if, indeed, they can think of one. It is *sandwich*. That word, like *club* and *bar* and *taxi* and others, is fully naturalized by now in Uruguay and most other Latin American countries. You can't make a conversation out of just four nouns, but they help.

The season! Rental prices for shoreside apartments and residences jump 150 per cent overnight. Buses need a perpetual S.R.O. sign. The sun can burn as intensely as anywhere in the hemisphere. Small tots can get just as tired and just as lost as anywhere else. But at the Montevideo beaches and at fifty others around the curving coast, Uruguayans, through all the long- and sunny-dayed months of December, January, and February, prove by the hundred thousands that they know how to live the good life.

For those who enjoy sailing, there is the Plata. Most sailing, however, is done in the winter, when a south wind, storming in for two or three days in succession, can pile up the water on the Uruguayan side for four or five feet beyond its normal level, temporarily leaving endless mud flats across the river on the Argentine shore. In the summer season, when the Plata is too calm, sailing is done from one of the several yacht clubs at Montevideo. Biggest of them is the Uruguayan Yacht Club. Its several-storied club building at Buceo is built to resemble the prow of a ship. Fronting the clubhouse is the enclosed harbor where dozens of yachts, sloops, and other small craft find haven.

Many of the vessels are small, one- and two-man sailboats. On a breezy Sunday morning the Plata off the Montevideo shores is dotted with trim, triangular sails almost as far as one can see. Dozens will be out in the water at once. Annual regattas are held: the yearly race from Buenos Aires to Montevideo is tops for Uruguay's spiritual kinsmen of Thomas Johnstone Lipton.

Like game fishing? Uruguay has it! Of course, there are fish and fish. Getting fish out of the ocean for a food supply is usually a prosaic business and Uruguay presents no exception. International authorities have said that the fourth or fifth best commercial fishing waters in the world are to be found off Uruguay. The country doesn't do much with them but even if it did that would all be commercial business, anyway.

As far as Uruguay's internal rivers are concerned there is not so much to be said. For that matter, the interior rivers are not very big anyway. The Río Santa Lucía flows down into the Plata near Montevideo, and incidentally gives the capital its water supply. What the modern descendants of Isaak Walton are more interested in, however, is the excellent *criolla* fishing in parts of the Santa Lucía. The *criolla* may tip the scales at a very respectable seventy-five pounds.

South America's largest artificial lake, created by the giant power project previously discussed, has yet to be fully developed as a source of piscatorial and nautical amusements.

In the Atlantic and the Plata River to the east and south and the Uruguay River to the west, however, fishing that *is* fishing may be found. Along the Atlantic coast you can hook sharks sometimes ten feet in length or rays weighing as much as sixty-five pounds. Off Punta del Este, Piriápolis, and other south-coast resort spots, the *lenguado, pompano,* salmon, and *corvina* are choice game fish. Some of the rivers contain exotically named fish: the *pejerrey,* caught in the winter months, and, during the summer fishing season, the *pacú, surubí, tararira, mandubí,* and many others.

The prize of them all for the fisherman who loves a good fight, however, is the *dorado.* This fish is built somewhat along the architectural lines of salmon. He is a golden yellow with lines of broken dots along his sides and with fins and tail of an orange-reddish hue. He may weigh as much as sixty pounds although that is unusual. At any rate, he is just so many pounds of finny dynamite. He is most likely to be found in the leaping waters just above and below the Salto Grande or "great falls" in the Uruguay River a few miles north of the city of Salto.

The *dorado* will lie in the depths of a turbulent pool but will rise to "take" a spoon. The fisherman then has a mad and incredibly swift rush on his hands that may relieve his reel of a hundred yards of line in no time flat. He shouldn't try to stop that first rush—it just isn't done. And he must plan for a good long fight before the *dorado* can be brought to gaff. He is worth it, though; the flaky white flesh makes a dish for a king—or a fisherman.

There are wild fowl, but they aren't numerous. The best of them all is a big duck, the *pato real,* and he is truly a royal bird. The duck many Uruguayans know best, however, is *el Pato Donald,* but to get a fowl of that kind you need a movie ticket, not a hunting license. The far upper Uruguay River has alligators but they are not much hunted.

Anyone who wants to organize a big-game safari would do well to look up schedules to central Africa rather than central Uruguay. There are such beasties as the *mulita,* a toy armadillo with succulent flesh; the *carpincho,* a water hog; the nutria, a water-loving rodent; the fox, deer, and a few others. Partridges, wild turkey, and quail are also there. But, on the whole, wild life played a losing game with civilization in Uruguay. Animal life is protected and some hunting seasons are short.

As far as meat is concerned, one of the best treats in Uruguay is to be had at an *asado*. The *asado* is an institution. It is cousin to a barbecue but done up with all the finesse and variety that only a meat-loving and -producing land can supply. The meat may be lamb or it may be beef. The iron grill is tilted at an angle over the slow fire and the savory aroma merely whets an appetite that was good to begin with.

Perhaps the best form is the *asado con cuero*. The beef (it is always from a fat yearling heifer) is grilled with the hide left on it to seal in the juices and double the tastiness of this best of Uruguayan dishes. Chunks of bread, usually in the form of hard rolls, ample supplies of good, red wine, and possibly a green salad—what more could one ask? Except for variety, Lucullan is the word for it.

If it isn't an *asado con cuero* the meat used is normally sides of ribs. They are preferred to meatier cuts. No seasoning except coarse salt is used. Uruguayans don't often season with hot pepper but some people make a sauce from fresh cayenne pepper, parsley, and vinegar.

A *churrasco* is a grilled beefsteak. It is usually served in slices, broiled, or, in emergencies, fried. Grilled, broiled, and roasted meats in all their glory can be obtained in Montevideo, of course, especially at the *parrillas* or neighborhood grills which are found all over the city. In general, however, the cuisine of Montevideo is sophisticated and reflects the best of France and Italy.

The swankier night spots are also sophisticated. Montevideo has some of them, such hotels as the Rambla, the Parque, and the Carrasco, and they are found, too, at the eastern resorts, Atlántida, Piriápolis, and Punta del Este. Sophistication is not necessarily synonymous with formality. Formality prevails at a spot like the Hotel Carrasco, but at Punta del Este slacks and other sportswear are definitely in order.

In the hotels which have casinos there is usually an atmosphere of casual ease. Roulette is the favorite game and wagers are often high. Daily "life" begins about five in the afternoon with horseback riding or cycling, dinner is late (ten or after), dancing or a turn at roulette or in the game rooms follows.

All the resort spots are well equipped with tennis, golf, stables, and other *divertissements*.

Punta del Este is the classic example of resort life in Uruguay—and its symbol. A tourist-conscious government has parlayed Punta del Este into one of the world's famous resorts, and properly so. The annual summer (January and February, remember) motion-picture festival centering at Punta del Este has won a good press for the spot, and the publicity, while sometimes garish, has been translatable into coin of the republic. Dollars, Brazilian cruzeiros, Argentine pesos, all have been welcomed but all have come for value received. One of the big North American steamship companies now makes Punta del Este a brief port of call for some of its liners during the season so that passengers can get a quick look-see at what is best in South American resorts. Hotels and casinos, lovely summer homes and beautiful avenues, shops that tend to change into shoppes, all these are making Punta del Este the gleaming star of the Uruguayan Riviera. Life there, as the Uruguayans well know and as increasing numbers of foreigners are discovering, can be lived at its leisurely best.

Out toward the northern edge of Montevideo is the great Maroñas race track, the Hipódromo Nacional. It is a development of the Montevideo Jockey Club. While not on as grandiose a scale as the Buenos Aires Jockey Club's racecourse and grounds, it is elaborate and stylish. Races are held throughout the year but the important meets come in January and February; it is then that the international classics occur. The big races at Maroñas attract the top officialdom and the top society of the country and many from across the river as well. They also attract the thousands of people who ride out in buses at a few centésimos each and who enjoy horse racing as much as the North American enthusiast.

Polo has some devotees in Uruguay and there is a club only a short distance from Montevideo. But the better ponies and the more famous teams are those in Argentina. After all, Argentina is more socially sophisticated.

The Maroñas track, or the one a little farther out, at Las Piedras, is a symbol of a certain segment of Uruguayan playland. A more common, though, paradoxically, less apparent, symbol is the ubiquitous social club in Montevideo. There are actually more than 500 (repeat: 500) of these organizations in the capital city, most of which have varied athletic programs for their members. Some have elaborate grounds and go in heavily for tennis or golf. Others are but humble neighborhood organizations which have budget-plan programs for more modest pocketbooks.

The clubs are an earnest of Montevideo's sportsmindedness. Their pattern is not to be equaled anywhere else in Latin America. They are the best evidence of the progress of the average Uruguayan from spectator sports to participation sports. Basketball, handball, *pelota vasca* (a cousin of jai alai), fishing, rowing, even aviation, all have their organized *aficionados* or fans. *Beisbol*, however, has not taken hold in Uruguay as it has in Mexico, Cuba, and Venezuela.

This growing addiction to sports which do not have a Spanish or near-Spanish origin—bull fighting or *pelota*, for example—plays havoc with the purity of whatever corresponds to the king's English; the *caudillo's* Spanish, maybe. You can't borrow an English or North American sport without borrowing and naturalizing some of the terminology or shop talk that goes along with it.

The sports pages of a single issue of a typical Montevideo newspaper, for example, yielded these locutions which doubtless would have left Cervantes somewhat dizzy: *amateur, básquetbol, bowling, boxeo, club, coach, cocktail, country club, cracks, decathlon, field, footing, fútbol, goles, golfista, halfs, hockey, juniors, links, match, performances, players, racing, récord, score, sporting, team,* and *training.* The ultimate in something or other was reached several years ago, however, in a law debated in congress, the purpose of which was to regulate *el match de box.* It didn't deal with lights for cigarettes, just with boxing matches!

The *ne plus ultra* of all Uruguayan athletics—of all Uruguayan life, mayhap!—is *fútbol. Fútbol!* capitalized, underlined, exclamation pointed. (Football, it must be remembered, means soccer in Uruguay.)

Football was introduced about the end of the nineteenth century by the English. British residents were partly responsible and crews of visiting British naval vessels shared the credit. British names dominated the game at first but soon the Latins began to take over. Football caught on. Spanish and Italian players got in the game, and then Uruguayans themselves; today practically no English names are among the rolls of the famous.

The first enclosed football field was laid out in a Montevideo park by the electric tramway company in 1900 (it boosted the transportation business). The field had attached only one small stand, "For Members Only," and the whole arrangement was highly cozy. Three decades later, on July 18, 1930, 100,000 spectators packed a Montevideo bowl to watch an Uruguayan team win the first world's football championship. Soccer had really made the grade in thirty years.

"The House that Football Built," or, more prosaically, the Centenary Stadium, was inaugurated with that famous game on the hundredth anniversary of Uruguay's first constitution. There doubtless would not have been a stadium if it had not been for two organizations whose names, to the ardent fan, are practically synonymous with that of Uruguay itself. They are Peñarol and Nacional.

Nacional and Peñarol (it's better to reverse the names occasionally to preserve a precarious neutrality) are the two greatest football clubs in Uruguay. They are the Dodgers and the Yankees, the Green Bay Packers and the Rams, Rockne's Notre Dame and Zuppke's Illinois, or whatever else occurs by way of fervid superlatives.

A North American visitor to Montevideo saw some miniature flags in a bazaar window, which he decided to purchase as souvenirs. He bought the national flag and one carried by Artigas, "father of his country." He then asked for a replica of another historic flag of which he knew. "I don't have that one," the shopkeeper answered, "but those"—pointing to some others and chuckling—"are the important ones here, anyway." The foreigner didn't recognize them and inquired what they were. "Oh, those are the Nacional and Peñarol flags," was the answer.

That foreigner had been remiss. Anyone of as much as a week's residence in Montevideo is expected to have become an ardent fan of either Peñarol or Nacional. Neutrality is just a word for the dictionary.

The two clubs are venerable. About 1890, employees of the

then British-owned Uruguayan railways organized the Central
Railway Cricket Club in the vicinity of the company's yards
and repair shops in the Peñarol section of northwestern Montevideo. Cricket ultimately gave way to soccer and Britishers
to Uruguayans. About ten years later the Club Nacional de
Football was born. Its original players were students under
twenty. Soon Nacional shared the public favor with Peñarol
and today each is an institution. The names are known far
beyond Uruguay's borders.

Agitation for a big colosseum began about 1920 under the
aegis of the Football Association of Uruguay. Hundreds of
clubs, thousands of players, and hundreds of thousands of fans
were able to celebrate a grand climax a decade later. The great
bowl in Batlle Park seats 80,000 people (the extra ones for
that first big game just jammed in), and any Peñarol-Nacional
clash is almost automatically a sellout.

Uruguayan teams have several times won South American,
Olympic, or world's championships in soccer. That is enough to
make even a reasonably calm *latino* run a patriotic tempera-
ture, of course. In mid-1950, when an Uruguayan team won a
world's championship from Brazil at Rio several people died in
the victory celebration crush at Montevideo. The plane returning the team had to land at another field—the national airport
at Carrasco had been completely taken over by the milling
thousands of delirious fans.

So, it pays for a boy to bat and kick around even a home-
made ball with his head, knees, and feet. He may grow up to be
a *futbolista*—might even make Nacional or Peñarol!

The football season ends with December but by then the fun
is just beginning. Beaches are all ready to open. An international fishing contest is scheduled for various beaches. National
regattas are in the offing. Contests in horsemanship are coming
up at the military academy. Carrasco will soon be the scene of
an international shooting match. The big season at the Maroñas
track is about to open. Some international tennis matches are
due soon, and a national swimming competition at the Plaza
Trouville municipal pool. Then there are motor races and a
South American basketball tourney. A volleyball tournament,
some yacht races, and a national track and field meet follow.
Then it is time for an international swimming match, some pro-

fessional boxing contests, and a rodeo. Polo is coming along, and the hunting season will soon be open.

The maddest and gayest of all these gay, mad days are those of *carnaval*, just preceding Lent. Officially, it is three days; actually, Montevideo stretches it out a week longer. Rio's carnival is better advertised but Montevideo's sons and daughters of Momus don't yield to Rio, Lima, New Orleans, or any other city in the wholehearted and imaginative abandon with which they celebrate the pre-Lenten period.

Carnival is a maze of arches of colored lights over Montevideo's Main Street, the Avenida 18 de Julio. Carnival is endless public balls at the clubs, hotels, and theaters. Carnival is thousands of masked people, men and women, girls and boys, joining in confetti and serpentine battles, duels of flowers and perfumed water. Carnival is fantasy and floats, clowns and queens, masques and mummers. But, best of all, carnival is the *tablado*.

This all takes planning. Even spontaneous madness must be planned. Weeks and months before carnival season, city authorities have been organizing for the *tablados*. Each neighborhood section of the city builds a low platform or stage in some reserved section of a street; that stage is literally the *tablado*. On it, musicians, mummers, clowns, and all the local talent the neighborhood can muster will perform. The community *tablados* are prefaced by a grand parade of all the performers of the city, marching in seemingly endless columns down the capital's main thoroughfare.

At the end of the carnival season the city fathers award substantial prizes to the *tablados* judged best. Artistry in decoration and imagination and talent in performance have their material rewards, but the even greater compensation is in the glow of community pride and achievement. It is a significant development in terms of social psychology.

During the carnival season costumed mummers, dancers, and jugglers work a gentle racket by forming strictly amateur and none too melodious bands (running principally to drums) to serenade the residential sections. It is a sort of "treats or tricks" proposition and usually a few small coins are forthcoming, partly out of the gaiety of the season, partly to get the musicians to move on to the next block. The drumheads are nailed to the drums and so, if they need tightening to improve the tone, the practice is to build a small fire of papers in the gutter and allow the heat from it to stretch the head more tautly. Small boys continue the pleasant practice of serenading even after the regular carnival season ends, as if reluctant to abandon its carefree days for the psychological austerity of Lent.

Uruguay has learned to play. It also likes for its visitor to play, offering him every facility to enjoy playtime in playland.

# 6

<center>~~~~~~~~~~<br>~~~~~~~~~~</center>

# *Uruguay Has Two Tyrants*

Uruguay is a democratic country. It has freedom of speech, it respects civil liberties, it has an excellent voting record. Yet, it has two tyrants. They dominate, directly or indirectly, virtually all Uruguayan activity. Politics is to a considerable degree a product of their rule. The social landscape is largely conditioned by their continuance in Uruguay. They live in the country, but even the capital city of Montevideo lies at their mercy. Their names are Cattle and Sheep.

Travel almost anywhere over the Uruguayan countryside, sheep and cattle are in evidence. Journey back into Uruguayan history for three centuries and more, cattle and sheep, especially the former, are the pillars of the economy. Of hogs, goats, oxen, burros, there are few; hogs, for example, number only about 250,000. Of horses there are about half a million, but they are, by and large, simply an adjunct of the livestock industry. Uruguay has, for better or worse, an essentially monoculture economy. If sheep and cattle could vote, the human population of Uruguay would be hopelessly outnumbered in determining the country's destiny. For every man, woman, and child in Uruguay there are more than three cattle and more than nine sheep.[1] The Department of Montevideo, almost ex-

---

[1] The livestock census of May, 1951, showed 23,408,648 sheep and 8,154,-609 cattle. Sheep and cattle population in selected earlier years was as follows:

clusively urban, counted in 1951 only 11,094 cattle and no sheep; that of Tacuarembó in the north, 790,174 cattle and 2,297,802 sheep.

Natural conditions have been good to Uruguayan livestock. Native pasture is normally excellent. The rainfall, though irregular, averages from thirty-nine to forty-one inches annually. Temperatures in humid, subtropical Uruguay are almost always moderate; they usually range from 50° to 72° (Fahrenheit), and the lowest and highest ever recorded were 23° and 109.5°. Frosts are infrequent and light. Wild animals that might claim a toll of livestock have been very few indeed.

Soils in most parts of Uruguay are entirely adequate. The almost bottomless depths of soil in parts of the Argentine pampas are not found in Uruguay; rock outcroppings in the latter country are much more common. The thinner soils necessarily have an important bearing on the cultivation of crops but they are less important from the standpoint of grazing.

The physical and economic cards are stacked in favor of a livestock industry and against cropping. More than 90 per cent of Uruguay's area is agriculturally utilizable; less than 10 per cent of it is in crops.[2] Of the total value of Uruguay's

| Year | Sheep | Cattle |
|---|---|---|
| 1852 | 796,289 | 1,888,622 |
| 1860 | 1,989,929 | 3,632,203 |
| 1900 | 18,608,717 | 6,827,428 |
| 1908 | 26,286,296 | 8,192,602 |
| 1916 | 11,472,852 | 7,802,442 |
| 1924 | 14,443,341 | 8,431,613 |
| 1930 | 20,558,124 | 7,127,912 |
| 1937 | 17,931,327 | 8,296,890 |
| 1943 | 20,288,756 | 6,255,976 |
| 1946 | 19,559,325 | 6,883,811 |

[2] The breakdown of land use, according to the 1951 agricultural census, was as follows:

| Category | Acreage |
|---|---|
| Range grassland | 34,497,845 |
| Cultivated land | 3,024,184 |
| Land in fallow | 565,262 |
| Planted pastures | 1,168,270 |
| Natural woodland | 966,689 |
| Planted woodland | 233,082 |
| Vegetable gardens | 147,716 |
| Orchards and vineyards | 137,129 |
| total | 40,740,177 |

exports in 1950, agricultural products represented 97 per cent, worth 317,400,000 pesos. Of that sum, the value of the first three exports, all from the livestock industry, were: wool, 177,900,000 pesos; meat and its derivatives, 61,000,000 pesos; and hides and skins, 41,900,000 pesos. The total value of all agricultural produce (including livestock and wool) in 1951 was estimated at 588,000,000 pesos. The tyranny of cattle and sheep is a prosperity producing one, despite the fact that a preliminary estimate of the value of agricultural produce for 1952 dropped the figure about a hundred million pesos below that for 1951. It is by no accident or coincidence that the cabinet post having to do with the rural economy is not Agriculture and Livestock but rather Livestock and Agriculture (*Ganadería y Agricultura*).

Livestock—cattle, horses, sheep—were turned loose in the Banda Oriental, or colonial Uruguay, by the Spanish during the seventeenth century. They throve fabulously. Colonial Uruguay was indeed well characterized as the Age of Leather. Leather made much of the clothing, some of the furniture, and occasionally a part of a dwelling. Cattle skulls were used as seats. Cow dung served as fuel. The free-ranging gaucho was not merely the principal human cog in the Uruguayan economic mechanism for decades and generations, he was romanticized in song and story and gave rise to a whole literary genre. He was related to the vaquero of southern Brazil, the *sertanejo* of the Brazilian hinterland, the *llanero* of Venezuela, even to the cowboy of the western plains. "Wars" between cattlemen and sheepmen were less an element than in the western United States, but the gaucho had nothing but contempt for the city.

Early cattle skinners usually made camp along some Uruguayan stream where they established themselves for some three or four months in the late fall and winter. The camps were "staying places" and hence the people of Uruguay and other

| | | |
|---|---|---:|
| Sand dunes | | 61,646 |
| Rocky land | | 713,032 |
| Swamps | | 141,585 |
| Alkaline flats | | 21,860 |
| Lakes | | 58,411 |
| Roads, farmsteads, etc. | | 188,160 |
| | total | 1,184,694 |
| | grand total | 41,924,871 |

Platine regions called them *estancias*, from *estar* "to be (located or situated)." The "*estancia*" later gained a different connotation but the cattle industry thus contributed at an early day to the language. The gauchos would hamstring, kill, and skin all the available cattle in the vicinity and then move on to another location. By the middle of the eighteenth century most of Uruguay was under some sort of vague individual land claims. *Estancias*—estates, as the word had by then come to mean—were huge: of areas up to 250,000 acres.

This general picture of rural Uruguay continued essentially unchanged until the second half of the nineteenth century. Cattle were valued for their hides. Tallow and jerked meat—the *charqui* of the pampas or the jerky of the American Southwest; usually now called *tasajo*—were usable, but distinctly secondary, parts of the animal. The jerked meat played an interesting part in early international trade. It was sold in reasonably large quantities for consumption by slaves on the Brazilian and Caribbean sugar plantations. The opening of the Liebig meat-extract plant at Fray Bentos in 1863–65 may be said to mark the beginning of a modern period in the history of the Uruguayan cattle industry. Prior to that time the salting of beef had attained a small-scale importance because the meat of the tough, lean animals of the Uruguayan plains could be processed only by this means.

The fencing of the ranges (and the introduction of the barbed-wire fence), the development of refrigeration ships for the European trade, the improvement of breeds and the introduction of new ones, all these developments went hand in hand to remake the picture of the cattle industry in Uruguay in the second half of the nineteenth and first half of the twentieth centuries.

The Uruguayan cattle industry is inevitably compared or contrasted, or both, with that in Argentina. In general, the Argentine industry is in advance, both absolutely and relatively, of the Uruguayan. Argentine soils are deeper and richer with the result that grasses are better. Argentina has done more with stock breeding than has Uruguay. (And yet, a Hereford bull sold at the national livestock exposition at Montevideo on August 28, 1951, for a record price of 80,000 pesos or about $33,000.) In some respects Argentine feeding practices have been superior, especially in regard to the use of alfalfa. But Uruguay has, over a period of years, been second as a beef-exporting country only to the vastly larger Argentina.

In the latter part of the nineteenth century the *saladero* began to give way to the *frigorífico*. The former had salted the meat it processed; the *frigorífico* prepared chilled, frozen, and canned meats and hence demanded a better grade of beef. The development of the *frigorífico* meant the coming of big business to Uruguay. As the price of cattle increased, the meat-extract industry declined in importance because it was geared to a low-priced source of supply.

England provided the first and, indeed, most of the breeding stock introduced into Uruguay. The first Shorthorns were imported in 1859, the original Herefords about 1884; at present four-fifths of Uruguayan cattle are principally Hereford. There are now 80,579 registered Herefords and 15,439 registered Shorthorns in the country. The introduction of Zebu cattle is prohibited by law in order that a tropical breed, considered unadapted to Uruguay, will not become mixed with the established breeds. For many decades almost the whole emphasis in breeding was on beef cattle; no real dairy industry existed in Uruguay before about 1930 when considerable numbers of Holstein-Friesian cattle began to be imported from Argentina and the Netherlands.

The nature and extent of the livestock industry necessarily determine the pattern of landholding. It is impossible to separate cattle-raising areas from those given over to sheep since in most parts of Uruguay cattle and sheep graze together—*estancieros* claim it is better for both. The lands of Uruguay can be classified in other ways, however. The Río Negro, flowing across Uruguay from northeast to southwest, is a stock-raising demarcation line of sorts. South of the river is found virtually all of the relatively small amount of cropped land. South of the Río Negro is the better grazing land for fattening cattle. To the north lie the tick infested areas of Uruguay. To the north, also, are the bigger *estancias* and the better areas for breeding.

Although the era of the giant *estancia* has not entirely passed, Uruguay is not now to be considered as a nation of large farms. The agricultural census of 1951 showed 85,258 farm units. Almost three-fourths of them were holdings of under 250 acres each.[3] The three-fourths had less than one-tenth of the area of all farm units, however. The units of more than 12,500 acres were negligible in numbers but contained almost a fifth of the total area.[4] Perhaps a dozen individual or family holdings run more than 100,000 acres in extent. The Martiricorena lands in the Department of Artigas, the Romay Salvo *estancias* in Río Negro, and the Damboriarena holdings in Rivera, some of them almost corporate in character, are classic examples of the lordly domains which used to be more characteristic of the pattern of land tenure. Allegedly thirty-five proprietors own more than half of the Department of Artigas.[5]

It would be difficult to make any exact correlation between the size and character of *estancias* in Uruguay. In general, however, the rural units where a diversified or mixed farming is carried on have heretofore tended to be somewhat smaller; they are located chiefly in the better soils in western and southern Uruguay, particularly near Montevideo. The *estancias* devoted more exclusively to grazing, larger in size, are located principally in the poorer soils of central, northern, and eastern Uruguay. The area available for stock raising and cropping will be increased if and when an ambitious flood-control and drainage project, involving more than 2,200 square miles of

---

[3] The Uruguayan unit for agricultural area measurements is the hectare, which is here arbitrarily translated at 2.50 acres to preserve some degree of roundness.

[4] The breakdown was as follows:

| Size | | Number | % of number | Area | % of area |
|------|------|------|------|------|------|
| Under 12.5 | acres | 10,953 | 13 | 71,939 acres | |
| 12.5–25 | " | 11,117 | 13 | 189,350 " | 2 |
| 25–50 | " | 13,771 | 16 | 476,441 " | |
| 50–125 | " | 16,910 | 20 | 1,321,485 " | 3 |
| 125–250 | " | 10,375 | 12 | 1,809,127 " | 4 |
| 250–500 | " | 7,814 | 9 | 2,725,936 " | 7 |
| 500–1,250 | " | 7,241 | 9 | 5,611,875 " | 13 |
| 1,250–2,500 | " | 3,475 | 4 | 6,036,623 " | 15 |
| 2,500–6,250 | " | 2,452 | 3 | 9,409,969 " | 22 |
| 6,250–12,500 | " | 763 | | 6,381,672 " | 15 |
| 12,500–25,000 | " | 316 | 1 | 5,099,932 " | 12 |
| Over 25,000 | " | 71 | | 2,790,522 " | 7 |
| | | 85,258 | 100 | 41,924,871 | 100 |

[5] *El País* (Montevideo), Aug. 18, 1951, p. 3.

land in the eastern Departments of Rocha and Treinta y Tres, is completed.

Various causes contributed to a decline in the average size of land holdings. Two of major importance were the legal prohibition, adopted during the administration of President José Batlle y Ordóñez, on entailed estates and, second, the relative absence of the social pressures which have operated to maintain large *estancias* in Argentina as a matter of family pride.

The pendulum may now be swinging in the opposite direction, however. The long-range trend seems to be for holdings to become larger, especially in the mixed-farming areas where use of modern equipment and methods puts a premium on large-scale operations. This is statistically borne out by a comparison of the farm sizes reported in the 1951 agricultural census with those reported in the 1943 census. Thus, farms under 250 acres constituted 13 per cent of the area in 1943 but only 9 per cent in 1951; farms over 12,500 acres totaled 15 per cent of the area in 1943 but 19 per cent in 1951.

The pattern of land tenure in Uruguay is even yet rigid. It is one of the major points at which the socially and economically advanced program of the Uruguayan government, a program which has made the country's name a byword for intelligent progress, has lagged and stumbled. The 1951 agricultural census revealed that half of the 85,258 farm units were fully owned; this is probably a record. Tenant farming is especially prevalent in the mixed cropping and grazing areas northwest of Montevideo. Renters occupied 38 per cent of all farm units in 1937 but only 29 per cent in 1951. The increased ownership over fourteen years is to be credited primarily to greater general prosperity.

The position of the tenant depends upon his bargaining power vis-à-vis the landowner. If that does not exactly represent a bargain between a lion and a rabbit, it still places the tenant at a decided disadvantage. The large degree of farm tenancy has come about as the peon climbed the agricultural ladder to the level of a *medianero* or tenant farmer and found that there the ladder ended. The only legal guarantee made the sharecropper is an initial contract for four years which can be renewed for a like period. In a typical situation the sharecropper is provided with *estancia* land from which the *estan-*

*ciero* gets 30 per cent of the crop or livestock yield. The tenant must provide all the machinery or equipment he uses.

The result of this relative insecurity is that the tenant farmer tends to "mine" the soil, take the maximum return from it without improvements, and build the cheapest sort of housing. The advantage of the system, to the agricultural picture in general but especially to the *estanciero*, is that it provides a stabilized and adequate labor supply for the big operator.

Mechanization of the rural economy has proceeded, especially recently, about as far and as fast as is practicable. The number of tractors in use in the middle of 1950 was estimated at 9,000, almost three times the number used four years earlier. Uruguay now has a more favorable situation with respect to the mechanization of agriculture than any other country in South America.

Even without mechanization the labor needs on the part of the large-scale operator, especially if he concentrates on grazing, are not great. On a typical large *estancia* of, say, 65,000 or 70,000 acres the owner will carry on operations in perhaps four geographic areas. Each will be under the supervision of a *capataz* or foreman over livestock. Each of the foremen will have the assistance of a *puestero* (call him a ranger) and from fifteen to twenty peons or hired workers. Additional hands will be needed at sheepshearing time. If there is much cropping undertaken—and many *estancieros* prefer a rude system of rotation that alternates grazing and cropping—the crop foreman will have from ten to a hundred workers, depending on the seasonal work load. This means an average, then, of only about two employees (of all levels) per thousand acres; even a large *estancia*, consequently, may have very few permanent residents. It is a significant footnote to the sparseness of rural population in most parts of Uruguay.

The *puestero* is a peon who has climbed one step up the occupational ladder. He lives almost continuously in the saddle and his responsibilities are to check the livestock, repair fences, brand cattle, and vaccinate both cattle and sheep. He is the nearest institutional descendant of the gaucho that Uruguay now possesses but he has been fenced in, both literally and figuratively, to a degree that makes him but a pale reflection of the historic gaucho.

Cattle and sheep graze freely at all seasons of the year. Livestock gets almost no alfalfa or concentrates of any sort because range feeding is usually found adequate. This dependence on Nature can come a serious cropper when the *estanciero* is shortchanged by rainfall. A drought in 1916 resulted in the death of 1,000,000 cattle and 15,000,000 sheep; other heavy livestock mortality occurred for the same reason in 1942–43 and 1949–50. There are other hazards. Foot-and-mouth disease is widely prevalent but not virulent; its chief effect is not to kill the cattle but to keep down their weight. A little, but not enough, has been done to manufacture vaccines for it. A top-flight international agricultural mission which made a thorough study of the Uruguayan rural economy in 1950 concluded that losses, in reduced weights and deaths, from foot-and-mouth disease, tick fever, brucellosis, tuberculosis, and other livestock diseases were needlessly high.

Despite the various difficulties confronting the cattle industry, the slaughter has not shown enormous variations over about half a century. Since 1940 the slaughter has varied from high figures of 1,516,000 head in 1943, and an estimated 1,500,-000 in 1952, to lows of 922,000 head in 1945 and 930,000 in 1947. When there is a variation in the slaughter, it reflects weather conditions (especially droughts), diseases, international prices, a fluctuating practice of holding cattle off the market until they are as much as six years old, etc. The producers, except the small ones, generally sell their cattle at public auctions which become institutionalized social affairs of a sort. They are generally held in a community center and the neighborhood gathers to discuss business and politics and to eat the barbecued beef ribs and hard rolls (washed down with wine) which the *estanciero* has provided.

Who eats Uruguay's meat? In general, the country exports one-third and eats two-thirds of the roughly 190,000 tons of dressed meat it annually produces. Most of the exportable surplus of meat is sold under contract, much of it over a period of years to Great Britain. The United States has become an increasingly heavy purchaser since World War II. Montevideanos are heavy beef consumers. They have been estimated to eat more than a pound daily per capita and the annual needs of the city total about 450,000 head of cattle. Meat eating in

Montevideo thrives under governmentally fixed and relatively low prices. A period of inflation, when unfixed food prices are skyrocketing, simply turns the people more strongly toward a meat diet. The cattle slaughter in 1951 dropped off somewhat, however, with the result that Montevideo experienced some shortage of beef, which in turn caused minor black market operations on the city's outskirts.

The inhabitants of the capital will eat mutton when they can't get beef. The meat diet in the interior, on the other hand, runs more strongly to mutton; some *estancia* workers, it has been stated on excellent authority, actually eat the fantastic average of four pounds of meat daily. Few cattle are killed to be eaten on the *estancias* because the meat of the larger animal would spoil before being consumed and because the cattle are more expensive than the sheep. Beef is generally reserved for feast days, but beef consumption is increasing, both in Montevideo and the *campo*.

A systematically fostered Uruguayan dairy industry is less than a quarter of a century old. It now is based on about half a million head of dairy cattle, almost 80 per cent of which are in the Montevideo milkshed extending for about seventy-five miles west, north, and east of the capital. Milk production per cow is low: it is estimated not to exceed about five quarts daily on an annual basis. The dairy cow can't take the hard life sometimes facing her beef-producing cousin. Summer droughts and rainy winters at times pose a problem. Financial losses from foot-and-mouth disease are relatively much higher for dairy than for beef cattle. Still, the tastes of the Montevideo public have been educated to include more and more milk. Consumption more than doubled, within a dozen years, from roughly 16,000,000 gallons in 1936–37 to about 38,000,000 in 1948–49. A part of the explanation lies in the low fixed prices for milk and related dairy products. The government's double-barreled milk-pricing program—subsidies both to producer and consumer—meant a net loss to the government of about five cents a gallon.

The monopoly distribution agent in Montevideo is Conaprole (*Cooperativo Nacional de Productores de Leche*), which is not organized as a true co-operative but operates under an industrial privilege granted by the government. People in the

Ministerio de Instrucción Pública

*Avda. Agraciada leading to the Legislative Palace* (below), *an architectural landmark of the capital designed by Cayetano Moretti.*

Moore-McCormack Lines

*Juan Zorrilla de San Martín, Uruguay's great XIXth century Romantic poet.*

*Dancing the Pericón Nacional, inspired from gaucho folk music.*

interior buy milk in bulk from horse-drawn carts; how many germs they get with it is probably a matter of entire uncon-cern. For that matter, the international mission sponsored by the United Nations' Food and Agricultural Organization and the International Bank concluded that the average milk re-ceived by Conaprole for Montevideo distribution had a re-grettably low quality.

For two centuries wool has been one of Uruguay's most important products. Sheep were a tyrant in the colonial period as well as more recently. The first of them were introduced, about 1670, from Spain. The Spanish sometimes liked to do things the hard way: to bring the sheep to Uruguay they drove them over the Andes from Peru. Wool has always been the main concern of the sheep raising industry; even now the pro-duction of commercially sold lamb and mutton is only of minor importance. Most Uruguayan wool is of a fine grade; little carpet wool is ordinarily produced. The most popular breed of sheep is the Corriedale. Rapid progress has been made, espe-cially in recent decades, in improving breeds of sheep, although breeding to improve wool quality began as early as 1851.

Sheep, like cattle, get a more or less cavalier treatment on Uruguayan *estancias*. They graze freely, they get no concen-trated feeds, they have no sheepherders. A concession to science is made by dipping and deworming them. Beginning in October the fleecy gold begins to come in to the *estanciero* in the form of the annual wool clip, removed by power shearing. The ap-proximately 70,000 to 85,000 long tons of wool available each year will usually have a minimum value of about 90,000,000 pesos or, say, about $36,000,000, depending, of course, on the rate of exchange. This means that sheep are annually worth more than fourteen dollars to every man, woman, and child in Uruguay. Wool prices began to skyrocket in the second half of 1950, probably due principally to the Korean war, and the average price for that year was almost three times the price level of 1940; prices dropped sharply in 1951 but recovered later. Wool serves Uruguay well in the international markets because it is durable for shipment and, having high value in proportion to weight, easily pays its freight rates.

Economic Cassandras would have us believe that the devel-opment of orlon and other synthetic fibers may well spell the doom of the Uruguayan wool industry. They point to the blows earlier given by rayon and nylon to natural fibers. Those who know the wool industry in Uruguay and Argentina profess not to be alarmed, however. There may be an ultimate competition which will force prices down, to the advantage of the consumer, but growing populations and growing demands for wool for mixed-fiber textiles will make the industry indefinitely a pillar of the Uruguayan economy.

Cattle and sheep still remain enthroned, then, in Uruguay. That country has more of those animals per land area than any other in all of Latin America. Production costs are low and quality is comparatively high. Ranges are often overstocked, it is true. The foreign experts who studied Uruguay's rural economy in 1950 made some fundamental and broad recommendations for improvement but, basically, Uruguay's livestock industry appears as sound as its democracy.

The raising of crops offers other problems. Crop production has in general been primarily for domestic consumption and has kept pace with the increasing population. There is no evidence of population pressure on the land and malnutrition is never a national problem. In a situation like that of Japan, where population pressure requires the land to be intensively cultivated to feed the people, the problem is of one sort. Uruguay really presents the reverse of that: how to utilize ample land in the most effective way to get satisfactory returns. This fundamentally involves the pattern of population distribution.

Population is concentrated in the south of Uruguay. This has meant that crop raising, agriculture in a narrow or literal sense, has, almost perforce, been confined largely to the southern departments despite the occasional tendency of some *estancieros* to alternate grazing with cropping. Crop raising in Uruguay faces certain difficulties. The often thin soils are less suitable for crops than for pasturing. Soil nutrients, especially calcium and phosphates, are frequently depleted, and good techniques of farm management, including scientific and extensive fertilizing, are not widely enough practiced. Scientific soil conservation studies are less than a decade old in Uruguay and it has been estimated that three-fourths of the crop land needs such attention; even on natural grasslands considerable gullying and erosion exist because of overgrazing. Insect pests affect the crops, especially because there are virtually no winter freezes to keep such pests under partial control. A more serious difficulty is the erratic and unpredictable rainfall.

Crop raising is, then, somewhat of a gamble. The area in crops usually averages less than 5,900 square miles, which is barely more than 8 per cent of the country's total area. The area in a specific crop will vary greatly from one year to another, however, depending on the fluctuation in rainfall, the cost-price relationship, locust invasions, and other factors. Wheat, corn, and flax have been the chief crops. The acreage of the first of those has remained fairly constant; the other two have somewhat declined in area under cultivation. Uruguay now supplies all its own wheat needs and even exports small amounts from the approximately half million acres sown annually. It is a far and fortunate cry from the situation in 1946 when drought conditions forced Uruguay to try to buy Argentine wheat and the Perón government, wanting its pound of flesh, demanded payment in dollars. An emergency shipment from the United States relieved Uruguay from a tight situation but taught the importance of self-sufficiency. Flax production, about 100,000 long tons annually, is used for linseed oil rather than fiber.

Until recent years relatively little attention was paid to the introduction of improved seed varieties. The work of Uruguay's one agricultural experiment station, north of Colonia, is now beginning to change that picture.

Truck farming is almost entirely economically tributary to Montevideo. It shows a long-range tendency to increase. Unpredictable rains are causing truck farmers to drill deep wells for irrigation. Only seven-tenths of one per cent of all Uruguayan land in agricultural use is devoted to producing vegetables, fruits, and wine grapes, but this infinitesimal fraction of the land has usually been responsible for from 17 to 20 per cent of agricultural income. It has been estimated that as recently as 1949 the value of such products probably exceeded that of all slaughter animals sold. Government agencies have encouraged experimentation with sugar cane and rice culture in the northwestern departments. Sugar production increased from about 1,500 long tons in 1947 to 5,850 tons in 1950. The northwestern corner of the country also has a growing importance as a citrus area. The raising of sunflowers has recently increased in southern Uruguay. Despite the greater variety and importance of fruit and vegetable production, Uruguay still has to import a number of such products and other foods: the ubiquitous yerba maté, coffee, bananas, cacao, sugar, and potatoes.

Uruguay has almost no indigenous forest. Only about 3 per cent of its area even now carries trees, and most of them, or their ancestors, have been hand planted. Chief among these species are eucalyptus and pines; in addition there are willows, acacias, and poplars. The principal uses of such trees as Uruguay has are for firewood, fence posts, and windbreaks. Logs and lumber for construction purposes have to be imported, principally from Brazil and Paraguay. Only in the approximately 42,000 acres of state-owned forests is any scientific arboriculture practiced. The government as yet has done nothing to carry out high-level, scientific recommendations for a large-scale afforestation policy.

Uruguay has two prominent organizations of livestock farmers, the Rural Federation and the Rural Association. Both are organizations of *estancieros*, of, by, and for the big operators. The Federation is the more politically minded of the two, and many of its members are congressmen or important officeholders in the executive branch of the government. The Federation frequently has a considerable influence on legislation and the government's agricultural policy; it has been especially concerned with policies affecting commercial agriculture and meat production and marketing. The Rural Association functions as an official registry body for blooded and pedigreed livestock; pedigree records have been kept since 1887.

A relatively insignificant but recently spectacular organization is the Federal League of Rural Action. Its members are largely businessmen and *estancieros* described as reactionary and its chief activity in 1951 was a series of daily radio broadcasts by one "Chicotazo" by which it sought, unsuccessfully, to influence wool prices and marketing policies.

Another small organization, and one with relatively little prestige and influence, is the Uruguayan Grange Confederation. It is composed of small farmers carrying on diversified operations, principally within about 125 miles of Montevideo.

Its political concern is chiefly with governmental legislation and policies affecting production and marketing problems of the fruit, truck-crop, poultry, and egg producers. Another (and influential) organization is the National Commission of Rural Development, which represents the interests of many small farm granges and similar organizations.

An Uruguayan equivalent of the 4-H Clubs is the *Movimiento de Juventud Agraria* (*Farm Youth Movement*) which operates through the rural schools on a volunteer basis. It began only about 1946 but in order to encourage it the Uruguayan congress appropriated 50,000 pesos in July, 1950, for its support.

In a country where governmental regulation is as common as it is in Uruguay it is not to be expected that the rural economy would be free from it, even though the government's orientation has been more toward urban problems. The recent tendency has been for the government to participate more rather than less in the farmer's affairs. Most regulative activity having to do with stock raising and agriculture has been in the area of prices: production and consumption subsidies. The subsidy program has been a flexible one and has been definitely used by the government as a major instrument of policy. Its main professed purpose has been to promote small and medium-sized farms and to encourage production of fruits and vegetables. Viewed from another angle, the objective has been to boost production beyond what the natural prices obtainable would promote or to provide consumers (usually in Montevideo) with staple commodities below the cost of production. After the near-disastrous experience with Argentine wheat in 1946, the government began subsidy of wheat production to achieve the now successful goal of self-sufficiency in that grain.

The whole subsidy program has been severely criticized by foreign experts as an artificial, unsound, and jerry-built structure. It is claimed that the net effect of the program is to distribute income (with the taxpayer footing the ultimate net bill) rather than to curtail costs or modernize the food-producing industry. Critics argue that the subsidy pattern establishes the philosophy that "the government owes the farmer a living," that it consequently lessens rural initiative, and that it contributes to inflation and increases the price of imported items. Subsidies, they say, are potentially dangerous on an economic basis but are politically expedient as an easy way of placating pressure groups (usually consumers). The economic dangers of the subsidy program were vividly illustrated in 1951 when subsidy obligations ran about 38,000,000 pesos more than the funds (chiefly from foreign exchange profits) available to pay them. The result was a necessary consideration, late in 1951 and early in 1952, of a retrenchment in the program.

Admittedly, the program has been expensive: the ministry of finance estimated that total subsidy payments in 1950 were more than 60,000,000 pesos, including 25,000,000 for wheat, 20,000,000 for meat, and 11,000,000 for milk.

The rural economy has usually been profitable for Uruguay and has contributed substantially to giving it the second highest per capita income in Latin America, a figure that United Nations experts estimated in 1950 to be $331 per year.[6] The major part of the investment and of the profits, although not a proportionately large share of the latter, are, of course, in stock raising. The value of Uruguayan ranch land has been estimated at 1,200,000,000 pesos; of the country's cattle, 500,-000,000 pesos; of the sheep, 200,000,000 pesos; and of the buildings, fences, and other improvements, 100,000,000 pesos. The industry can consequently be appraised at some 2,000,-000,000 pesos or, say (depending on exchange rates), $800,-000,000. It is a tidy sum in any man's language. *Estancieros* have usually earned at least 7.5 per cent on their invested capital; many in recent years have had a 10 per cent return or better.

Perhaps, then, we should relabel Cattle and Sheep. They have been good to Uruguay. They turn out to be less tyrants than benevolent despots.

[6] For comparable purposes the figures for the other countries of the hemisphere were: United States, $1453; Canada, $870; Argentina, $346; Venezuela, $322; Cuba, $296; Chile, $188; Panama, $183; Colombia, $132; Costa Rica, $125; Mexico, $121; Brazil, $112; Peru, $100; El Salvador, $92; Nicaragua, $89; Paraguay, $84; Honduras, $83; Guatemala, $77; Dominican Republic, $75; Bolivia, $55; Ecuador, $40; Haiti, $40.

# 7

~~~~~~~~
~~~~~~~~

*Montevideo Is Manufacturing*
*and Business*

The tourist—or, for that matter, the permanent native resident—walking about the narrow streets of Montevideo's Old City is not aware that he is traversing a funnel. The configuration of a funnel is not physically apparent, even from a high-flying airplane. Figuratively, however, the Old City is the narrow inlet and outlet of the economic life of Uruguay. The tip of the funnel is the port of Montevideo; its valve is the multi-storied *aduana* or customs house. Through the port flow more than three-fourths of Uruguay's imports and exports. We have already seen that in the Old City are located the shipping firms, the banks, the stock exchange, the commercial houses which regulate that flow of goods and materials.

If the figure be changed, the Old City becomes at one and the same time the nerve center and the heart of economic Uruguay; through its streets as arteries pulses the economic lifeblood of the country; over its telephone wires as nerves pass the messages which control the nation's economic activity.

In terms of political expression Uruguay's capital city is Government. In economic terms it is Business, which is to say, in large measure, Trade and Manufacturing. Uruguay is still, of course, to be labeled a pastoral and agricultural country, with those tyrants sheep and cattle its basic economic pillars. Montevideo employs those pillars in building its own economic edifice, and the superstructure becomes industry and commerce.

It was calculated a few years ago (when the Uruguayan population was estimated at 2,350,000) that the number of employed people in the whole country was 776,000 or almost exactly one-third of the population. Of the roughly three-quarters of a million of employed persons almost exactly half were estimated to be concerned with livestock and agriculture, about one-fourth with trade and industry, approximately a tenth with government, a twentieth with construction work, and a twenty-fifth with transportation and communications.[1]

If we assume that none of those directly engaged in work with livestock and agriculture live in Montevideo but that nine-tenths of those concerned with merchandising, manufacturing, and government and three-fourths of all persons occupied with the other categories are residents of the capital, and if we further assume that the ratio of employed persons to total population is logically somewhat higher for Montevideo (say two-fifths instead of one-third), we arrive at a population figure of about 830,000 for the capital city. It is a figure very closely approximating current direct estimates of Montevideo's population.

About the only industrial activity outside of Montevideo, and most of it is distinctly small-scale, is at Fray Bentos, Paysandú, Salto, Canelones, Mercedes, and Puerto Sauce.

At any rate, an estimate of some third of a million employed persons in Montevideo necessarily presupposes an important role for both commerce and industry. Insofar as this involves a considerable degree of industrialization, it is the more surprising because Uruguay suffers in even exaggerated form several of the general handicaps which afflict Latin America as a whole in its almost desperate struggle to industrialize. In other respects, however, Uruguay is at an advantage as against other Latin American countries.

Among the elements which must be present and intricately

[1] More specific figures and percentages were: livestock and agriculture, 385,000 (49.7 per cent); merchandising, 100,000 (12.8 per cent); manufacturing, 90,000 (11.6 per cent); government, 76,000 (9.8 per cent); construction, 38,000 (4.9 per cent); transportation and communication, 31,000 (4.0 per cent); other activities, 56,000 (7.2 per cent).

geared together before a large-scale and especially a heavy industry can be successfully built are capital, raw materials, power supply, labor supply, industrial know-how, markets, and an adequate transportation system. Uruguay has or can easily attract ample supplies of capital, either domestic or foreign. It is singularly lacking in such important raw materials as iron and manganese, copper and aluminum, sulfur and rubber. The usual sources of industrial power—coal, petroleum, and hydroelectric power—are either absent or in woefully short supply in Uruguay; only four of the small northern Latin American states, for example, have a smaller hydroelectric potential than Uruguay. Labor supply involves an adequate reservoir of man power, preferably reasonably well fed and educated; Uruguay's population is small, but there is no complaint about the satisfactory filling of stomachs and minds. No problem is presented with regard to industrial know-how by Uruguay's intelligent and adaptable population. Markets, domestic, at least, depend on the size of the population and on its purchasing power; Uruguay's population, though small, has a relatively high purchasing capacity. The country's transportation system is reasonably good; compared with that of many Latin American countries it is excellent.

All factors taken into account, then, the shape of Uruguay's not inconsiderable industry is agriculturally determined. Uruguay's chief manufacturing industries are those processing some form of agricultural product, most of it of national origin. In 1947 the number employed in industries dependent on agriculture was almost two-thirds of the total employed in Uruguayan industry, and the gross value of production in such establishments was more than four-fifths of the total gross value.[2] The role of Uruguayan industry in the foreseeable future appears to be, then, in the processing of agricultural products and the manufacture of consumer goods for the domestic market.

The circumstances further, and in greater detail determine, the shape of Uruguayan industry. With a small population, a relatively high and widely distributed purchasing power, and a considerably developed though not chauvinistic sense of economic nationalism it is logical to anticipate that the second

[2] George Wythe, *Industry in Latin America* (New York, 1949), p. 130.

type of industry referred to above, *i.e.*, the making of consumer goods for the domestic market, would be primarily small-scale industry. The probability of this result in industrial organization is at least presumptively borne out by the 1936 industrial census (the latest one taken) which indicated that of a total of 11,470 manufacturing establishments no fewer than 10,374, or just over nine-tenths, employed fewer than nine workers.

The other portion of the picture is determined by the fact that the overwhelmingly pastoral economy of Uruguay produces relatively enormous supplies of wool, meat, hides, and skins for export. The industries growing out of this situation will, by the same token, presumably be few in number but much larger scale in operation. The same industrial census showed ninety-nine, or less than seven-eighths of 1 per cent, of the establishments making use of 100 or more workers. The statistics would be shown to have changed in detail by a later industrial census, but doubtless the proportions would be much the same, as would the deductions to be drawn from them. Dr. George Wythe, the foremost authority on Latin American industry, concludes that only a little more than a fourth of the industrial workers were employed in good-sized factories and that about half of these, or some 12,500, were in the single category of meat-processing plants.

It is the meat-packing and refrigerating plants that are symbolic of Uruguayan industry. A meat-processing factory was also the parent, or grandparent, of all modern Uruguayan industry. The Liebig Meat Extract Company of London established its famous plant at Fray Bentos on the Uruguay River in 1863–65. The meat-extract industry throve on cheap cattle, and as the quality and the price of cattle increased, that type of processing declined until it now has dropped to a relatively unimportant point.

The same course of ascendancy and decline characterized the jerked-beef industry. This form of processing, industrial descendant of the colonial preparation of *charqui* or *tasajo* for consumption by Brazilian and Caribbean slaves many generations ago, also prospered on a supply of cheap beef, often stringy and tough. The *saladeros* which prepared the jerked and salted meat were the backbone of the processing industry in the nineteenth century and at times used two-thirds of the cattle raised in the country. The gradually improving quality of Uruguayan beef spelled potential doom for the *saladero*, however, and by the early twentieth century both the Brazilian and Cuban markets were lost because of tariff walls and other obstacles. The industry inevitably passed to the present form of meat processing by the *frigorífico*.

The *frigorífico*, which is distinctly a large-scale type of operation, dates from 1904. At present one British-owned, the "Anglo" *frigorífico*, two American, Armour and Swift, and the Uruguayan government's Frigorífico Nacional (or, to use the common practice of telescoping words, the Frigonal) almost completely monopolize the canning, chilling, and freezing of meat.[3] The first three are concerned primarily with the export trade and the Frigonal with the domestic market, especially that in Montevideo. The *frigoríficos* operate by distinctly modern industrial methods and, while their production falls much short of their larger-scale counterparts in Argentina, they form a type of industry of which Uruguay may well be proud. The four *frigoríficos* have a capacity of some 4,000 cattle and 7,000 sheep a day; mutton is a far less important product of the industry, however, than is beef in its various forms. As by-products the *frigoríficos* produce beef extract, fats, dried blood, guano, glue, and others—using everything but the moo and the baa, as a North American packing-house man might put it.

The food wealth of the sea has been tapped by Uruguay but with only a minimum of success. One of the government's autonomous entities or public corporations is the Servicio Oceanográfico y de Pesca, or Soyp for short, which was dedicated to the end of providing abundant and cheap fish for the Uruguayan table. To date, however, the people have refused to become fish conscious: the annual per capita consumption as recently as 1949 was only about three and a half pounds. Soyp's canning of fish and preparation of fish oil and meal has definitely not been big business nor has it been financially profitable.

The government's successful efforts to stimulate wheat production have naturally opened the way to increased milling ac-

[3] The Anglo *frigorífico* ceased operations, at least temporarily, in 1952, because of the difficulty of contending with governmental and economic obstacles.

tivity. Most of the wheat flour mills—rice and corn mills, too, for that matter—are small-scale establishments. Montevideo's domestic cuisine puts a premium on vegetable oils—a glance at the shelves of half a dozen neighborhood *almacenes* would convince one that the Uruguayan navy could be floated on a sea of vegetable oil. Its processing, principally from sunflower seed and peanuts, is really a war-born industry though the shutting off of olive oil imports during the Spanish Civil War was a contributing factor. Packaged food production is increasing in Uruguay though the Montevideano and, needless to say, his country cousin eat much less out of tin cans, cellophane bags, and cardboard cartons than do their North American opposite numbers.

Beverages, especially wine and beer, are made in quantities large enough to supply the Uruguayan demand. It is Uruguayan-grown grapes and barley that furnish the raw materials. Some 3,000 tons of locally grown sugar are refined annually—only about 2 or 3 per cent of what Uruguay uses—but if governmental stimulus to cane growing in the northwest proves successful, the raw material sources, hitherto limited to beets grown in two southern departments, will be considerably augmented.

Since wool is Uruguay's most valuable dollar export, it is conceivable that a gigantic woolen textile industry might emerge. There is such an industry but it does not deserve that optimistic adjective even though the more starry-eyed Uruguayans look forward to the day when all Uruguayan wool will be consumed locally, none exported. That day seems remote. Yarn making, knitting, and weaving received a wartime lift in Uruguay because of the difficulty of importing textiles. Uruguayan tastes still run to English woolens, however, and some Montevideanos will tell you that a suit made of Uruguayan-woven cloth will sell more readily if the maker or the merchant has sewed an "English" label on the inside pocket!

Most of the wool fabrics woven in Montevideo's mills are the lower- and medium-priced grades and they are now to some extent protected by tariffs. The early postwar industry counted over 60,000 spindles and a production of more than 6,000,-000 square yards of worsted and woolen fabrics and some 3,850 tons of woolen yarn.

Cotton weaving—most of the raw cotton is imported from Paraguay—is of long standing in Uruguay, but spinning was developed only during World War II. The finer cotton fabrics and yarns are imported, but the Uruguayan industry in the early postwar period included some 47,000 spindles and 1,100 looms and produced about 3,300 tons of fabrics and 4,600 tons of carded yarns.

Uruguay has long since given up making houses, doors, beds, and rope of leather, as was common in the early colonial period, but with hides and skins still among the country's foremost exports it stands to reason that much leather is even yet available for shoes. Uruguay manufactures them to the number of about a million pairs a year.

Other kinds of manufactures are numerous. The pacesetter in chemical manufacturing is the government's Institute of Industrial Chemistry which began during World War I as an experimental establishment but, because of the wartime inability to import needed chemicals, had to go into the manufacturing business. Gasoline and alcohol are now—and cement will later be—produced by the autonomous entity Ancap—the Administración Nacional de Combustibles, Alcohol y Portland. Funsa (the Fábrica Uruguaya de Neumáticos, S. A.) carries on a profitable business making tires, inner tubes, rubber sheeting, garden hose, and other rubber products; its capital is Uruguayan, but a large North American rubber company provides technical direction. Matches (not one of the manufactured products of which Uruguay can be proudest!) are all locally made. Metal working, electrical appliances, glassware, building materials, fertilizers, paint, paper, cigarettes, and pharmaceutical products provide other sorts of industrial activity.

If there is an economic elite or aristocracy in democratic Montevideo, it is composed, not of bored *estancieros* who have sought the more varied and attractive life of the city, but of the factory owners and industrialists who make the considerable variety of products suggested above. Many of these industrial barons—the scale of Uruguayan industry scarcely suggests a higher rank in the peerage—are of Uruguayan nationality; a few are of foreign birth or at least ancestry. Uruguayans, or at any rate Montevideanos, have not had the fear of, or at least the distaste for, industrial enterprise and investment which has characterized the wealthy class in many other Latin American lands.

In the other pan of the scales of industrial personnel is the laboring class. This group has been a politically favored segment of the Uruguayan population for most of the years of the twentieth century but much of the organization of labor has been of somewhat later growth.

It is true that the first Uruguayan labor unions date back as far as 1895. Some of the early ones were organized by European immigrants and followed either an anarcho-syndicalist or a Socialist line. The government at that time had no especial smiles for labor, and workingmen's unions did not prosper. President José Batlle y Ordóñez in the early twentieth century reversed the governmental attitude and established a policy which has since been maintained. Batlle's spectacular campaign for establishment of the eight-hour industrial working day, culminating successfully in the law of November 17, 1915, did much to encourage the more extensive organization of labor. Despite Batlle's dominance of his own Colorado party, that political group, as well as the major opposition party, the Blancos, took for a long time a dim view of labor unionization for fear that, if well organized, labor might form a third major political party with heavy voting power. As late as 1929 the number of union members totaled only about 25,000.

More recently, labor organizations have grown and prospered. The parent and largest of the now existing major organizations is the Unión General de Trabajadores. The U.G.T. dates back to 1940 and it has a mid-century membership of from 35,000 to 40,000 from some thirty unions. Enrique Rodríguez, a textile union representative, who has recently been its secretary, carried into it a Communist program; he was at one time a Communist deputy in congress. The principal international affiliations of the U.G.T. have been with the Confederación de Trabajadores de Latino-América, the famous CTAL dominated by the Mexican leftist, Vicente Lombardo Toledano. The CTAL has not spoken for Uruguayan labor as a whole, but the U.G.T. has occupied a strategic position in Uruguayan labor politics and has exercised considerable leverage and nuisance value. Communist efforts, through the C.G.T., to interject international politics into local Montevideo strikes and other labor troubles have sometimes backfired. In general, Communist influence in Uruguayan labor groups has declined but not disappeared.

As Montevideo workers increasingly came to realize that the U.G.T. had primarily political interests and would not hesitate to sacrifice labor if necesary, the union began (by 1951) to lose its hold over them and even to show some signs of disintegrating. A competing organization, the militantly anti-Communist Confederación General de Trabajo, was formed at the end of 1950, but it failed to gain much of the ground the U.G.T. lost. The C.G.T. soon developed a reputation for being pro-Perón, and many of its members, never more than 3,000, began falling away from it.

The most recent general labor organization in Uruguay is the Confederación Sindical del Uruguay. The C.S.U. has successfully steered a course between the lures of Communism and peronismo and has affiliated with the International Federation of Free Trade Unions and its hemispheric branch, the Organización Regional Interamericana de Trabajadores or O.R.I.T. Some of the most important and democratic unions, *e.g.*, that of the meat workers, have remained unaffiliated with any of the general organizations. The large and strategically placed dockworkers' group is syndicalist dominated.

Uruguayan laws give unions full rights to organize, assemble, and strike. The strike is legally prohibited to organizations of public employees but has been used by them with impunity. Through the years, as the government has designedly expanded its industrial and commercial enterprises, it has come increasingly to face a dilemma with regard to organized labor: the government's consistent attitude has been pro-labor, but it has itself become more and more an employer of labor; the two attitudes have at times come into basic conflict.

Uruguayan wages are determined piecemeal and with much government intervention. Salary councils and conciliation tribunals have been important cogs in the process but have not worked with complete success. In regard to both apparent and real wages, most Uruguayan workers have been generally better off than their opposite numbers in other Latin American countries, though in a less favorable position than their cousins in the United States.

Instances of governmentally decreed monthly minimum wages in 1951 were: for San José motion-picture theater managers, first operators, ticket distributors, and ushers, respectively: 319.25, 169, 108.75, and 72.50 pesos; for Fray Bentos retail merchandising managers, bookkeepers, clerks, delivery boys under fifteen years of age, window dressers, and cleaners: 300, 210, 85, 40, 125, and 55 pesos; for waiters, garage attendants, night watchmen, managers, and cleaners in Montevideo houses of assignation: 170, 160, 160, 350, and 80 pesos; [4] for general foremen, cutting foremen, finishing section helpers, and skilled designers in a Montevideo shoe manufacturing shop: 339, 274, 232, and 430 pesos. First-class mechanics, painters, electricians, carpenters, turners, and smiths were getting 8.50 pesos and ordinary laborers six pesos daily in 1950; stevedores received 5.80 daily and first-class stevedore foremen twenty pesos daily and double that amount for the night shift.

Strikes have been widely used by Uruguayan labor in recent years. Both the government and the public, with the former looked to for immediate relief by all elements and the latter footing the ultimate bills, have been plagued by crippling strikes of textile workers, bus drivers, Ancap employees, meat workers, and others. Spiraling inflation has been an understandable cause of many strikes, but some of the blame must be charged to a certain degree of immaturity and irresponsibility on the part of labor. Labor has, however, repeatedly won piecemeal wage increases. There is evidence, too, that the diet of at least Montevideo workers has improved.

The freedom of Uruguayan labor unions from legal regulation has traditionally been remarkably complete: no laws have been adopted to control or regulate unions in any way. The government has long considered a law to make it more difficult for unions to engage in political activity, to assure a worker's freedom to join or remain outside of a union, and to limit undemocratic elements within unions. The opposition of organized labor, based upon the assumption that any regulation is bad, has thus far been sufficient to prevent enactment of such legislation. There has been little governmental effort to protect the interests of the employer as against those of labor.

That Uruguay is one of the world's most advanced labora-

[4] *Diario Oficial,* No. 13331, April 30, 1951.

tories for political, social, and economic experimentation is well known. The economic policies of the government have been concerned in part with industrial activity to the end both that inexpensive basic products might be made available for Uruguayans and that dependence on foreign sources of supply would be lessened. From a strictly accounting point of view the government's experience has been varied. Some government industrial and business activities have operated regularly at a loss and have been maintained only by subsidies; other enterprises have consistently returned handsome profits.

This aspect of the whole question of government economic policy has developed two opposed, and quite conscious and vocal, schools of thought. The one maintains that government enterprises of the sort should plow back all profits into extending and/or lowering prices of their respective services or products. The other holds that such activities should be operated on a strictly business basis with the profits being used for general governmental purposes.

The usual device employed by the government for operating its industrial enterprises (as well as certain commercial, financial, and cultural activities) has been the autonomous entity or public corporation. Each has operated under a semi-independent bipartisan board of directors and hence has had more freedom from direct legislative or executive control or interference than would otherwise be true.

The prototype of Uruguayan industrial autonomous entities is Ancap. Its creation, on October 15, 1931, resulted from a long campaign, spearheaded chiefly by Batlle, to break the virtual private monopoly of the manufacture and sale of alcohol. The law also authorized Ancap to refine and distribute petroleum products and to manufacture cement. The initial emphasis was on manufacture of alcohol and alcoholic beverages; Ancap became an important maker of *caña*, an inexpensive white rum described as "the Uruguayan national drink" (though if other than alcoholic potables be included, yerba maté would undoubtedly take first place).

Ancap's emphasis was later put on the refining of petroleum and the sale of gasoline. It now monopolizes the refining of crude petroleum but controls only about half the volume distribution of gasoline; the other half is shared by Standard Oil, Texaco,

Shell, and Atlantic. The manufacture of cement has not yet been monopolized by Ancap. It does, however, exercise a monopoly over the importation and sale of coal.

Ancap has won a solid and respected place in the whole picture of Uruguayan industry. Its competitors charge that it operates only by virtue of a large annual governmental subsidy, but their charges have been mild, and Ancap, on its part, has not chosen to ride roughshod over all private competition. A former Uruguayan president, Baltasar Brum, perhaps the next greatest after Batlle, said of Ancap twenty years ago: "It is one of the finest economic achievements of recent times in Latin America. It is a step to the economic independence of Uruguay." [5]

The government's tariff policy has been geared primarily to revenue production, but with the growth of industry it has increasingly come to have protective rates as well. Not only have "infant industries" been given direct tariff protection but Uruguayan industry has been further encouraged by tariff exemptions on needed foreign raw materials, machinery, railroad equipment, etc. The legal device of an "industrial privilege" grants a new manufacturing industry exemption for a nine-year period from payment of certain internal taxes and, wholly or partially, from customs duties on imported materials or equipment. An Uruguayan economist estimated soon after the government's 1936 industrial census that about one-seventh of the country's manufacturing was uneconomic and existed only by virtue of tariff protection.

The shape of Uruguayan trade is the product of other economic factors, by far the most important of which is livestock production. Uruguay consumes only a small part of its production of wool, hides, and skins, and only about two-thirds of its meat. The remainders are available for export. In most years the products named have constituted roughly 97 per cent of the country's exports. The major imports have been petroleum and coal (in view of Uruguay's lack of fuel supplies), raw materials and machinery for Montevideo's factories, and consumer goods and vehicles.

Uruguay has usually had a favorable balance of trade; in

[5] Quoted in Simon G. Hanson, *Utopia in Uruguay* (New York, 1938), pp. 97–98.

only two years between World Wars I and II (1929 and 1931, when depression readjustments affected it adversely) was it unfavorable. During the 1920's the United States was Uruguay's principal supplier but European countries were the chief buyers. The destination of Uruguay's exports, however, showed a far greater disproportion than did the source of her imports. In the depression years of the thirties the source of imports showed a tendency to shift slightly to Europe.

Britain bought heavily of Uruguayan meat during World War II but could export very little to balance her purchases. The result was the accumulation by Uruguay of a sterling balance of about £17,000,000. The war blocked virtually all trade with continental Europe and hence the United States became the most important buyer of Uruguayan wool. In the post-World War II period most Uruguayan wool continued to go to the United States and most meat to Great Britain; the United States, however, has recently bought heavily of Uruguayan canned meat. Higher wool prices and increased United States purchases after the outbreak of the Korean war contributed to the establishment of a dollar balance of more than $100,000,000 by the end of 1950. At the same time, sterling balances were declining because of Uruguay's heavy purchases from Britain and her acquisition of the British-owned railways.

The government has closely controlled the flow of foreign exchange for trade purposes, operating through the Bank of the Republic. The bank sets peso exchange rates for different classifications of imports and exports and determines the amount of foreign exchange periodically available for use.

Uruguay and the United States signed a reciprocal trade agreement on July 21, 1942. Recent bilateral trade treaties have been negotiated with various states including Belgium, Brazil, Czechoslovakia, France, Italy, Japan, the Netherlands, and Western Germany. Some of the European arrangements involved barter deals—for Italian tractors and Yugoslavian lumber, for example. Exports to the United States have been additionally valued recently because the resulting dollar exchange was usable in any markets.

Uruguay's total foreign trade has not at any time seemed enormous, but compared to that of the other Latin American countries it has measured up well. A study made a few years ago by the United States Tariff Commission showed the value of Uruguayan foreign trade to be in seventh position among the Latin American group of states although the population rank was only thirteenth among the twenty. Total imports in 1948 were valued at $200,430,000 and exports at $178,938,-000. This unfavorable balance of about $21,500,000 is one of the few instances when the net result has been in the red for Uruguay; by 1950 imports were valued at $200,900,000 and exports at $254,300,000. Per capita imports in 1948 were valued at $85.30 and exports at $76.15.[6] The principal suppliers in that year, with the percentages of Uruguayan imports which each provided, were: United States, 33.7; Great Britain and Northern Ireland, 12.1; Brazil, 9.8; Argentina, 8.3; and Belgium, 4.6. The chief buyers and the percentages of exports which they took, respectively, were: United States, 28.4; Great Britain and Northern Ireland, 18.2; Belgium, 8.9; the Netherlands, 7.2; Italy, 6.8; Brazil, 5.6; and Argentina, 2.3. The United States has consistently led both categories.

It might seem odd at first thought that Uruguay trades no more than it does with its immediate neighbors, Argentina and Brazil. An important part of the explanation as it involves Argentina is the competitive nature of the Argentine and Uruguayan economy. Lack of good overland transportation between Uruguay and Brazil retards trade between those countries. Montevideo early in 1941 hosted a first Economic Conference of the River Plata, attended by representatives from Argentina, Bolivia, Brazil, Paraguay, and Uruguay. The conference was aimed at the possibility of organizing a customs union among the states represented. That objective was not realized, but several new bilateral trade treaties were negotiated in consequence of the conference. An Uruguayan-Brazilian barter arrangement concluded April 14, 1952, provided for Brazilian acquisition of 20,000 tons of Uruguayan frozen and chilled beef, 40,000 tons of wheat, and 80,000 tons of wheat flour in exchange for Brazilian coffee, yerba maté, cocoa, lumber, etc.

[6] For comparative purposes the per capita imports and exports of certain other countries in 1948 were: Argentina, $92.75 and $101.15; Brazil, $22.90 and $24.00; Chile, $47.50 and $58.20; Cuba, $101.55 and $136.65; Haiti, $9.20 and $8.90; Mexico, $21.45 and $19.35; Venezuela, $150.80 and $221.35; and the United States, $48.60 and $83.33.

A not completely orthodox item in the trade picture, but one which normally forms an element of real importance in Uruguay's balance of payments, is the tourist traffic. The attractions of Montevideo and, above all, those of the incomparable beaches along the southern and eastern shores of the country customarily draw tourists by the tens of thousands. In 1949, for example, 184,859 tourists entered the country. The large majority of them, however, usually come from across the river in Argentina; but as has been pointed out earlier, the austerity program later adopted in Argentina, plus that government's successive reprisals against Uruguay, later reduced the flood of Argentine tourists to a trickle. Brazil may provide at least a partial revival of the tourist traffic.

Two essential handmaidens of the economy of Montevideo, both of industry and trade, are the banking structure and the transportation and communications system. Both are oriented almost entirely in terms of Montevideo.

The great cornerstone of the Uruguayan financial system is the state-owned Bank of the Republic. Its huge, classic edifice deep in the heart of the Old City is a pillar of respectability and figurative as well as literal solidity. Established in 1896, it was completely nationalized in 1911 and now operates several branches in Montevideo and sixty or more in other parts of the republic. It is operated as an autonomous entity. The bank has two main divisions, the department of emission and the commercial department. It has a present authorized capital of 70,000,000 pesos and on the basis of that now carries on approximately two-thirds of the commercial banking business of Montevideo. The total gold and silver holdings of the Bank of the Republic early in 1951 were almost 450,000,000 pesos and its total note issue approached 400,000,000 pesos.

Despite the intimate connection of the bank with Montevideo's economy, one of its chief purposes has been the provision of cheap rural credit. It also engages in the construction and administration of granaries, the financing of rural industries, the marketing and exporting of certain agricultural products—and the operation of a pawnshop! Its management has been intelligent and imaginative as well as sound. "By the thirties," wrote an eminent student of the Uruguayan economy, "the Bank had demonstrated that it could make available the most comprehensive banking service the country had ever known at low rates and in addition produce large revenues for the State." [7]

The remaining two state-owned banks, each operated as an autonomous entity, are the Mortgage Bank and the Insurance Bank. The former was converted in 1912 from a private to a government-owned and -operated status. Since that time it has been active, though by no means monopolistic, in mortgage financing both in urban and rural areas. The State Insurance Bank was opened early in 1912. It immediately assumed a prominent role in the fields of fire and workmen's compensation insurance and later branched into other fields; life and marine insurance have been especially important categories of its operations.

The third of the commercial banking business of Montevideo not dominated by the Bank of the Republic is shared by some thirty private banks, most of Uruguayan but a few of foreign control. Though their credit activities and certain other operations are to some extent controlled by laws which are administered by the Bank of the Republic the relations of the private banks with the great, state-owned bank are generally good.

The money market in Montevideo enjoyed especially prosperous times after the outbreak of the Korean war because of the flight of "scare capital," amounting to many millions of dollars, from various European countries to Uruguay. One consequence was a rapid drop in the dollar exchange rate; between June 23 and December 20, 1950, the dollar declined from 2.86 pesos to 1.90 although it later made up most of that loss.

Uruguay moves its goods internally chiefly by adequate railroads and highways. The railway system, as noted earlier, fans out from Montevideo; there are few cross-country lines. Some of the facts about railways which we have already touched upon can bear expansion: The first railway was opened in 1869 and from then on it was primarily British capital which was responsible for extending the system. By 1911 it had been completed substantially in its present form. The mileage by 1948 was 1,874 of which 1,490 was British-owned, the re-

[7] Hanson, *op. cit.*, p. 78.

mainder belonging to the government. This total figure gave Uruguay a better mileage-area ratio than any other country in South America: Uruguay had one mile of track to each 38.5 square miles of area; its closest competitors were Argentina and Chile whose comparable figures were 40.4 and 50.0. The mileage-population ratios, however, find both of the latter countries more favorably situated than Uruguay, which has one mile of track for each 1,334 people; Argentina has one mile for each 603 and Chile one mile for each 981 people.

Railway policy was a matter for governmental considera- tion from the time of the second Batlle administration (1911–15) on for many years. Government plans finally culmi- nated at the end of 1948 in the purchase of British railways with £7,150,000 of accumulated sterling. All mileage is hence now government-owned and -operated. The government in Oc- tober, 1952 completed the amalgamation of the railways as a single system. Deficits were incurred in railway operation in both 1949 and 1950 and in the latter year the government ap- propriated about 6,500,000 pesos to cover the deficit. None- theless, passenger traffic was at a high level: the number of passengers carried in 1949 was 8,158,000.

It is as freight carriers, however, that the Uruguayan rail- ways find their chief importance. Therein lies their fundamental problem of rates and profits. Most of Uruguay's imports (*e.g.*, industrial fuel, raw materials, machinery, and consumer goods and vehicles) stop at Montevideo and are not transported in- land. The freight traffic from interior points to Montevideo (livestock, meat, wool, etc.) is hence uncompensated by return freight as a well-balanced traffic pattern would necessitate.

The highway network supplements the railroad mileage. It is more extensive—the country claims 3,051 miles of im- proved highway. The mileage-area ratio for all Uruguayan roads is more favorable than in any other country of all Latin America. The country's most publicized road is, of course, its share of the Pan American Highway, almost 400 miles in length, from Colonia, opposite Buenos Aires, via Montevideo, to Aceguá on the Brazilian border. Roads in the northern de- partments are generally much poorer, and of course traffic is much less. The number of Uruguayan motor vehicles is re- ported at 78,200; the automobile-population ratio is likewise more favorable than in any other Latin-American country, 31.9 persons per car.

Highways, especially in the southern departments, were often located as a means of control over the railways. The government intended for the frequently parallel routes followed by roads and railways to force down rail rates, but the policy boomeranged after the government's purchase of the British rail lines. Thereafter two governmentally operated systems of transportation were thrown into competition with each other; the position of certain privately-owned trucking companies then tended to deteriorate.

Improvement of the port of Montevideo began about the turn of the century. Plans have been developed since 1948 for the expenditure of about 50,000,000 additional pesos on port improvements. The port is a busy one: in 1950 a total of 2,072 ships with a tonnage of 9,241,136 entered it. As usual, British and United States vessels predominated, in that order. Normally, in addition, Argentine, Dutch, Italian, Norwegian, Swedish, and Panamanian flags will enter in annual numbers of at least a hundred each. Uruguay's own merchant marine is very small.

The National Administration of Ports, another autonomous entity, has exercised monopolistic control over Montevideo's port facilities since 1932. The facilities themselves—tugboats, lighterage, stevedoring, warehouses—are, on the whole, adequate. The rub comes in the fantastic delays encountered in clearing goods through the Montevideo customs house. At one period in recent years the accumulated backlog of merchandise awaiting clearance reached the incredible value of 250,000,000 pesos.

Country-wide telephone facilities and service are a monopoly of another autonomous entity, the Administración General de las Usinas Eléctricas y los Teléfonos del Estado (understandably telescoped to Ute). The number of telephones by 1952 had reached 95,080, a phenomenal increase from the 29,378 reported in 1932. Uruguay's per capita telephone figure of one instrument per 26.3 persons is second only in South America to Argentina's figure of 24.7. Ute now not only operates the country's telephones but it also has a monopoly over all electric services and hydroelectric power development in

Uruguay. Ute's electric and telephone services were designed to be virtually the only beneficiaries of a $33,000,000 loan made to Uruguay in 1950 by the International Bank for Reconstruction and Development.

Uruguay's economic development—industrial and commercial, financial and communicational—is mature, even sophisticated.[8] But to say "Uruguay's economic development" is a misnomer. It is Montevideo's. The economic growth of the city has been achieved only at the cost of an extraordinary imbalance. It is an imbalance which is at once economic, social, political, cultural, psychological. It pits Montevideo against Uruguay, capital against *campo*.

---

[8] At the same time, some of the government's price-fixing and other regulative policies appear to have broken down and the government seems to find it very difficult to face hard economic realities.

# 8

# Capital against Campo

Uruguay is a land without war—and yet war goes on constantly. There is no slavery in Uruguay—but two-thirds of the nation is enslaved. Uruguay has practically no poverty—but countless thousands of its inhabitants are impoverished to the point of destitution. Uruguay is a healthful land—but yet it is desperately sick.

True, the war is a conflict without casualties in terms of bloodshed and corpses. The slaves are not held by chains or bars. The poverty is not that caused by lack of bank accounts or sufficient media of exchange, and the sickness is not the sort that fills hospitals and mortality tables. But the war has very serious casualties in terms of social and economic dislocation and distortion. The enslavement puts roughly two-thirds of the population in subjection to the other third (or, in terms of area, subordinates some 99.65 per cent to the other .35 per cent). The impoverishment is spiritual and psychological; the sickness is that of the body politic, social, and economic.

Probably the gravest indictment to be made against Uruguay is for its failure to solve the perennial and growing problem of capital against *campo*, of the relations of Montevideo with the interior, the hinterland, the departments. Intelligent Uruguayans are well aware of the situation and deplore its existence. It is so subtle a problem, however, so almost invisibly casual, so lacking in dramatic coloration and overtones, that the line of least resistance for the vast majority is simply to ignore it. Even those in high places have been inclined, at least until recently, to adopt a shoulder-shrugging attitude.

Nowhere else in the world is there so extreme a comparable case of what the population scientist might call demographic megalocephaly as in the instance of Uruguay's capital city. The layman would not use the five-dollar term; he would call it, literally, at least, the bigheadedness of Montevideo. It affects in subtle, even insidious, ways virtually every aspect of Uruguayan life. Let us see, before going further, what kind of problem we face. Gravitation of population toward a national capital is a natural phenomenon. In Latin America, despite the predominantly agricultural character of most of the countries, the phenomenon of urbanization is especially noticeable. It has been heightened by the degree of industrialization which has taken place here and there but it is by no means solely the product of the trend toward the machine. Latin American urbanization is a deeply rooted movement; certain of the roots are more than two thousand years long.

As the table on page 108 shows, Montevideo's estimated population of 850,000 gives it more than a third of the people of all Uruguay. If anything, the figures err on the conservative side. Some persons guess that greater Montevideo has more than two-fifths of the country's people. Paysandú and Salto are almost equal in population but neither of them has more than about one-seventeenth of Montevideo's inhabitants. Among the Latin American countries (which do, after all, have a considerable common denominator) Argentina is usually cited as the outstanding example of megalocephaly although, as will be seen from the table, Santiago actually has a slightly higher percentage of Chile's population than Buenos Aires does of Argentina's. But even if Santiago's and Chile's populations are more comparable in size to those of Montevideo and Uruguay, the comparison of the latter city and country with those across the Plata is more valid because of a general, even if somewhat misleading, similarity of economic and social conditions in Uruguay and Argentina.

Buenos Aires with 3,371,000 of Argentina's 17,424,926 people is far ahead of Rosario's 467,937, but Buenos Aires has

## COMPARATIVE POPULATION RATIOS *

| Country | Capital | *Its Percentage of Total Pop.* | *Next Largest (or Largest) City* | *Its Percentage of Capital's Population* |
|---|---|---|---|---|
| Uruguay (2,500,000) | Montevideo (850,000) | 34.0 | Paysandú (50,000) | 5.9 |
| Argentina | Buenos Aires | 19.3 | Rosario | 13.9 |
| Bolivia | La Paz | 7.5 | Cochabamba | 26.6 |
| Brazil | Rio de Janeiro | 4.7 | São Paulo | 92.0 |
| Chile | Santiago | 20.4 | Valparaiso | 16.5 |
| Colombia | Bogotá | 4.3 | Medellín | 49.2 |
| Costa Rica | San José | 10.0 | Guadalupe | 20.0 |
| Cuba | Havana | 14.8 | Santiago | 19.0 |
| Dominican Republic | Ciudad Trujillo | 8.5 | Santiago de los Caballeros | 30.9 |
| Ecuador | Quito | 6.5 | Guayaquil | 117.4 |
| El Salvador | San Salvador | 6.7 | Santa Ana | 41.3 |
| Guatemala | Guatemala City | 8.1 | Quezaltenango | 14.9 |
| Haiti | Port-au-Prince | 4.5 | Cap Haitien | 17.6 |
| Honduras | Tegucigalpa | 4.1 | San Pedro Sula | 39.2 |
| Mexico | Mexico City [1] | 11.8 | Guadalajara | 12.4 |
| Nicaragua | Managua | 13.9 | León | 36.3 |
| Panama | Panama City | 18.2 | Colón | 37.2 |
| Paraguay | Asunción | 9.2 | Villarica | 23.9 |
| Peru | Lima | 11.9 | Callao | 10.0 |
| Venezuela | Caracas | 9.9 | Maracaibo | 46.8 |
| Australia | Canberra | .24 | Sydney [2] | 7729.1 |
| Austria | Vienna | 25.6 | Graz | 12.8 |
| Belgium | Brussels | 15.0 | Antwerp | 61.3 |
| Denmark | Copenhagen | 17.1 | Aarhus | 14.7 |
| England | London | 20.3 | Birmingham | 13.3 |
| France | Paris | 6.4 | Marseilles | 23.3 |
| Switzerland | Berne | 2.9 | Zurich | 263.7 |
| United States | Washington | .52 | New York City [3] | 983.8 |

\* All calculations based on census statistics or population estimates taken from *Britannica Book of the Year, 1952* (Chicago, 1952).

[1] The federal district.

[2] Ratio of Sydney's population to that of Australia: 18.6 per cent.

[3] Ratio of New York City's population to that of the United States: 5.1 per cent.

less that a fifth of Argentina's population, and Rosario, even though declining in size, still has more than an eighth of the inhabitants of the capital. Furthermore, Rosario, Santa Fe, Tucumán, Córdoba, and Mendoza have a historic tradition

which no amount of population disparity can wipe out. It is
the sort of tradition which no city in Uruguay other than
Montevideo even begins to share.

Australia, to take a non-Latin American example, is also
mentioned as an urbanized country. But its population of
8,315,799 includes the two large cities of Sydney with 1,550,-
000 and Melbourne with 1,288,000 people. Clearly there is no
single head outgrowing the body, and even the combined population of Sydney and Melbourne is a lesser proportion of Australia's population than Montevideo's is of Uruguay's. Austria
provides the classic example of disproportion in Europe, but
Vienna with 1,760,784 people has only just over a fourth of
Austria's 6,881,100. Uruguay is sometimes compared, for one
reason or another, to Switzerland, Denmark, or Belgium, but
the comparison cannot extend to population ratios. Such countries as the United States, England, Germany, France, and
Japan, though each has a largest city more than twice the size
of the second largest, patently give no examples of single-city
disproportion.

It boils down, then, to noting (referring to the table again)
that the Uruguayan figure in the first column of statistics is
much the largest figure in that column and that the Uruguayan
figure in the last column is much the smallest. With such statistical evidence to undergird it, the broad statement may be
repeated, to pose and focus the problem anew, that nowhere
else in the world does there exist so extreme an important example of disproportion between a country's metropolis and the
rest of the country.

In the Uruguay-Montevideo case, at least six main factors
can be cited by way of explanation. In most instances they are
not only causes but also contemporary facets of the problem.
They are the historical, the geographic, the economic, the social, the cultural, and the political. The capital's megalocephaly is explained in terms of an intricate complex of all these
factors.

Montevideo is not Uruguay's oldest city, but the circumstances of its early existence helped give it the pre-eminence it
has always maintained. During the era of colonial rivalry between Spain and Portugal it was inevitable that Montevideo,
the Spanish settlement, should receive all the impetus which

Buenos Aires, the Spanish metropolis across the river, could give it in the contest with Portuguese-settled Colonia. The pastoral economy of the hinterland effectively prevented the growth of large inland settlements and hence Montevideo continued its unchallenged supremacy even though all towns of the colonial period were but minuscule compared with today's metropolis. Montevideo was the unquestioned and constant hub of activity during the revolutionary period; it was the great goal of the various military forces, Spanish, Uruguayan, Argentine, Brazilian. Control of the hinterland was largely incidental. *Campo* suspicion of Montevideo dates in part from the exigencies of the revolutionary period; the capital seemed even then to concentrate the aristocracy and wealth of the country, while the interior prided itself on monopolizing the rude and unpretentious patriotism of the time. It seems inevitable for province to suspect metropolis.

The bitterness of the Colorado-Blanco wars of the nineteenth century was projected in part as a capital-*campo* feud. The rhythm of reform introduced by President José Batlle y Ordóñez early in the twentieth century even contributed to the problem. Batlle was detested by the large *estancieros,* some of whom had led the revolt against him in 1904, but as long as pastoral prosperity continued, they were willing to tolerate those of his reforms which did not upset their rural social and economic order. Batlle seemingly deemed it prudent not to antagonize the great *estancieros* further and hence he made no effort to redistribute the land or even seriously to tax it. Social legislation inspired by Batlle was applicable in considerable measure in practice to the capital only; the rural workers remained in large degree untouched and inert.

In terms of geographic pre-eminence Montevideo can claim the best natural and artificial port of all Uruguay; indeed, as noted earlier, the capital has the only port of consequence in the entire country. The capital is at the extreme south of Uruguay but in terms of population distribution it is centrally located. The seven departments making up the northern half of the country have 48.9 per cent of Uruguay's area but only 22.7 per cent of its population. The five departments fronting on the Plata River contain 11.9 per cent of the area but 53.0 per cent of the population. The single department of Montevideo has only .35 per cent of the area of Uruguay but 33.5 per cent of the population.[1] The highway and railway systems of the country fan out from Montevideo. Well over a fourth of the farm units in Uruguay (mostly among the livestock *estancias* in the center and north) are more than fifteen miles from a railroad station or a port, and almost an eighth are more than thirty miles distant. Highway facilities are also much more inadequate in the north.

It cannot be too often emphasized that the economic control of Uruguay centers overwhelmingly in its capital. The very large part of the country's industrial output is Montevidean. Its banking and its major commerce are almost entirely in the capital. Though much of the wealth of Uruguay is agricultural, especially in the form of cattle and sheep, the channeling of that wealth and the processing of the agricultural products are concentrated in Montevideo. More than three-fourths of Uruguay's imports enter through Montevideo and an even larger fraction of her exports go out through the same port.

The social landscape of the capital is far more varied, attractive, and flexible than that of the *campo*. The middle class, for which Uruguay is justly noted among Latin American countries, lives in large part in the capital. The rural areas, even though they lack literal slavery, still possess much of the social stratification and rigidity which characterized the pre-Civil War southern planter society in the United States. If a *campesino* wishes to escape the heavy hand of social tradition, effectively re-enforced by economic organization, his usual recourse is to pull up stakes and move, not the few miles to the nearest departmental capital, but to make the slightly more distant move to Montevideo. Social and familial relationships are more conventional in the capital; the percentage of illegitimate births—customarily more than 25 per cent for the country as a whole—regularly runs much higher in the northern departments, in some cases roughly twice as high as in Montevideo.

Uruguay's single university—all its faculties or schools—is located at Montevideo. For that matter, most of the compo-

[1] These calculations are based on official departmental population estimates of December 31, 1944; the disproportions are now greater.

nents of the so-called Labor University are also situated in the capital. Forty of Uruguay's eighty-one *liceos* or secondary schools are in Montevideo. Almost all the indices by which general schooling can be measured—physical condition of buildings, quarters for teachers, preparation of teachers, attendance, financial assistance to schools, and others—show conditions to be notoriously worse in rural areas, despite recent improvements, than in Montevideo. The capital has fifteen daily newspapers, large and small, in Spanish and in other languages. All other parts of the republic have sixteen daily papers. Montevideo's papers, however, monopolize some 90 per cent of the total sales of daily papers for the entire country. Of forty-five medium-wave radio stations in Uruguay, twenty-four are in Montevideo. The single government broadcasting station, Sodre, which has a reputation extending far beyond the borders of the country, is inevitably in Montevideo. Uruguay's single theater for the presentation of opera, the Teatro Solís, is in the capital. The National Library and the Legislative Library, the country's most notable collections of books, are in Montevideo. All but two of the country's museums are in the national capital. Of some 16,000 hospital beds, about two-thirds are in Montevideo institutions. The capital city has about one-half of Uruguay's doctors; up until a few years ago, at least, some sections of the northern departments of Artigas, Salto, and Tacuarembó had no physicians closer than sixty miles.

As a small state, with a centralized government and extensively developed social welfare services, it is inevitable that both governmental machinery and the political processes would center in Montevideo. An overwhelming majority of the estimated 145,000 governmental employees (including those in the government corporations) are located in the capital. The departments are in large degree only administrative subdivisions of the central government, and they lack both the considerable structural extent and the tenacious political vitality and consciousness which characterize states in the United States. The differential between the Department of Montevideo and the other eighteen is constitutionally recognized by the establishment of a larger size for both the executive board and the legislative council of the Department of Montevideo. A disproportionate amount of public works funds is spent in the capital.[2]

These are but the physical and measurable symptoms—geographic, economic, political, and so on—of the disparity between capital and *campo*. Above and beyond them are the far more subtle and often invisible psychological distinctions which exist. Attractiveness and variety of life, opportunity, power, often the chance for wealth, all in large degree the monopoly of the capital, cannot help but affect the ego of the individual. In the same way as much of Latin America has a colonial economy in relation to the outside world so the Uruguayan *campo* has a colonial psychology in relation to Montevideo.

The problem of the *campo* is one of social statics. The stable, though artificially rigidified, rural social order is in turn a by-product of the rural pastoral economy. That economy has three effects: it dilutes the rural population, both qualitatively and quantitatively; it retards the growth of cities throughout the *campo;* and it makes inevitable the growth of the capital disproportionately to the rest of the country.

The stock-raising economy is one which typically lends itself to large-scale landownership, small and nonmechanized employment, casual but poor working conditions, and an unbalanced family life. The problem resembles that of the corresponding rural portions of Argentina across the river. Few Uruguayan *estancias* contain more than 100,000 acres, but roughly half the agriculturally used area of the country is in farms of more than 2,500 acres. On large numbers of these, employment will not average more than two workers per thousand acres, which in considerable measure helps to account for the sparseness of population in the northern departments of Uruguay. The life of the ranch hand ostensibly resembles that of the gaucho who was his institutional ancestor, but despite its carefree appearance it is hard, generally cheerless, and monot-

[2] A footnote to the preponderance of emphasis on the capital is to be found by making certain simple deductions from the Uruguayan entries in the third edition of *Who's Who in Latin America, Part V: Argentina, Paraguay, Uruguay* (Stanford, California, 1950). A total of 254 biographies of Uruguayans is included. Information in a few cases is incomplete, but from the data given it appears that 155 persons were born in Montevideo, sixty in Uruguay outside of the capital, and fifteen abroad. Present residences show that eight live abroad, five in other parts of Uruguay than its metropolis, and 236 in Montevideo. The cityward drift as a result of Montevideo's greater opportunities is startlingly underlined.

onous. About the only opportunity for mechanization of the work is in sheepshearing.

The tradition that the colonial gaucho was a single man carries down to the contemporary *estancia* in the almost universal practice that rural workers (except foremen and the office staff) may not have their wives and children with them on the *estancia*. This practice is not solely a matter of tradition and prejudice. In the mixed-farming areas in the south, where the labor needs are more varied, there is much more economic use for the wife and even the minor children. On the *estancia*, however, those persons are largely economic dead weight.

The resulting unnatural situation means that, especially in the northern departments, the families of the rural workers must often live in a shack town thrown together along some stream bank, in an arroyo, or at some other undesirable location. This is the infamous *rancherío* or rural slum. It is inhabited by squatters who exist, rather than live, in squalor, idleness, and hopelessness. They are the people of Uruguay, above all others, who are ill-fed, ill-clothed, ill-housed. Many of the personal unions which are established are on an irregular and sometimes temporary basis; a single *rancherío* may be composed of the descendants of but one family, though most such settlements will have from twenty to 200 families. The customary absence of many resident men (except boys and old men) makes for a sort of *de facto* matriarchy.

The *rancherío* presents the Uruguayan census taker or statistical worker with his hardest job. A survey some years ago enumerated 613 rural settlements not classed as towns; these did not include suburban *rancheríos* which were satellites of recognized cities and towns. Of the 613 settlements 515 were located in the departments devoted primarily to stock raising, *i.e.*, all except Montevideo, Canelones, San José, and Colonia. All 515 were classed as *rancheríos* and of that number 460 were composed of *estancia* day laborers' families. The total *rancherío* population was estimated at 250,000.[3]

Promiscuity, concubinage, prostitution, illegitimacy, and venereal disease are common in the *rancheríos*. The simplicity, monotony, and irregularity of social life have made chronic

[3] Juan Vicente Chiarino and Miguel Saralegui, *Detrás de la Ciudad* (Montevideo, 1944), pp. 179–80, 182.

and long-standing problems of drinking and gambling in many such places.

A report of 1920 by the Blanco party leader, Dr. Luis Alberto de Herrera, described the *rancherío* vividly: "These rachitic centers, of shameful birth, graphically labeled towns of rats, mark a subversion which demands serious examination and urgent correction. They are established as heads of a tumor. . . . The *rancherío* constitutes a public calamity, a den of malignancy and thievery, the center of disease of all kinds, without hygiene, without schools, without conduct. [The people] live by night and sleep by day; it is an everlasting snare spread out against what is good, whether it be shelter or health. At that place is rooted the rural cancer; from there come degenerate youth with a horror of honest work; there grow wasters." The same description would not, except for educational progress, be greatly overdrawn now, more than three decades later, for some areas.

The study made several years ago indicated that of the more than 600 rural settlements only twenty-one had adequate drinking water, only nineteen possessed electric lights, and only fifty-three had the permanent, or even the weekly, services of a physician but that, on the other hand, only eighty-nine were without a primary school. The result of the deplorable health conditions is that disease, especially tuberculosis and syphilis, is rampant.

The problem of the *rancherío* will doubtless persist for some time to come. The old-school *estanciero's* attitude is characterized by a rude sort of democracy, but it is reflected largely in his treatment of the worker with personal dignity and does not extend to a cognizance of the social problems involved in the substandard housing and the irregular family relationships. It is a personal rather than an economic or a social democracy. The government's attempt to solve the problem of the *rancherío* has as yet made little headway.

Although from 75 to 80 per cent of the *campo's* population live in small settlements rather than actually on the *estancias* in individual dwellings, great barriers in social intercourse still prevail among different classes of workers; they have little to do with one another except in a working relationship. Rural life has developed few if any important community aspects.

Very little community self-government, creative participation in local affairs, responsibility for law and order, or interest in educational advancement exists. In a word, the average rural worker does not think in terms of community interests or institutions.

Unskilled rural workers between the ages of eighteen and sixty must, by law, be paid a minimum wage of thirty-five pesos monthly. Actually, most peons receive forty-five to sixty pesos monthly plus living quarters and food. For years Uruguay has had a retirement pension system for urban workers but those in the *campo* were given similar security only by a law of October 20, 1950, which, even yet, is not fully in operation. Such mechanization as is possible operates to relieve the drudgery of *estancia* labor, but it also brings into play a vicious circle: it decreases the demand for human labor. In view, then, of the low wages, the monotonous and unbalanced diet, the lack of diversion and excitement, the still incomplete security on retirement, and the threat of lessened employment due to mechanization, it is no cause for surprise that the growing industrialization and consequently better wages of Montevideo, plus the general lure of the metropolis, win out over the drabness of life on the *estancia*. The cityward drift from the *campo* continues at a steady, if partially invisible, pace, so that some people assert that almost all of Uruguay's gain of population is that of its capital.

Statistics do not bear this out. The strictly rural population increased between 1916 and 1937 by an estimated 72,603 but its percentage of the total population declined from 19.56 to 16.35. Urban population between 1910 and 1939 increased 164 per cent; rural population in the same period gained 17 per cent or at about one-tenth of the urban rate. Births in Montevideo are usually about one-third of the total for the whole country, but the capital's marriages consistently run to almost a half of Uruguay's total. The birth and death rates seem to conspire against the *campo*. In the statistical analysis made some years ago by the United States Bureau of the Census, it was shown that the Department of Montevideo, which is for practical purposes the national capital, had a lower birth rate than that of the country as a whole in every year from 1900 to 1919 inclusive, but that in every year from 1920 to

1941 inclusive, its birth rate had been higher than the rate for Uruguay and that in only one year, from 1925 to 1941, did the Montevideo rate fail to be the highest of those of all the departments. The general death rate of Montevideo is often higher than the country average but the childhood death rate (those under five years) is consistently lower than that of any other department.

It is not only the peons who drift to Montevideo. The *estancieros* themselves often make a Mecca of the capital. To the extent that their profits are paid and spent and they and their families live in Montevideo, they tend to have the lessened concern of the absentee landlord for the social problems of the countryside. "Montevideo's port has been improved," wrote an Uruguayan years ago with slight but understandable exaggeration, "its castles have been built, its streets have been paved with the beef, wool, and hides of the provinces." The meat and wool processers of Uruguay operate in Montevideo, and their payrolls stay there. It is with grim aptness then that certain Uruguayan writers refer to Montevideo as the "suction pump" of the country.[4]

In the southern crop-raising departments the position of the rural worker is better. Inasmuch as he participates in a more flexible type of agriculture and is more within the immediate economic orbit of Montevideo, he is to that degree released from the dead hand of a pastoral economic and social tradition which, farther north, would condemn him to a probably permanent psychological subordination. His diet is not solely the endless mutton of the peon on the livestock *estancias;* it is varied with butter, cheese, honey, fruits, and vegetables. The agricultural routine in such regions is less restricted, the demand for agricultural labor is greater, and the threat of mechanization to employment is consequently less. The workers of these regions are sometimes afflicted by poverty, seldom by misery.

That crop zone (plus the cities such as Paysandú, Salto, Melo, Rocha, and a few others) provides a sort of transition area, even though the interior cities are in many cases only isolated enclaves in the *campo*, between the social and cultural fluidity of the capital and the static character of the *campo* it-

4 *E.g.,* Julio Martínez Lamas in *Riqueza y Pobreza del Uruguay* (Montevideo, 1946).

self. As one approaches Montevideo by such a social path—through the crop zone or by way of the other cities of Uruguay—the various criteria by which progress is measured all reflect higher standards: roads are paved or are more passable if unpaved, schools are better and more accessible, health services are more efficient and more widely available, the diet is more varied and palatable.

The crop-producing transition zone does not play the role of mediator, however. One does not mediate between overlord and vassal. The zone's economic prosperity is so dependent on the metropolis—its milk, vegetable, fruit, and cereal markets are almost entirely in Montevideo—that it cannot, if it would, be independent. Indeed, it does not choose to; it lies too much within the magnetic field of Montevideo which, to change the figure, attracts it as the flame the moth. The real contest is that between the capital and the *campo*. Despite the greater population of the latter, and the more basic character of its economy in relation to Uruguay's total prosperity, the capital still has advantages in the struggle. It is geographically more compact, socially better knit, politically more vocal. Industrialization, one of the pillars of the Montevidean economy, thrives in part by virtue of government policies adopted by a regime dominated by a party oriented toward the city. The tourist dollars, pesos, and cruzeiros are spent in the capital and its satellite areas. The instruments of communication and the elements which mold public opinion are all but wholly controlled by Montevideo. The urban rhythm is faster and more varied than the rural. The conflict is even one of disparate eras: it is the twentieth century fighting the nineteenth.

The whole problem can be broken down into various segments, *e.g.*, the need for greater and more efficient rural production, the deficiency of adequate roads in the north, the state of public health in the *campo*, the abnormally high illegitimate birth rate, the problem of the *rancheríos*, still inadequate rural education, and others. It cannot, however, be solved except by a major, sustained, and integrated attack.

A frequently suggested solution of the question of the *campo* is to give land to the landless. This has merit but it is only a short and halting step. Many landless workers, for one thing, are not interested in landownership; they would rather

go to the city. A first period of land reform lasted roughly
from 1913 to 1923. Two laws passed in that decade established
ten agricultural "colonies" totaling about 75,000 acres, divided into farms averaging about 100 acres in size. Government
loans of up to 85 per cent of the appraised land values were
authorized. A second period of land reform began with the
creation in September, 1923, of the Rural Development and
Resettlement Division of the government's Mortgage Bank, financed by a 3,000,000-peso bond issue; resources for the program were later increased by 8,000,000 pesos in new bonds.
Prior to 1948 the Bank acquired 418,855 acres for the colonization program; this represented only about 1 per cent of Uruguay's area. A third period began with a law of January 12,
1948, establishing the National Colonization Institute. It has
operated with 21,000,000 pesos of capital. One of its aims is to
break up large estates. Up to March 31, 1952, the Institute
had acquired 123,870 acres by expropriation and direct purchase. The program has thus been a modest one. Prices paid
have been considered fair and owners have not been pressured
into selling their land.

Other legislation has provided for the more liberal extension of credit by the Mortgage Bank and the Bank of the Republic to small farmers. Conditions under which tenant farmers
can be evicted have been tightened. The government's National
Institute of Economic Dwellings has taken beginning steps toward improving deplorable rural housing conditions in certain
areas. The most extensive and significant developments in public housing, however, have been in Montevideo—again the capital wins at the expense of the *campo*.

Thus far, the attacks on the whole problem have been piecemeal and essentially unintegrated. The government's own policies have in part been basically contradictory: it has sought to
foster colonization programs aimed at making rural living and
working conditions more attractive to halt the cityward exodus, and at the same time it has encouraged industrialization
schemes which could result only in pulling more people from
the *campo* to the capital. Some fundamental agricultural production problems have been neglected by failing to take adequate steps to lower production costs, decrease animal disease
losses, increase labor efficiency, conserve the soil, improve for-

age, etc. Tens of millions of pesos could well be spent on better roads and schools in the stock-raising departments. The better provision in rural areas of running water and electric light, medical services and hospital facilities, wholesome diversion and more varied diet are elementary steps which are yet to be solved satisfactorily.

So greatly is the control of public policy in Uruguay influenced by the political parties that the solutions must come by the intervention of those agencies. Private organizations, such as the Rural Federation, have neither the prestige nor the political leverage to undertake a frontal attack on the problem though the Federation's reports and congresses have called needed attention to specific phases of the situation. The Rural Federation, being composed exclusively of *estancieros*, is, of course, an interest group and would not relish certain sorts of reforms. Nor can single individuals, even if in official position, really solve the problem, though such persons as Julio Martínez Lamas, Miguel Saralegui, Juan Vicente Chiarino, and Francisco Gómez Haedo, as authors, and Daniel D. Vidart, as director of the Department of Rural Sociology of the Ministry of Stockraising and Agriculture, have done yeoman work in helping focus public attention on the problem.

The position of most of the various parties on the problem of the *campo* is affected by certain limiting factors. The orientation of the Blanco or Nationalist party is toward the rural area, but the party's backlog of strength is the *estancieros* and hence it must be regarded as taking a not completely impartial view. The dominant Colorado party has faced toward the urban centers, especially Montevideo, in terms of interests and support and is consequently less conscious of and interested in rural problems than would otherwise be true. Inasmuch as the government for almost ninety years has been dominated by the Colorado party, it is in part, then, a Colorado favoritism, conscious or unconscious, which has increased the prestige and prominence of the capital at the expense of the interior. The Socialist party has been professedly socially conscious, but its orientation, like that of the Colorados, has been Montevidean; however, its veteran and respected leader, Dr. Emilio Frugoni, has advanced constructive reforms for rural problems at various times. The Communist party has alleged an interest in rural questions, but whatever it proposes in such a direction may almost automatically be assumed to be insincere. It is probably the Unión Cívica, the Catholic party, which has taken the most consistent, constructive, and penetrating interest in the problems of the *campo*. Its newspaper, *El Bien Público,* and its leaders, Dr. Dardo Regules, Tomás Brena, and others, have long sought to get at the roots of the situation.

So large and so involved is the question that Uruguay's most conscious students of it were led some years ago to cry out passionately that "The *campo* must be for us something more than the picturesque stage of the gaucho and the creole and the characters of the stories of Javier de Viana to be the living heart of our country, of our creole and rural country, of that which we are, economically and socially. And we must feel that country and that *campo* as ours and not as a distant foreign region, as our authentic way of life and of historic fulfillment and not as a simple geographic appendage of a riviera (*costa azul*). . . ." [5]

At bottom the solution lies in freeing the *campo* from its psychological serfdom. This is simple to state but tremendously difficult to achieve. Its attainment will be in part a product of the winning of material improvements which will make life more worth living in the *campo*. In part it will depend on a remodeling of rural social mores and relationships and a revision of the *estancia* employment pattern. In large part, too, it must be a result of a change in attitude of mind by the people of both Montevideo and the hinterland.

It is the chief point at which integration now fails in Uruguay.

[5] Chiarino and Saralegui, *op. cit.,* p. 402.

# 9

## The Lengthened Shadow of a Man

Someone wrote years ago that the history of Europe in the first decade and a half of the nineteenth century was the history of France and the history of France was the biography of Napoleon. For a different era the second part of that figure of speech might be transplanted to Uruguayan soil and applied to the country's foremost son.

Probably in no other country in the world in the past two centuries has any one man so deeply left his imprint upon the life and character of a country as has José Batlle y Ordóñez upon Uruguay. Perhaps the only comparable situation was to be found in the impact of Mustafa Kemal on recent Turkey. For a half century past the course of Uruguay's history has been turned, the policies of its government have been molded, the thinking of its people has been oriented by the vision, the courage, the crusading fervor of the man Batlle.

Two decades and more after his death one must ask not only, who was Batlle? but also, what is Batlle? For he has become, in that short time, a legend, almost a cult. Batlle is still a candidate in every election. He is the Cousins Roosevelt and Woodrow Wilson rolled into one, with a liberal admixture of Andrew Jackson and Grover Cleveland as well. Through their countless reproductions his leonine figure and features are probably more familiar to even the younger generation of Uruguayans than those of the succession of contemporary presidents or national councillors. On the windowless side wall of a downtown business building a three-story mural of Batlle stands ruggedly and stares challengingly out over Montevideo's busy streets.

No discussion of a man, even a prominent man, should deteriorate into mere fulsome adulation or hero worship. Batlle was no saint, but a very human man, subject to failings and frailties. Nor was his final legacy solely the work of Batlle himself. Capable lieutenants, Baltasar Brum, Domingo Arena, and others, re-enforced Batlle's work and carried his banner after his death. It must be admitted, too, that deep-rooted economic and other currents beyond the control of any single individual would inevitably have brought Uruguay in time a considerable measure of advancement. But the fountainhead of inspiration for what Uruguay accomplished in the early twentieth century remains the great depths of moral faith, the dreams and hopes and convictions of Batlle himself.

To so great a degree is this true that some of the discussions of Batlle which one hears today in Uruguay are altogether too likely to take on lyrical overtones and be suffused with an air of discipleship which presumes the infallibility of the master. Where the cult of Batlle may lead in another generation, as the memory of him recedes into an aureate perspective, is difficult to say. At any rate, that trend would seem to do the man a disservice. Along with being a man of great strength of character and vivid personality Batlle was a practical politician, an effective assessor and molder of public opinion.

It is a truism that great men are the products of their times. Usually these times must be ones of struggle or flux. Great men seldom come from lands or times that are passive, quiescent, stagnant. Batlle was no exception. His name appears, to an English-speaking person, as if it were but a misspelling of "battle." The similarity is not without symbolic significance. José Batlle's life was a battle, a succession of battles, against the essential medievalism that still persisted in Uruguay when he got his cue to go on the stage for the long and Wagnerian role he was destined to play.

What was Uruguay in the days when Batlle came to man-

hood? It was basically a land still waiting to find itself. A land
and its people must, of course, go on living from day to day.
Babies are born, people eat, sleep, and carry on their daily
occupations, procreation goes on, other people die. These
things occur every day, every minute, and yet they do not mean
that much of a reason for being necessarily exists on a national
scale.

Uruguay was in just that transitional stage in the early
1880's. The ordinary personal life processes and activities went
on apace, but the country, as a country, had not yet developed
any full, mature personality or purpose. The pointlessness and
restlessness of adolescence still marked it. The wild, gaucho-
esque anarchy of Uruguay's national childhood was past—maturity was yet to come. Comtian positivism was making an increasing intellectual impact in Mexico, Brazil, and elsewhere
in Latin America. On the more material side, the population
of Europe was growing rapidly—and demanding constantly
more food. As that population grew and strained against the
trammels of space in certain European countries tens of thousands of persons, who could not all find haven in the United
States or Canada, readied their possessions to sail for southern
South America. What Uruguayans call "the New Spirit" was
fermenting in the land, waiting the hands that could give it
form and meaning. Uruguay was ripe to profit by these potential changes, psychological and material, but a catalytic agent
was needed to start the process. Batlle would, in large measure,
become that agent. Between his birth and his death Uruguay
made vast strides.

By the time this subtle chemistry of national maturing had
been completed, some decades later, Batlle's touch had been felt
on virtually every phase of Uruguayan activity. His interests
had been as catholic as those of Leonardo or Jefferson, his constructive restlessness as far-ranging as that of Franklin or
Voltaire. His "reforms" altered the whole current of Uruguayan life. Unlike Benito Juárez, he happily missed most of
the dregs which were the lot of that Mexican with whom he has
been compared. Unlike Lincoln, he escaped a tragic martyr-
dom.

Uruguayan biographers have spilled much ink trying to
answer the question as to what Batlle's ancestry, childhood,

and youth contributed to his remarkable career.[1] Like a similar question about anyone, it must always remain partly unanswerable. What Batlle's principal biographer calls, in a commendable admission of uncertainty, his "possible remote ancestors," can be traced back to Mallorca and Catalonia in the thirteenth and fourteenth centuries. The name Batlle—it was apparently originally spelled Balle—was in Catalan equivalent to *alcalde* in Spanish, perhaps to "judge" or "mayor" in English. Some of these early ancestors were royal councillors or bishops in Catalonia, others were in more humble positions. The lineage can be traced back with more certainty to the early eighteenth century. Batlle's grandfather transferred at the end of the eighteenth century to the New World: a passport exists dated November 26, 1799, issued at Barcelona to Josef (who became José across the Atlantic) Batlle y Carrió by the "Knight of Justice of the Order of San Juan, Lieutenant General of the Royal Armies of His Majesty, Governor and Captain General of the Army and Principality of Catalonia, President of the Royal Court, etc., etc." A century later grandson José Batlle y Ordóñez would have none of such trappings.

Batlle y Carrió established commercial, social, and political ties in Buenos Aires. In 1803 he founded in Montevideo a mill and, comments a biographer, "In 1903, José Batlle y Ordóñez, his grandson, was founding in Montevideo a Democracy and building a nationality on postulates of justice."[2] A son of Batlle y Carrió, Lorenzo Batlle y Grau, became president of Uruguay, but his chief claim to fame was that he fathered José Batlle y Ordóñez. Despite all his long career as a man of public affairs, both military and civil, Lorenzo Batlle was unable to master the strife, the ill will, the near bankruptcy that marked the Uruguay of the mid decades of his century. The report was not yet ready for a catalyst.

José Batlle y Ordóñez was born into that sort of an Uruguay, at Montevideo, on May 21, 1856. His childhood, despite the fact that his father, shortly before José's twelfth birthday, became president of Uruguay, was not especially distinctive.

[1] Interestingly enough, no definitive biography of Batlle has yet been written, in Uruguay or elsewhere. It is perhaps because his life has not yet settled into any agreed perspective; he is still a highly controversial figure.

[2] Enrique Rodríguez Fabregat, *Batlle y Ordóñez, el Reformador* (Buenos Aires, 1942), p. 19.

His early education was at the English Academy and other Montevideo schools. Astronomy and other physical sciences especially attracted him. In 1873, at the age of seventeen, Batlle entered the University to prepare for law. This course he abandoned in 1879, without completing it, and at that point his formal education was terminated except for brief courses he took the following year at the Sorbonne and the College de France in Paris. By this time the twig was bent—and bent primarily toward journalism.

Batlle and a friend had founded in 1878 a rationalistic journal, *El Espíritu Nuevo*, whose courageous and ambitious mission was "the total emancipation of the American spirit from the tutelage of the Old World." To the review Batlle contributed scientific articles and poetry. Later in the same year he began contributing to a Montevideo newspaper. His first political article, published three days before his twenty-third birthday, was an attack on the dictatorship of Colonel Lorenzo Latorre.

In the turbulent politics of the early 1880's Batlle continued his vigorous journalistic campaigning, now on one paper, now on another. He developed a terse and trenchant style and fearlessly turned his guns on a dreary succession of dictators. Of one of them, General Máximo Santos, he wrote: "The national sovereignty, honor, and dignity were crucified by his henchmen." On various occasions he became the object of personal attacks, persecution, and temporary imprisonment. In 1885–86 he engaged in a brief period of revolutionary plotting and fighting against Dictator Santos. He was winning service stripes in the political wars.

One of the significant milestones of Batlle's career came on June 16, 1886, when there first appeared *El Día*, the newspaper he founded as his own enterprise to give him freer rein in inveighing against dictatorships. *El Día* gave Batlle a position of leverage, but it was punctuated by brief periods of imprisonment and exile. By the autumn (March) of 1887 Batlle was ready to launch upon a new aspect of his life's work, that of reorganizing and revivifying the Colorado party. The departure from an exclusively journalistic career (with which his new objective geared nicely) was almost simultaneous with his entry into a life of public service. Several years in the thick of the journalistic battle had convinced Batlle that the Colorado party still had a "powerful vitality"—a conclusion some of his more disillusioned compatriots were reluctant to share—but that it was seriously discredited and compromised by the several recent dictators who had carried the Colorado label. It was time for a scrub brush.

The sordid state of Uruguayan politics had produced a kind of party accommodation. Colorado strength was mainly urban, that of the traditionally oppositionist Blanco party was chiefly in the rural areas and came especially from the great landowners. The chronic disorder of the country had been partially ended by the "buying off" of Blanco leaders by giving them practically undisputed political control in half a dozen interior departments. These "fiefs" the Blancos regarded as virtually their own private domains.

In May, 1887, Batlle became political chief (roughly, governor) of the Department of Minas, the first of a long series of public posts which thereafter adorned his career. In the several months he held the office his administrative and political success was considerable. Back in Montevideo he returned to the fray and began the organization of Colorado party clubs based on "grass-roots" democratic assemblies. In 1891, he became a national deputy for the Department of Salto and within six weeks had presented a bill for obligatory voters' registration. The democratic mind and will were at work. The middle 1890's were a political struggle between Batlle, leader of the reformist element in the Colorado party, and the cynical and corrupt Juan Idiarte Borda, president of Uruguay from 1894 to 1897. Batlle strove to arouse a public conscience. "The evil, the great evil of the country," he wrote, "is not in the laws: it is in the apathy of the people."

At the end of 1895, circumstances led Batlle—never a theoretic politician—to adopt his thereafter permanent pro-labor orientation. Montevideo workers, seeking to shorten their hours of labor (fifteen to nineteen hours daily) and to improve their wages, organized and went on strike. The government, Colorado though it was, labeled the strikers as "rebellious workers" and brought all its force to bear to break the strike. Batlle and *El Día* strongly supported the strikers: "if this working day ought to be considered suicide for the workers,"

Batlle wrote, "it is, on the part of the employer, an assassination." *El Día* began a permanent department, "The Working Movement," as a forum for the employed classes.

The closing years of the century saw Uruguayan political turmoil reflected in a good deal of fighting—attempted revolts and civil war—led by the Blanco *caudillo*, Aparicio Saravia, an unpolished but magnetic leader in the interior, who thus began the last period of civil turbulence. Meanwhile, Batlle was ever forging to the front: in November, 1898, he was elected a senator from the Department of Montevideo. The middle of the following February he was unanimously named president of the senate, which carried with it the *ex officio* vice presidency of the republic. Since the national presidency would be vacant until the inauguration of a new term soon afterward, Batlle therefore filled that office, too, for the two weeks following.

The highest office in the land, the national presidency, came to Batlle by election by the congress on March 1, 1903. His election was the cue for a further revolution by Blanco forces under Saravia. For a year and a half the expensive (and in 1904 the bloody) rebellion continued. It was brought to an end by a decisive defeat of the rebels on September 1, 1904, in which Saravia suffered a wound from which he died several days later. In the meantime, most avenues of constructive activity had inevitably been closed to President Batlle. Indeed, the liquidation of the rebellion's aftermath retarded the accomplishment of much permanent reform during Batlle's first administration.

A beginning was at hand, however. A Colorado legislator in May, 1905, introduced a bill legalizing divorce. The conservative classes, and especially the orders of nuns, opposed the bill vehemently and proclaimed the imminence of social chaos. Batlle, through *El Día*, supported the bill fervently. A few months later it became law. The passage of the divorce law in 1905-07 was only a first step that Batlle took to elevate the status of women. That sex now enjoys a greater degree of social and economic emancipation in Uruguay than in any other Latin American country primarily because of the impetus Batlle gave that emancipation.

Late in 1905, Batlle decreed the abolition of income taxes on the salaries of the lowest-paid public officials and on the incomes of those receiving small pensions. The loss to the national treasury was 460,000 pesos annually, but that same fiscal year was the first in Uruguay's history to show a budgetary surplus.

It was during Batlle's first term as president that he began his many contributions to the remarkable educational achievement that Uruguay was to make. The University curriculum was expanded, foreign professors and technicians were brought in, scholarships for study in the United States and Europe were established. Batlle began his favorite technique of educating the public to acceptance of another of his great principles: that education must be absolutely free at all levels. He obtained from the congress an appropriation of a million pesos for new school buildings. He proposed the creation of night schools for adults. He sponsored the establishment of a *liceo* or secondary school in each of the eighteen departmental capitals in the interior. He prepared a plan to guarantee the autonomy of the national university.

Within the last three months of his first term in the presidency Batlle began one of the great battles of his career. It was his effort to express the Uruguayan social conscience by passage of a law providing for a maximum working day of eight hours and an obligatory weekly rest period. "The battle for the eight hours," Uruguayans are fond of saying, in retrospect, "required eight years to win"—actually, a longer period was necessary. The proposal struck not only Uruguayan employers but most conservatives as both fantastic and revolutionary. Batlle was never one to approach a reform obliquely, however. In the specifications of a platform on which he might run for re-election to the presidency in 1911, he prescribed (in August, 1910) advocacy of an eight-hour day as one of the planks.

Four months of his second term in the presidency had not passed before Batlle sent to the congress a new message calling for an eight-hour day and an obligatory weekly rest. The message was thrown into bold relief by a transit workers' strike begun a few weeks earlier to seek to reduce the fourteen hours of daily work. Batlle's contest for the eight-hour day continued vigorously through the several years following; all conservative elements in the country closed ranks in opposition to him.

The climax finally came on November 17, 1915, with congressional approval of the bill. Big industrial employers attempted to sabotage the law by reducing wages and organized labor countered by going on strike. For some days a tense situation existed, with Argentine and other international repercussions, but by the end of February, 1916, the employers had accepted the inevitable and one of Batlle's greatest victories was conclusively won. By that time he was in the thick of a still greater fight. But that is getting ahead of the story.

Batlle's first term was concluded in 1907 with few other reforms undertaken. He did, late in 1906, succeed in converting the foreign debt from a 6 per cent to a 5 per cent basis, thereby saving the treasury more than half a million pesos annually. At about the same time he promulgated a law establishing the unattachability of wages. In a sort of valedictory at the conclusion of his term Batlle stated, with justifiable satisfaction: "There are great surpluses in the treasury. The State fulfills all its pecuniary pledges. All rights, all liberties are guaranteed. The Republic has faith in the Future." Even then Batlle was a man more concerned with the future than the present.

Some three weeks after surrendering the presidency, Batlle and his family left for an extended tour of Europe and other foreign parts. Even the European interlude was not without its public and quasi-public service. One of Batlle's main purposes in making the trip was to study the political and economic problems of Europe. With widely opened eyes and ears he visited France, Belgium, the Netherlands, Switzerland, Spain, Italy, and Egypt. At the Hague he headed the Uruguayan delegation to the Second Peace Conference in 1907, and made one of the notable addresses delivered there. He proposed a plan for a society of nations to maintain the peace—a full dozen years before Woodrow Wilson, Jan Smuts, and others achieved the ideal. After the Hague Conference adjourned, Batlle proceeded to Switzerland, where he became peculiarly and profoundly interested in the contributions that little state had to make to the science of government. Afterward, he visited other countries, including a trip to his ancestral home in Catalonia.

The campaign for the presidential election by the congress in 1911 began shaping up some fifteen months before the inaugural date. By December of 1909, the Colorado party had begun agitation to make Batlle the party's candidate in 1911. As the months of 1910 passed, the movement grew, despite Blanco threats that the re-election of Batlle meant civil war. A small conservative anti-Batlle sentiment within the Colorado party was lost in a growing tide of enthusiasm for a renomination. The national committee of the party on July 3, 1910, unanimously proclaimed Batlle's candidacy.

Batlle's letter—he was still in Europe—stating to the party's committee the kind of platform he could stand on was a veritable creed of batllismo. In addition to his reiterated advocacy of the eight-hour day, he took a stand for popular instead of legislative election of the national president; for proportional representation of parties in the congress; for assurance of such workers' rights as those to life, health, and culture; for full protection of children, women, the ill, and the aged; for free and assisted immigration; for free public instruction in all its levels and obligatory education at the elementary level; for assistance to stock raising and agriculture and the stimulation of national industry; for the organization by the state of all services of social interest. Truly it was a broad platform, hewn to a political design far in advance of its time.

True to earlier threats, a Blanco revolt did break out in December, 1910, but it was neither formidable nor long. A more spectacular development was Batlle's return to the country on February 12, 1911, and the delirious welcome accorded him in the weeks thereafter. His election to a second term in the presidency by the congress on March 1 was almost anticlimax.

Before two months of his new term had passed, Batlle sent to the congress a bill providing for a state monopoly over insurance and for the creation of a state insurance bank. In rapid order he followed this in ensuing weeks with a proposal for creation of agricultural research stations, a project for the complete nationalization of the Bank of the Republic, a plan for creation of a section of rural credit, a bill for the establishment of a women's university, a decree freeing agricultural machinery and tools from all import duties, a decree abolishing official honors to symbols and persons of a religious character, a renewed advocacy of the eight-hour day, promulgation of a law creating a national commission of physical education, a proposal for the creation of a national orchestra and an experimental school of dramatic art. Such were Batlle's labors in his first six months in office.

Highlights of Batlle's reform program of the following year (1912) included the division of the country into new military zones, the issuance of regulations for a school of nursing, approval of an urbanization plan for the city of Montevideo, decreeing of a law of literary and artistic copyright, a bill for suppressing bullfights, promulgation of a law making the supply of electric light and power a country-wide state monopoly, and creation of an institute of industrial chemistry. In the late winter and spring of 1912 (August to November), Batlle and the congress took the necessary steps looking to the election of a constituent assembly to reform the Uruguayan constitution, by then more than eighty years old. The president kept his trump cards for that trick concealed for a few months longer, however.

Those cards were laid on the table on March 4, 1913—a date that saw another reformer inaugurated as president in a larger northern republic—when Batlle published in *El Día* his ideas of constitutional reform. The basic problems of Uruguayan government, he felt, were those stemming from dictatorship and instability. Both, in turn, could be blamed on the all too common Latin American phenomenon of a dominating president. The answer, Batlle thought, was to be found in the Swiss practice he had studied so assiduously a few years earlier. Hence, he now made the super-revolutionary proposal that Uruguay abolish its presidency and substitute a nine-member national plural executive. Thus began Batlle's greatest and bitterest battle.[3]

The Colorado reaction was immediate, violent, and, in its parts, diametrically divergent. An important fraction of the party repudiated Batlle's leadership and formed a dissident wing which maintained opposition consistently thereafter on the issue of the collegiate executive, though supporting Batlle's reforms in most other respects. The bulk of the party followed the president's lead. Much of the country exhibited that apathy of which Batlle had complained years before. The violent inter- and intra-party feuds continued to the time of the assembly

[3] Cf. Russell H. Fitzgibbon, "Adoption of a Collegiate Executive in Uruguay," *Journal of Politics*, November, 1952.

elections on July 30, 1916, when the antireform coalition was triumphant.

Both before and after that time Batlle himself had participated in a number of duels growing out of the violent recriminations produced by his proposals for constitutional change. In the last of these, on April 2, 1920 he killed his man. The victim was Dr. Wáshington Beltrán, co-director of an opposition Nationalist paper which had been needling Batlle for a long time. Ask a loyal batllista his feeling about this tragic incident and he is apt to shrug, or perhaps chuckle, and say that, well, Batlle was *muy hombre* [quite a man]. It must be remembered that dueling was neither legally nor morally outlawed in Uruguay and while it was a declining practice it had by no means disappeared. The fact that no duel in the United States involving similarly important people had occurred for well over a hundred years must be set in a matrix of changing moral concepts and attitudes.

The setback for Batlle's hard-fought plan registered by the assembly elections of July, 1916, was the cue for opposition political editors to begin writing his political obituary. They were premature. Batlle did temporarily withdraw from all official connection with his party, and, although he was a member of the constituent assembly, he did not attend its sessions. The work of the assembly represented a compromise. Batlle's followers, while they could not dominate the assembly, could still checkmate majority action if they so wished. Their threat to bring about a congressional re-election of Batlle to the presidency in 1919 for a third term was sufficient to persuade the hostile majority of the constituent assembly to make a virtue of presumed necessity. The resulting new constitution retained the presidency but created an independent and parallel national council of administration to divide with the president the functions of the executive branch.

Batlle's major work was now done. The fight for the collegiate executive had overshadowed all else during the closing years of his greatest activity, but he found time in his second term in office to prepare a bill establishing pensions for the aged, to sponsor a law providing equality of rights between legitimate and natural children, to initiate a state-owned railway system, and to direct the negotiation of a number of arbitration treaties. Following his retirement from the presidency, further Colorado party defections occurred, but the batllista nucleus which remained as the dominant fraction became more devoted than ever to Batlle's ideals and leadership. Twice during the 1920's, in 1920 and 1926, Batlle was elected president of the national council of administration. Colorado party dissensions continued during that decade; the magic of Batlle's living leadership proved less potent as a unifying influence than that of his memory in later decades.

In mid-September, 1929, Batlle entered a Montevideo hospital for major surgery. He died, in the same hospital, on October 20 of that year. Though he had been a tenacious opponent of the Church, two Sisters of Charity who had attended him in his last illness offered their prayers before his body resting in state in the Legislative Palace. The congresses of neighboring countries paid extraordinary tribute to him. Foreign officials—President Herbert Hoover and many others—sent their condolences. And in Uruguay the great and the humble mourned.

Alfredo Palacios, the eminent Argentine public figure, had earlier called José Batlle "without doubt, the foremost South American statesman." The lowly in Uruguay were less concerned with any rarefied and abstract statesmanship than with the fact Batlle had, year after year, proved himself their friend. He had once said in a public address: "Our party [*agrupación*] has a great flag: the flag of love for mankind, the flag of social justice." His deeds as well as his words had long since proved that it was his personal banner as well.

One of the greatest of Batlle's guiding principles was his consistent and persistent concern for what a spiritual cousin in a northern republic would later label "the forgotten man." Another was his abiding faith in the democratic process. Another was his firm belief that political affairs must be controlled secularly and not by any ecclesiastical authority or influence. Another was his conviction that a modified state socialism would free Uruguay from foreign economic domination and exploitation. In pursuance of this policy, which became perhaps the most pervasive and significant part of his program, Batlle made Uruguay the foremost political laboratory in all of Latin America for social and economic experimentation.

The Scandinavian countries, or New Zealand, or some of the North American states had become such laboratories, but on the Latin American scene a development of the kind was so rare as to be almost nonexistent.

Two problems Batlle did not solve—or even tackle. One was the overwhelming, and gradually worsening, problem of the relation of Montevideo to the rest of the country—capital against *campo*. It is true that many of the reforms Batlle undertook reflected in rural as well as urban areas, but there is little to indicate that he was even aware of the almost pathological economic, social, and cultural disparity between the two parts of the Uruguayan whole. A second important problem, related to the other, was that of the huge *estancias* or landed estates. Their social and economic impact on the Uruguayan scene was not so great, absolutely or relatively, as was the case with the Argentine *estancias* across the river, but, nonetheless, Batlle did nothing, and subsequent governments have done little, to break them up. There is, of course, a case to be made for the economic soundness of the large landed unit in Uruguay. It would seem, though, that Batlle's inattention to the problem was more by way of default than because of a reasoned satisfaction with the situation as it existed.

A possible explanation of these seemingly blind spots may lie in the fact that the static countryside provided less fertile soil for batllista reforms and hence attracted less of Batlle's interest. Montevideo, as one biographer puts it, "is the batllista city, with its great working masses, the student groups, a powerful middle class, intellectuals of revolutionary ideas, and the multitude of public employees who from the first administration of Batlle have experienced dignification from his social function." [4]

Batlle's hold on his followers was the kind one finds only once in a century or more. Time after time after time the history of the years of Batlle records a manifestation, a demonstration, a eulogy, a poem or hymn of tribute, all of which went far beyond the dictates of a sober and logical agreement with his political ideas, even far beyond what might have been expected of a typically emotional Latin response to dynamic and fervid leadership. The wide and ardent discipleship was

[4] Justino Zavala Muniz, *Batlle, Héroe Civil* (Mexico City, 1945), p. 216.

the result of Batlle's combination to an unusual degree of intelligence, sincerity, practicality, and magnetism.

That devotion to Batlle and to batllismo seems in some ways even to have increased since his death twenty-odd years ago. An evidence of the persistent influence of batllista ideas and ideals was the readoption of the collegiate executive in 1951, in purer form than even Batlle could originally obtain. Talk to a loyal batllista about one or another point of Batlle's program and he is likely to respond, "There are some things we just do not discuss; Batlle's ideals are an article of faith with us." Attend a convention of the batllista wing of the Colorado party and learn that the mere mention of his name is likely to be the cue for a thousand voices to break out in a chant, "Batlle—Batlle—Batlle—Batlle." Kept up for ten minutes or more that cannot have other than a sort of hypnotic effect. On the other hand, Batlle's enemies still characterize him by such epithets as "atheist," "a morally loose man," "usurper," "traitor," "dictator."

In the course of time Uruguay would have achieved much of its progress anyway. Nor can the full credit be given to Batlle; he had able, young lieutenants both before and after his death. Indeed, one criticism sometimes heard of Batlle was that he gathered round him a group of brilliant young men who sat adoringly at his feet and uncritically accepted his leadership. The criticism can be taken for whatever it may be worth but it by no means invalidates the solid achievement of Batlle. It was his lot to lift Uruguay by her bootstraps, as it were, to give form and vocality and impetus to the ferment that was in the making at the turn of the century.

The impress of José Batlle y Ordóñez is written large and ineradicably upon the face of Uruguay.

# 10

## Parties and Politics

It is well to begin a consideration of things political by establishing a premise or two. Let us recognize, for one thing, that there are democracies and democracies. It is not even necessary to admit consideration of so vicious a fiction as the "people's democracies" such as are alleged to exist behind the Communist curtain to contend successfully that various persons will have varying concepts and definitions of democracy. "Government by the people" is about as condensed a definition as can be proposed. But Lincoln's formula leaves something to be desired. Who are the people? How much government is there?

"The people" may be the highly restricted electorate of an ancient Greek city state—in which case we have an aristocratic democracy. Or they may be "the peepul," that vastly expanded electorate to whom some Huey Long will make a demagogic appeal. What should the particular government do? Some will tell you that it isn't a democracy unless limited to some narrow ambit such as Jefferson would have approved. But the English—some English, anyway—contend that their "Democratic Socialism" is democracy as fully as it is Socialism. And, if we return to our capsule definition of government by the people, perhaps they are right, because, after all, the people voted it in and, subject to qualifications which space limitations preclude being discussed here, could vote it out.

After two such paragraphs (which a hundred years ago might have been labeled An Inquiry into the Nature and Limitations of Democracy) let us turn for equally brief treatment to that devil-word Socialism. It has been suggested, by reference in the preceding paragraph to the English contention, that the dividing line between democracy and Socialism is hard to draw. If we take as a basic tenet of Socialism that the government shall control the agencies of production and distribution, then a nationally controlled mail service, municipal light plants and garbage disposal, state-owned railways (in many countries), city-operated tram and bus lines, all are Socialism of purest ray serene. All of which we tend to forget. TVA and government production of atomic energy are newer developments and will be a little longer in shedding their label of "Socialism." William Allen White put an editorial finger characteristically neatly on the trend when he wrote just after the 1936 election in the United States that, regardless of the party in power, the long current was toward a more and more inclusive sphere of government action, i.e., that Socialism constantly gained while Socialists did not.

In addition to being a form of government democracy is a process and an attitude. But of that, more later.

All of this is not so far apart from the Uruguayan scene as it might seem. For Uruguay is one of those countries which, like the Scandinavian, has seen its Socialism come slowly, peacefully, in almost an evolutionary fashion. As of today the government owns and operates the light and power plants and the telephone system of the country. The great hydroelectric project of the Río Negro (or Rione—another of those telescoped names) is a government enterprise. The Administración Nacional de Combustibles, Alcohol y Portland, or Ancap as it is universally known, has a monopoly over the refining of petroleum though not over the distribution of gasoline and other petroleum products. The state-owned chemical manufacturing monopoly is an important part of the picture of government enterprise. Several hotels and casinos are owned and operated by the government.

The "banks of the state" are three in number: the Bank of the Republic, a mortgage bank, and an insurance bank. Each is relatively a giant in its own field; the Bank of the Republic

controls some 65 per cent of the commercial banking business
of the country. The government is a heavy factor in the business of slaughtering, processing, and distribution of meat, operating chiefly through the agency of the Frigorífico Nacional,
the Frigonal. All of the railway mileage of the country is government-owned and -operated. Borrowing a leaf from the book
of Mexican precedent, the government, at least in theory, controls all mineral deposits. These, then, are some of the com-
ponents of the picture of Socialism in Uruguay.

If we employ the euphemism of "the welfare state" and pre-
suppose substantive, even if fine, distinctions between it and a
Socialist polity we can add to the evidence: Uruguay was the
first of the Latin American states to adopt a forty-four-hour
week and an eight-hour day and to make them applicable to
rural and domestic labor. An old-age assistance program dates
from 1919, a pension system for workers in many private industries from a few months later. The country was a pioneer in
requiring compulsory liability insurance, in providing compensation for industrial accidents, and in instituting government
inspection of factories. Vacations with pay have long been part
of the labor pattern. Labor union organization is encouraged
and the law provides for tribunals for conciliation and arbitration of labor disputes. The poor have free medical services and
all children and youth have absolutely free educational opportunities in the public schools all the way through the university
faculties. Illegitimate children have a recognized legal status
and are entitled to inherit property; the law requires investigation of paternity in doubtful cases.

If we look at what we may call merely liberal legislation,
the evidence continues to pile up. The legal position of women
is an advanced one, at least among Latin American states.
Women have the vote, divorce is permitted them, they may hold
property in their own names. The law of criminal procedure
provides for parole and probation. Uruguay has abolished the
death penalty. The constitutional bill of rights is extensive and
goes considerably further than the merely conventional provisions found in some Latin American constitutions.

All these—and more items might be cited—betoken what
by any yardstick might be called an advanced state and political system. Is it democracy? If we revert to our thumbnail

definition of government by the people we are justified in calling the Uruguayan system a genuine democracy. The people, in
approving three constitutions and a number of constitutional
amendments in the past generation and a half, in electing a
succession of administrations devoted to furthering the program of advanced and even socialistic legislation, in registering
their solemn judgment through the subtle but powerful voice
of public opinion, have declared in favor of what the Uruguayan government is today. Foreign specialists, too, regard
that government as highly democratic. A poll was taken among
a number of them in the United States in 1945 and repeated in
1950, the results both times ranking Uruguay first among all
Latin American states in the sum total of achievement according to various criteria devised for measuring democracy in
Latin America.[1]

Uruguay's constitutional and political path toward this
contemporary democracy has been, to say the least, rocky.
After the little Banda Oriental had for three years been a territorial football pushed around in an ironic game of international soccer by Argentina and Brazil, there still remained the
problem of laying a constitutional flooring under the newly independent republic. The fledgling state did have the advantage
of being able to draw on other Latin American constitutional
experience. Various ones of the new Latin republics had diligently studied the United States' two constitutions, the Articles
of Confederation of 1781 and the permanent basic law following it eight years later. They also had as models the liberal
Spanish constitution of 1812 and various French revolutionary
documents. In Uruguay's case, as well, there was a Chilean
constitution of 1828 to draw on and one written at Buenos
Aires in 1826, in addition to various earlier ones in southern
South America.

The resulting constitution of 1830, Uruguay's first, was
not a long basic law, as Latin American constitutions go, and
was, withal, relatively simple. It established the basic unitary
or centralized pattern of governmental organization which
Uruguay has followed uniformly ever since. The territorial

[1] *Cf.* Russell H. Fitzgibbon, "The Measurement of Latin American Political Phenomena: A Statistical Experiment," *American Political Science
Review,* vol. 45, pp. 517–23 (June, 1951).

departments—they are more than counties, less than states—
have only such powers as the central or national government
gives them. They cannot thus set themselves off against the
central government in that seeming equipoise that a federal
system permits. In this wise, Uruguay has departed from the
federal example set her by both her larger neighbors. Both
Argentina and Brazil are theoretically federal in organization,
though at times a Perón or a Vargas seems to make a mockery
of that relationship. The Uruguayan constitutional atmosphere
is just not favorable to the flowering of any such political
growth as Dixiecrats with their deeply rooted states-rightism.
This basic fact of a unitary government helps explain the
subordination of *campo* to capital, that megalocephaly of
which Montevideo gives us the world's most extreme example.

It is not cynics in the United States alone who can say,
"What's the constitution between friends?" Indeed, it seems as
if many of the early Latin American politicos must have put it
merely, "What's the constitution?"—period. The sordid short
of it was that in the early days of Latin American independence, even the best constitutions were often honored only in the
breach. Uruguay's was no exception. An intelligible and intelligent constitutional provision for peaceful succession of administrations did not prevent frequent political inquietude,
civil war, almost chronic near anarchy. The followers of rival
political chieftains inaugurated their feuding and the melancholy story of nineteenth-century politics was fairly begun.

It was in the Battle of Carpintería on September 19, 1836,
that followers of Oribe and Rivera, respectively, first used their
white and red hatbands as marks of distinction one from the
other. Thus were humbly, almost trivially, born the Blancos
and the Colorados, Uruguay's two great long-lived political
parties. In few other countries indeed in Latin America, perhaps
only in Colombia, have political parties shown the longevity
and tenacity of organization that these majority Uruguayan
parties have exhibited. As in the United States, politically-
minded men in Uruguay are born into one party or the other.
A Colorado can be one as much by inheritance as can a Re-
publican in the United States.

The next two decades of party development, as was true of
the government itself, were a sorry saga. Lust for power led

more than one politico to rise in revolt and the political panorama dragged its dismal way through one year and one administration after another. Dictatorships and governmental irregularities were common coin. A ten-day Blanco presidency in early February, 1865, gave way to a Colorado dictatorship. This in itself would not have been unusual but for the fact that it was the last (it seems scarcely necessary to say "latest") time a Blanco ever occupied the presidency in Uruguay. Since 1865, an unbroken period of more than four score years, Colorados have controlled Uruguay's highest executive office. Some were enlightened and progressive, others the worst sort of military dictators. Blancos, in 1872, definitively took the name of Partido Nacional, one they had used unofficially since 1857.

Party differences of ideology were never sharp in the nineteenth century. The same amorphousness characterized the social and geographical location of the membership of the two parties. But in the latter decades of the century the Colorado strength began to gravitate cityward while the Blancos or Nationalists found the nucleus of their support chiefly among the great estate owners or *estancieros*. It will be remembered that on more than one occasion in the late decades of the century the dominant Colorados reached a modus vivendi with the minority Blancos by which cash payments and control of offices in certain departments were given as a, shall we say, bribe to preserve the peace. Ultimately six of the departments thus fell under Nationalist sway and to all intents and purposes became the fiefs of the minority party.

The great Nationalist leader of the closing years of the century was a provincial gaucho, Aparicio Saravia, a wealthy *estanciero* whom the late Professor Percy Martin characterized as "a man of little culture and no political education." [2] Saravia's Nationalist following was a fanatical one and went faithfully with him into Uruguay's last full-dress rebellion in 1904. Saravia and many others paid with their lives. The blood sacrifice may have appeased the god of chaos who had held so heavy a hand on Uruguay. At any rate, political history thereafter followed a much more conventional pattern.

[2] Percy A. Martin, "The Career of José Batlle y Ordóñez," *Hispanic American Historical Review*, vol. 10, p. 415 (November, 1930).

The revitalization of the Colorado party was one of the early accomplishments of the great Batlle y Ordóñez. Sterility, a creeping cynicism, the incubus of the military dictatorships of recent years, all combined to put the Colorado party in almost as unenviable a position as that occupied by the Blancos. Batlle sold his party on its need for idealism and a program of reform, on the importance of intra-party democracy, discipline, and cohesiveness. The Colorado program, as Batlle thus evolved it, might have been a Latin archetype for the pattern of the New Deal in the United States a generation later.

Batlle's proposals for constitutional reform, made in 1913, dropped like a bombshell into the Uruguayan scene. They stemmed in large measure from his long-gestating conviction that the root of Uruguay's ills lay in the overwhelming dominance of the presidency in the governmental system of the country. A president who could, and as a matter of course did, overshadow both the congress and the courts would in all likelihood hand-pick his own successor. The opposition's only recourse, as ballots would in normal event fail it, would be bullets. Thus was born, Batlle reasoned, the dreary, deadly cycle of revolution, disorder, dictatorship, and repression. A plural executive, which Batlle had found and liked in Swiss practice, might be the answer. Executive authority, thus consciously decentralized, would be less of a temptation to resort to the pathological remedy of revolution with all its train of attendant evils.

The current constitution was by then more than eighty years old and many Uruguayans who were bitterly opposed to Batlle's specific proposals for change were willing to admit that revision was due, even overdue. There is a curious dichotomy of attitude on this score in the Latin mind. Latin, or at least Latin American, constitutions are normally more symbolic than instrumental, in contrast to those of Anglo-Saxon lands. But a persistent Latin American line of thinking has it that, even as symbols, they should be periodically refurbished, brought abreast of the times. Hence, it was not constitutional revision *per se* which aroused much of the violent opposition but rather the specific proposals for revision as made by Batlle. The Nationalists were naturally in opposition. Batlle's own Colorado party split. A dissident wing, the riverista

Colorados (so named from Fructuoso Rivera, the party founder of eighty years before), went off the range on the issue of the collegiate or plural executive.

Exigencies of politics precluded a clear-cut batllista control of the constitutional convention elected in 1916 even though Batlle's followers still dominated the congress. Hence, the convention of 1916–17 was forced to compromise the issue of Batlle's proposed collegiate executive. The compromise, which took the form of the so-called Pact of the Parties, was induced by the threat by Batlle's followers to push through the congress (which, by the constitution of 1830, elected the president) his election in 1918 to a third term in the presidency. The Nationalists regarded this possibility as horrendous and accepted a modified form of plural executive. The result, as embodied in the 1917 constitution, diluted though it was, was perhaps the most significant and unique governmental experiment ever undertaken in a Latin American country.

Batlle would have discarded the presidency entirely; the compromise provided for keeping it. The president was to be elected for a four-year term by a simple popular plurality (no longer by the congress) and would have within his power the appointment of the ministers of foreign relations, war and navy, and interior. Alongside and co-ordinate with the president the new constitution established a National Council of Administration, a popularly elected body of nine members chosen from the two major parties and renewable by thirds each two years. This body would have complete control over the ministries of public instruction, public works, finance (with certain exceptions), labor, industry, public welfare, and hygiene. The setup made for a vertical bifurcation of the executive branch, something definitely new under the governmental sun in Latin America, perhaps (in such a form) anywhere in the world.

Other features of the new constitution were less novel as well as less controversial. Municipalities and territorial departments were given a considerable autonomy, various state-operated commercial and educational services were placed under autonomous councils, Church and state were separated, the secret ballot and proportional representation were introduced, obligatory inscription of voters was provided, tentative steps

*From Playa Ramírez, near the heart of Montevideo, gleaming
white beaches extend like a string of beads along the Plata River
and the Atlantic Ocean, all the way to the Brazilian border.*

*Kiosk in the Plaza Constitución, Montevideo.*

were taken looking toward suffrage for women. But easily the most significant feature of the new constitution was its reorganization of the executive power.

As might have been expected, the operation of the new system was as controversial as its proposals had been. Its opponents claimed that the duality of authority made confusion and stupidities inevitable, that friction and acrimony were a natural outgrowth of the bifurcation, that the National Council of Administration concerned itself too greatly with petty details, and that "with its regulations similar to those of the Senate, its presidents, vice [presidents], agents, secretaries, assistants, stenographers, etc., it functioned more as a third chamber than as a branch of the government."[3] On the other hand, Professor Martin reported that "most foreign observers are agreed that this, the most spectacular of Batlle's innovations, has more than justified itself."

Party lines in the 1920's began to shape up much as they are today. The Colorados continued to dominate the political scene, often divided among themselves but cannily combining their votes for choice of a president and vice president. By the early 'twenties the Blancos or Nationalists were strongly led by Dr. Luis Alberto de Herrera, a hardy perennial in the political garden. So complete was this leader's control of his party that Nationalists came almost as commonly to be referred to as herreristas. Nationalists suffered certain splits and the schismatics—the Independent Nationalists were later the most important such group—thereafter proved unable to combine votes with the parent party. A party weed which entered the garden in 1921 was the Communist organization. It was thereafter quite active, vocal, and consistent in following the inconsistent party line. Socialists, with much more respectable leadership than that of the Communists, were also active in the field. The fate of party politics brought Herrera to the presidency of the National Council of Administration in the mid-'twenties, but in later years the Nationalist vote suffered a relative decline.

Gabriel Terra, a Colorado of batllista persuasion, was elected president in 1930. So far had party fractionation gone

[3] Pablo Blanco Acevedo, *Estudios Constitucionales* (Montevideo, 1939), p. 68.

by that time, however, that he represented a wing—perhaps a feather!—opposed to the so-called "unadulterated" batllistas who were grouped around the sons of the late José Batlle y Ordóñez. Party differences, both among Colorados and Nationalists, were deepening. The world-wide depression, with its uncertainties and economic strain, added to party acerbities. The dramatic upshot of the accumulated disaffection, particularly of Terra's dissatisfaction with the functioning of the National Council of Administration, was the president's coup d'état on March 31, 1933, by which he dissolved the congress and the council and made himself a dictator.[4] A tragically dramatic consequence of this coup was the suicide of Dr. Baltasar Brum, brilliant former president of the republic and at the time president of the National Council of Administration. By the narrow margin of one day his action failed of being a macabre All Fools' joke.

Dictatorship fell strangely on the Uruguayan scene. There had been no such thing for more than a third of a century. Terra, however, almost immediately took steps toward the election of a new constitutional convention. This assembly in 1933–34 drafted Uruguay's third constitution. Inasmuch as anti-Terra groups boycotted the election of delegates, it went almost without saying that the new document would reflect the president's basic ideas. The primary change was the abandonment of the National Council of Administration: a more conventional type of presidential control was thereby established.

Perhaps the most novel feature of the new constitution was the specification that half of the thirty senators should represent the ticket of the largest fraction of the majority party and the other half the strongest branch of the next largest party. This open invitation to party deadlocks in voting threw a correspondingly greater responsibility on the vice president, who was made the senate's presiding officer and given both voice and vote. The new "half and half" senate was equally divided between terrista Colorados (the followers of Terra) and herrerista Nationalists; batllista Colorados and anti-herrerista Nationalists continued in active opposition and in January, 1935, attempted an abortive revolution; some of the leaders of

---

[4] Cf. Philip B. Taylor, Jr., "The Uruguayan Coup d'Etat of 1933," *Hispanic American Historical Review,* vol. 32, pp. 301–20 (August, 1952).

this "anti-marzista" [5] marriage of convenience thereafter found the political climate temporarily healthier in Brazil or Argentina.

Elections in 1938 were almost a cozy little family affair. The two presidential candidates within the Colorado party were the brother-in-law and the son-in-law of the incumbent President Terra. The brother-in-law, General Alfredo Baldomir, won. A civilian, Terra had diverted Uruguay to its interlude of dictatorship; it fell to a general, Baldomir, to lead it back to its traditional democratic course.

But politics, as well as circumstances, alters cases. New presidential elections were scheduled for March, 1942, but in February of that year Baldomir, who had begun to disagree with the herreristas (they were being called pro-Nazi) and who had showed a clear wish for a rapprochement with the batllistas and the anti-herreristas, undertook a coup of his own. He dissolved the congress and named a council of state to draft a constitutional amendment terminating the famous "half and half" senate. The lapse from democracy was only temporary: the following November saw a new president chosen, the senate revamped on a more practical basis of proportional representation, and women voting for the first time.

The path of democracy has been followed faithfully during recent administrations. A political bomb of a kind was dropped in mid-1951 with the announcement that representatives of the two major parties, Colorados and Nationalists, had agreed to support a constitutional amendment re-establishing a collegiate executive. With both major groups supporting it, the proposal seemed an odds-on favorite to win, but it carried in December, 1951, by only a relatively small majority. For the Colorados it was simply a return to the old love of Batlle himself. The basic explanation of the Nationalist *volte-face* allegedly lay in the fear that it would always be runner-up to the Colorados and by thus sponsoring a collegiate executive it might at least share in the control of that branch of the government.

Until the rise of Batlle y Ordóñez the traditional parties had been distinguished from each other, in reality, only by the

[5] Terra's followers, of both major parties, were called marzistas because his coup had taken place in *March,* 1933; his opponents were, therefore, anti-marzistas.

color of their emblems. They were parties of men rather than
of ideas. The Colorados were the men who were "in," the
Blancos the men who were "out" and sometimes revolted to get
"in." Batlle's social revolution gave his party an ideology, but
after his death in 1929, it tended to revert to a large measure
of personalism. The prevalence of personalism is easily footnoted by citing the common use of leaders' names to identify
party wings or fractions: batllistas, herreristas, baldomiristas,
blancoacevedistas, terristas. This also suggests, as is unfortunately true, that a few families and a few individuals often exercise a disproportionately large influence within a given party
organization.

The Colorado party is the most extensively organized of
any in Uruguay. This, too, was initially the work of Batlle, but
of course even yet the party's organization feeds to a significant extent on patronage. Party headquarters in Montevideo reflect an air not only of prosperity but also of importance: the various offices carry on their work with a full
realization that it is the activity of the country's dominant
party. Conventions of the batllista wing of the party [6] are
likely to be mass rallies of dedicated devotees for whom the
name of Batlle is still a magic symbol.

The internal organization of the batllista Colorados is, on
the whole, democratic. Major party matters are decided in
convention. Montevideo has scattered over it sectional clubs of
the Colorado party (and to a lesser extent of the Nationalists),
some of which operate "schools for citizenship," a euphemism
for drumming up party enthusiasm.

The liberal ideological position assumed by the Colorados a

[6] The Colorado party's family tree is slightly complex. The majority of
Colorados are followers of Batlle's position and tenets—hence, batllistas.
But the batllistas are divided into two groups, one following the lead of
Batlle's sons, the other, and smaller group, that of Luis Batlle Berres,
nephew of José Batlle and himself president from 1947 to 1951. The
riverista Colorados were a more conservatively inclined group, which split
away from the parent trunk in 1913 over the issue of the collegiate executive. Terristas and baldomiristas were the subordinate fractions of Colorados who respectively followed the lead of Presidents Gabriel Terra and
Alfredo Baldomir. A group of independent Colorados felt, after Baldomir's
election in 1938, that they had nowhere else to go and, under the leadership
of Eduardo Blanco Acevedo, split from the main body. They still operate
as independents. Appropriately, but ponderously, they are called blancoacevedistas.

half century ago under the drive of Batlle has forced the Blancos or Nationalists to become relatively more conservative in position. On the part of both major parties, however, many inconsistencies and many ideological subdivisions, temporary or permanent, occur. Each of the large parties has its conservatives and its liberals, and party lines are often difficult to hold in congressional debate.

The center of gravity of Blanco psychology is in the *campo,* though its headquarters, newspaper, and other main agencies and activities are in Montevideo. In terms of individuals composing the parties, the Blancos, especially the herreristas, are often regarded as more cultured and substantial than the batllistas; the former are "the better class of society" by such classification.

The Independent Nationalists are said to be antipersonalist but they do not thereby fall back on a consistent ideological position. To the extent that they could be considered to have a common body of ideas they have been described as the Uruguayan equivalent of New Dealing Republicans. A small group of Blancos formed the Social Democratic party, with a definite leftist orientation, but it had no congressional representation and little popular following.

The only really ideological parties operating in Uruguay at present are the Socialists, the Communists, and the Unión Cívica, a Catholic party. The Socialist party, now forty-odd years old, is largely the reflection of Emilio Frugoni, lawyer, poet, diplomat, legislator—the term statesman would scarcely be amiss. When Dr. Frugoni was arrested by Argentine police in Buenos Aires in the latter part of 1951 and deported to Uruguay for the heinous offense of visiting a prominent Argentine Socialist, the uproar in Montevideo was great. A civic reception was promptly organized, with representatives of all political groups except the herreristas and Communists participating. The Uruguayan Socialists give a slight impression of shabby gentility. Their orientation, like that of Colorados and Communists, is toward the Montevideo working classes. A practical program to appeal to those classes has been so much the monopoly of the Colorados, however, that the Socialists have been left little distinctive ground on which to stand.

The logic of democracy would scarcely allow Uruguay to

ban the Communist party. That party does operate freely there. That is not to say effectively, however. Uruguay possesses both fundamental advantages and disadvantages for Communist functioning. As probably the most politically free country in Latin America, Uruguay has put almost no hindrance in the way of Communist propaganda and other activity. But, as one of the most socially and economically advanced of all the Latin American countries, Uruguay has provided correspondingly poor soil for Communist proselyting.

When the Third International began its active propagandizing in Latin America in the early 1920's, it concentrated its work on the countries where the greatest discontent with the economic and political order was apparent. Those did not include Uruguay, but that state gained the dubious distinction of having the Communist international headquarters for Latin America. Agents and literature were sent from Montevideo to all parts of South America. A Soviet branch trading company in Argentina, the Iuyamtorg Corporation, was raided and closed in 1931 during the dictatorship of General Uriburu. It thereupon moved across the river, incorporated under Uruguayan law, and continued to do business.

This favorable situation was brought temporarily to an end during the dictatorship of President Terra. Under a tenseness increased by depression conditions Terra deported many radicals. Late in 1935 the Uruguayan government broke diplomatic relations with the Soviet Union because of the Russian legation's abuse of the hospitality granted it in Montevideo. With the re-establishment of diplomatic relations during World War II, the way was again opened for freer Communist activity in Uruguay. Despite the fact that the great weight of Uruguayan opinion has been consistently and strongly anti-Communist, the party during the War gained the sympathy of a number of idealists and intellectuals; even then, however, most Uruguayans remained indifferent if not hostile to it.

For twenty years or more the number one Communist leader in Uruguay has been Eugenio Gómez, an able, if rabble-rousing, speaker. He has been characterized as a field man rather than an original thinker. He is very commonly regarded in Uruguay as a professional demagogue and party liner, and he is accorded none of the respect widely given Emilio Frugoni, the top Socialist leader. Gómez is assisted in the high command of the Communist party by Sra. Julia Arévalo de Rocha, a labor leader and former senator, and Enrique Rodríguez, former representative and the secretary of the Unión General de Trabajadores, the biggest labor organization.

Uruguayan Communists have prided themselves on a professionally shabby and proletarian party appearance. Though the party has been reasonably well financed, its various headquarters have a designedly down-at-the-heels look. The card-carrying membership has been estimated at 5,000 to 8,000, with about 15,000 additional sympathizers. The peak vote was reached in 1946 when the Communist presidential candidate received 32,680 votes, about 5 per cent of the total vote cast; four years later the Communist vote declined to just over 19,000. Communist party ballots, ironically, have had to be printed in black because of the legal monopoly of the traditional red as the color of the Colorado party's ballots.

Communists have tried to make political hay with the Slav colony in Montevideo, estimated to include 25,000. There also has been a consistent and partially successful effort to infiltrate the ranks of organized labor. Several Communists or fellow travelers have gotten into the radio field. The most consistent party line in Uruguay has been hostility to the United States. The former Communist daily paper, *Diario Popular*, suspended in June, 1947, because of declining circulation. It was succeeded by the weekly *Justicia*, a typical party organ with flamboyant typography and illustration and sensational stories.

Despite its vocality and persistence, the Communist party does not prosper in Uruguay. Uruguay's social advances and general lack of poverty cut the ground from under its traditional appeal. Carnival, maté, the beaches, and *fútbol* are more immediate and filling to the Uruguayan spirit than stock Communist arguments about imperialist threats and capitalist responsibility for the high cost of living.

The Unión Cívica has consistently followed a Catholic position and has attracted only a Catholic membership, but many Catholics belong to other parties, especially the Nationalist and its offshoots because of the traditional batllista tenet of anticlericalism. The establishment of woman suffrage in the late

'thirties contributed, as might have been expected, to the benefit of the Unión Cívica. The Catholic party has had its internal
ideological differences but usually has presented a common
front and usually has been blessed with capable leadership.

Parties can be very easily organized: a legal minimum of
only fifty citizens is necessary to register a political party.
Occasionally an unconventional, even an eccentric, party will
appear momentarily on the political scene and nominate candidates. In the 1946 campaign one Domingo Tortorelli, a prosperous vegetable salesman, ran as a self-appointed presidential
candidate. His platform and campaigning were, to say the
least, different. He promised two fountains on every Montevideo
street corner, one flowing with milk for the children, the other
with wine for adults. The capital city should have a roof built
over it to protect its residents in rainy weather. Uruguay was
still in the throes of gasoline shortages: ergo, Tortorelli promised, a super highway from Montevideo to Colonia would be
built running downhill both ways in order to save gas! His
nightly speeches sometimes drew crowds estimated at as high
as 150,000. They often pelted him with vegetables, which he
professed to like as being good for his business. Unfortunately
for novel experiments in highway engineering, the vegetables
were far more numerous than the votes—he was very much an
also-ran.

# 11

## ¡Viva la Democracia!

Reference has been made to fractions of one party or another. Which raises the question of the strange and wonderful election laws of Uruguay. The proof of the pudding must lie in the fact that they work, and that Uruguayans, many of them, anyway, seem content with them. Some Argentines will occasionally comment privately, very privately, and with envy about the Uruguayan electoral system. Uruguayans have even adopted the principle of the system for certain private organizations. But to the foreigner it appears to be something that was dreamed up in a nightmarish moment, and at the very least it seems rigged to assure the continued dominance of the majority, that is to say, the Colorado, party. The system was devised by a Belgian named Borelly and was introduced into Uruguay in the mid-1920's.

The election system is based on what the Uruguayans call the double simultaneous vote. This means, in terms about as simple as they can be made, that the voter votes at one and the same time for the candidate and for the party of his choice. Each of the parties operating in an election lists its candidates under a *lema* or motto. This is usually simply the party name. To speak of the party *lema* is roughly the same as referring to the party ticket. Candidates for, say, the National Council of Government and for senators may be identical on two ballots, but the lists of candidates for representatives or for the electoral board will differ. The latter lists, then, will be printed under a *sublema*. If the necessity for differentiation goes still further, one group of candidates or another may be listed under a *distintivo* or distinguishing mark.

The *sublemas* and *distintivos* may be the names of party heroes or they may be ringing calls to party loyalty and triumph. For example: "For batllista ideals," "With Herrera, against collegialism," "Long live Batlle," "For suffrage, for economic democracy," "For Saravia, for Herrera, for Otamendi, for national reconstruction; down with collegialism." (That Nationalist inveighing against collegiate government is now ironic in view of the party's about-face on the issue in 1951.) The *lema* is the legal property of the party organization, which can grant or refuse its use to those candidates or subordinate groups which it chooses. Thus, the refusal by the Nationalist party to allow the use of its *lema* by the Independent Nationalists necessarily resulted in the latter group's organizing and operating as a legally distinct party.

The law provides for cumulating the votes of various *sublemas* and giving them all to the top candidate of the one party. Therein lies the grim joker for the Nationalist party. Thus, in the elections of 1950 three Colorado candidates ran for the presidency. Andrés Martínez Trueba received 161,262 votes; César Mayo Gutiérrez, 150,930; and Eduardo Blanco Acevedo, 120,949. The Nationalist candidate, the perennial Luis Alberto de Herrera, running for the sixth time, won 254,834 votes, or 93,572 more than the highest of the three Colorado candidates. But the three Colorados were running under the same *lema* and the total of all their votes was 433,454 (adding in about 300 ballots unassigned to any candidate individually). All these votes were consequently given to Martínez Trueba, the leading Colorado, which gave him a handsome plurality of 178,620 over Herrera. The Colorados might well jubilate privately, "How can we lose!" In effect, the system combines a primary election and a final general election. Its result has been to preserve a two-party dominance but at the same time to facilitate fractionation within the major parties.

The multiplicity of *lemas*, *sublemas*, and *distintivos*, especially in Montevideo, means that the voter is often confronted with making a choice from among several dozen lists. Since he has a legal limit of one minute in which to vote, he usually will have brought with him a ballot supplied by the party organization of his choice. To place the ballot in the official envelope (supplied by the government), seal, and deliver it to the election board requires, then, an average of only thirty seconds! The whole system is complicated but—it seems to work. The powerful and respected electoral court closely supervises elections; charges of electoral fraud are just not heard in Uruguay. President Baldomir reportedly said on one occasion during the War, "We have the costliest electoral system per capita on the continent but it is cheaper than revolution."

The be-all and end-all of party activity often seems to be the electoral campaigns for national council, senators, representatives, departmental and municipal councils, and other offices. Campaigns are frenetic affairs—a mélange of mass meetings, newspaper polemics, radio addresses, sound trucks, what seem to be millions of posters on walls of houses and business buildings, inscriptions and official numbers of *lemas* painted on walls, etc. Elections, as is all but universal in Latin America, take place on Sunday. The impartial electoral court keeps the official register of voters, which is revised *weekly*. Women have voted in encouraging and increasing numbers. The percentage of eligible voters actually casting ballots is not so high as it once was. In the presidential elections of 1926 and 1930, it was more than 80 per cent; in 1938, due probably to bitterness and defeatism engendered by the Terra dictatorship, it dropped to 56 per cent; in 1942 and 1946 it increased to 66 and 65 per cent respectively; and in 1950 it rose to 70 per cent. But statistics indicate that Uruguay at times has had a higher percentage of its total population voting than any other republic in the hemisphere.

It is a truism that all government tends more and more to gravitate into executive hands. Even democratic Uruguay provides no exception. In virtually all Latin American states the president is the personification of the government: the degree to which he falls short of that role is sometimes a rough measure of democracy in the given country. Government in Uruguay until 1951 revolved around the president from the day of his inauguration. The executive was, in reality, shortchanged for office buildings, one decides, when he contrasts the quite ordinary Government Palace with the costly and ornate Legislative Palace. But perhaps it was made up in the gay colorfulness of the presidential guard, the shakoed and sometimes mounted and helmeted military unit used as attendants at the Palace and as an honor guard on important ceremonial occasions.

The president's powers, while that office lasted, were carefully circumscribed both by the constitution and the laws and by tradition and the subtly effective control of public opinion. It was not always thus: W. H. Hudson wrote many years ago of "the throne of human skulls, styled in their ghastly facetiousness a Presidential Chair." The recent limitations, legal and extralegal, meant that the president secured whatever effectiveness he had through the intangible channels of party controls, through his influence with and over the people, and, as did the great Batlle, through sheer force of character and personality. It was a skillful president, for example, who, as Martínez Trueba did in 1951, could persuade a leading opponent in the presidential campaign of the preceding year to take a relatively minor cabinet position. Only once in more than half a century did Uruguay have a member of the military in the presidency and then under unusual circumstances.

The plan voted in 1951 for the re-establishment of the collegiate executive, and made effective March 1, 1952, provided for supplanting the presidency with a National Council of Government of nine members, six of them belonging to the major wing of the strongest party and three to the dominant fraction of the leading minority party.[1] Candidates for the national council are popularly elected. The involved provisions of the new 1951 constitution permit subordinate fractions or offshoots of a party to have representation on the council under certain circumstances. That provision was aimed at blanco-acevedista representation among the Colorados and at the possibility of including an Independent Nationalist among the minority bloc of three. It was the price paid for political support from those two subordinate party groups. The division of council seats between the two major parties is not true pro-

[1] Cf. Russell H. Fitzgibbon, "Adoption of a Collegiate Executive in Uruguay," in *Journal of Politics*, vol. 14, pp. 616–42 (November, 1952).

portional representation inasmuch as the smaller parties are, in effect, legally excluded from all representation. The practical operation of the system allows complete domination of the national council by batllistas and herreristas.

The presidency of the national council is annually rotative among the six majority-party members although a temporary provision in the constitution was designed to allow Martínez Trueba to hold the council's presidency as long as he would have been president of the republic, *i.e.*, until 1955. The powers given the council were almost identical with those previously held by the president.

In its first months of operation the new collegiate government, the first full-dress experiment of the sort ever tried in the New World, seemed to work reasonably well. An initial honeymoon between the two old rival parties, born of their cooperation in getting the 1951 constitution adopted, tended to wear off as 1952 passed. Party maneuvering for advantage gradually returned.

The principle of executive government by commission is also introduced by the new constitution into the nineteen departments into which Uruguay is divided. The single intendant which each department formerly had is now replaced by a bipartisan council of seven in the Department of Montevideo and five in each of the other departments. The departmental legislatures are retained as before but enlarged.

The cabinet is fixed constitutionally at nine members. At present they head the ministries of the interior, foreign relations, national defense, public instruction and social welfare, industries and labor, stock raising and agriculture, public works, public health, and finance. Political tradition forbids monopoly of all cabinet positions by any one wing of a single party; the new president in 1951, for instance, chose seven batllistas and two blancoacevedistas for cabinet positions; the first National Council of Government in 1952 prorated the cabinet positions on a party basis. In earlier administrations members of the Independent Nationalist party and the Unión Cívica had occasionally been included in the cabinet. Communists and Socialists have not been.

In addition to the ministries there are various special services, social welfare institutes, and other agencies operating in the industrial and commercial sphere. Some of these are known in Uruguay by the somewhat five-dollar term of autonomous entities; Stateside they would be called independent agencies or government corporations. The important autonomous entities administer various of the banking, industrial, commercial, and educational activities of the government. They are controlled by semi-independent, bipartisan boards of directors.

The ministry of the interior, which is perhaps more logically named than the department of the same designation in the United States (but ought to be called ministry of government, as most Latin American countries do name it), clearly occupies top position in the Uruguayan cabinet machinery, as is true elsewhere in Latin America. It supervises the police, maintains order, sees to the execution of laws and decrees, performs various other service functions. The ministry of foreign relations does what one would expect of it and in addition has the less conventional function of being responsible, in a way, for the important national tourism commission. Perhaps tourists promote good foreign relations!

The ministry of national defense does not call the tunes in Uruguay, as is unhappily often the case in other Latin American countries. That is by way of saying that Uruguay is *not* military minded and that its armed establishment has always been kept within due and modest bounds. It has been estimated that in case of a defensive war Uruguay could put 120,000 men in the field. This figure may represent a bit of wishful thinking. A law for compulsory military instruction is on the statute books but is honored in the breach rather than in the observance. The army establishment itself includes only nine regiments of cavalry, five each of artillery and infantry, six of "pioneers," and one of tank troops. The air force has some 200 planes. The navy includes two frigates, four patrol vessels, one surveying ship, four training ships, and four tenders; its personnel: 171 officers and 1,300 men. In 1951 Uruguay bought for 2,600,000 pesos two former United States destroyer escorts for use as frigates in its navy. Assuredly it is a law book rather than a sword on which Uruguay relies for defense of its international position. In addition to its more orthodox functions the defense ministry supervises certain national parks and monuments, controls military courts, and maintains a military library.

The minister of public instruction and social welfare is in the half-anomalous position of finding that education-wise the decisions are made almost entirely by four independent councils which largely control the various levels of Uruguay's excellent educational system. But he is responsible, more directly and effectively, for museums, libraries, historical archives, the development of fine arts, supervision of private instruction, and much that has to do with the broad field of social welfare, of which few, if any, countries are more conscious than Uruguay. The ministry of public works deals with more than meets the eye through the title itself: the formidable words of hydrography, marigraphy, and topography suggest some of the more unusual responsibilities. The ministry of public health reveals in its various internal ramifications a broad and advanced consciousness of the health problems and needs of the country as a whole.

The ministry of stock raising and agriculture reflects the importance of a primarily livestock-producing country. Among the less logical functions which fall to it are supervision of immigration and of the national observatory. Promotion of manufacturing and mining, development of commerce, and control over labor disputes are among the problems that fall to the responsibility of the ministry of industries and labor. And by no means least, even if last in this catalog, the ministry of finance must keep the governmental wheels turning by its collection of taxes and management and expenditure of public funds. The whole cost of an elaborate governmental mechanism is great, even in a small country like Uruguay, and the piper has to be paid. The tax structure has hence become a small-scale Pelion atop Ossa. If a new financial obligation is incurred, an easy out is to legislate a new tax of two per cent on this or three per cent on that. Movie admissions, matches, rentals, all and many more items are subject to percentage taxes of various kinds. Gasoline is the classic example: its cost is approximately *doubled* by the twenty-odd taxes levied against it.

Governmental costs are a relative matter. Those in Uruguay are expensive relative to other Latin American countries

—not so much so in comparison with the United States. The estimated governmental revenues in 1951 were 332,952,656.03 pesos and the estimated expenditures 332,096,967.71 pesos.[2] In terms of United States dollars (at an arbitrary conversion rate of 2.50 pesos to the dollar) this meant a governmental income of $53.27 per capita and an outgo of $53.14. Not too high, especially in comparison with the cost of government in the United States; Uruguay pays relatively little, of course, for past, present, and future wars. The per capita income in Uruguay was estimated in 1950 to be $331 as against $1,453 in the United States. Thus, the average Uruguayan was paying about one-sixth of his income for the support of his government; in the United States the fraction was about two-sevenths.

About 56 per cent of Uruguayan governmental revenues come from taxation, some 21 per cent from customs duties, and about 14 per cent from all types of governmental enterprises. The biggest percentage expenditures are for education and debt servicing, about 19 each; then follow public health and pensions, and national defense, about 10 per cent each; over-all administration, subsidies, and the ministry of the interior, about 7 per cent each; the treasury, 6 per cent; and public works, 4 per cent.

The large expenditures for debt servicing inevitably imply a large governmental debt. By the end of August, 1951, it has reached 1,005,076,163 pesos.[3] This represented a per capita public debt of 402 pesos or about $160.80, far smaller than the United States figure of $1,829 (federal, state, and local). Again, the conclusion is inevitable that war is an expensive business. The Uruguayan public debt has increased almost

[2] The principal items of revenue, in round numbers of pesos, were: import duties, 71,340,000; internal revenue, 44,910,000; industrial, commercial, and professional taxes, 81,729,000; business taxes, 22,991,000; property transfer taxes, 18,700,000; gambling taxes, 11,030,000; revenue from government enterprises, 39,565,000; debt service reimbursements, 13,587,000. The chief expenditures were: congress, 3,914,000; the presidency, 416,000; national defense, 34,861,000; treasury, 19,698,000; industry and labor, 9,549,000; educational expenditures, 63,521,000; interior, 24,187,000; public works, 12,-195,000; foreign affairs, 1,485,000; public health, 30,475,000; livestock and agriculture, 4,587,000; judiciary, 7,022,000; pensions, 15,835,000; debt servicing, 61,948,000; subventions, 24,262,000.

[3] This was broken down into roughly 106,596,000 of floating and 898,-480,000 of bonded debt; the latter was divided between approximately 783,241,000 of internal and 115,239,000 of foreign debt.

every year since 1860 when it represented a per capita debt of
only thirteen pesos.

In a governmental organism such as Uruguay's, where the
executive machinery becomes so expanded, the legislative
branch becomes, anomalously, similarly more important. Its
job is legislation, policy making if you will, but more basically
and more subtly it has the correspondingly greater responsibility of retaining fundamental control over the executive and
the administrative machine. Uruguay's parliament well realizes
and exercises that responsibility.

The two houses, senate and chamber of representatives,
have thirty-one and ninety-nine members, respectively. In terms
of internal organization, committees, and so on, the two houses
resemble in general what we would find at Washington or at
most state capitals. Legislators at Washington might, if transplanted to Montevideo, feel themselves abused inasmuch as the
Uruguayan congress meets for some eight or nine months a
year but, on the other hand, it often meets only two or three
days a week, so perhaps matters even up. The home of the Uruguayan legislature is the magnificent Palacio Legislativo dominating Avenida Agraciada. It is a fitting domicile. The houses
feel their responsibility in the Uruguayan political scheme of
things and the dignity of their locale is, then, in proper proportion.

The two houses normally meet at about four-thirty or five
o'clock in the afternoon. The day's papers will have carried
the order of business for the day and John Citizen will consequently know whether he wishes to attend. If he does he will be
politely but effectively "frisked" by a gallery attendant before
he is admitted. Debate is usually dignified, but it can on occasion become Latinly aroused and continue until four or five in
the morning. Murmurs, interruptions, calls for order, even a
temporary adjournment by the presiding officer, may mark
instances of the sort.

The veteran Communist legislator, Eugenio Gómez, has developed a particular and unenviable reputation as a gadfly. On
one occasion, years ago, he got himself temporarily expelled
for "making a disrespectful gesture toward the galleries," as
the *Diario* euphemistically put it (though, perhaps fortunately,
failing to specify the nature of the gesture). At times when a

Communist speaks in the congress, other members will walk out, read their newspapers, or openly visit with neighbors to indicate their disdain.

Debate is sometimes stodgy, at other times scintillating. Uruguayans still chuckle over a passage at arms a few years ago. It was on an occasion when the brilliant Emilio Frugoni was the object of a bitterly scurrilous attack by an opposition legislator who pulled all the stops in criticizing the Socialist leader. When the critic had done, Frugoni asked politely, "Are you quite finished?" "Yes, quite," was the surprised reply. "*Entonces*," answered Frugoni, "*tire la cadena*" ("Then, pull the chain"). Those familiar with the intimate details of Uruguayan domestic plumbing needed no explanation of Dr. Frugoni's metaphor.

The best organized and selected congressional group is often conceded to be the herreristas. They usually maintain a fairly specialized division among researchers, parliamentarians, negotiators, and orators. Batllistas are often regarded as the better cloakroom specialists and strategists.

The congress has an important degree of questioning and investigative power over the ministers. The latter officials can and on occasion do attend the sessions of one house or the other to debate or explain measures in which they are specifically interested. But the houses do not feel subservient to the ministers and at times have given them a rough going over. Usually the relations between legislature and executive are harmonious enough—there is, of course, the connective tissue of party affiliations—but the Uruguayan congress is fortunately and democratically conscious of its role as vigilant guardian of the public weal.

Congressional salaries are not large and, so tight is the party control, the members often have to "kick back" from 20 to 30 per cent of their salaries to the party treasury; as a consequence, the job frequently entails a financial sacrifice, especially since those lawyers who are members of the congress are legally prohibited from having any government business. The office does serve as a means of political advancement, however, and congressmen who are willing to surrender their legislative seats to their alternates are often appointed to more lucrative government positions or to the directorates of au-

tonomous entities. The congressman's primary political loyalty
is often to his party and he may not even live in the department he represents. He is frequently under great pressure from
job seekers.

The classic representation of Justice is that of the blind-
folded goddess, stern of mien, full of figure, holding aloft a pair
of scales. Blindness signifies impartiality. In more than one
Latin American state it takes on the substituted and ironic
meaning of inability to distinguish wrong from right, of ve-
nality (say, for example, holding out the scales for a measure
of gold), of subservience. In Uruguay, however, the Greek goddess can and does hold her head in unsullied pride. If any extraordinary significance is to be read into the blindfold it is
probably only that Justice is slow in finding her way—it takes
ages, seemingly, to get a court case settled.

The symmetrical and well-organized structure of the Uruguayan court system is headed by a dignified and able supreme
court of justice. Its five members are chosen, not by the executive, but by the two houses of the congress. They serve for ten-
year terms and cannot be re-elected except after a lapse of five
years. That ten-year service has a qualification: they (and all
members of the judiciary) stop judging at the age of seventy.
This provision, be it noted, antedated by about three years a
slightly similar proposal made by President Roosevelt in the
1930's. The constitution and the law give the supreme court
broad power, not only to act within its own orbit, but also to
supervise the lower courts.

Down the judicial ladder, which of course is the reverse of
the way a case goes, one runs into courts of appeal, the un-
translatable *juzgados letrados* (we had best call them just
courts of record), justices of the peace, and district judges,
which latter would find its closest counterpart in the United
States in the local police judge. There is more to the family
tree of the courts than that—special courts for minors, military courts, those for administrative matters, courts for certain financial cases. Some use is made of the jury but, for better or worse, it is neither hallowed nor hollow as is often the
case in the United States.

The majesty of the law is no empty phrase in Uruguay.
Lawing, as our great-grandfathers sometimes called it, re-

quires time, but a part of that problem is doubtless the more leisurely tempo characteristic of Uruguay which, after all, is not wholly removed from mañanaland. But, all in all, Uruguay's courts are a good complement to her congress and her executive branch.

Local government in Uruguay offers little that is either spectacular or unique. The constitution does give both the departments and the municipalities a greater degree of autonomy than is found at those levels in most Latin American states, but they still remain much subject to the national government. It is in part the old question of capital versus *campo*. Of the eighteen capitals of departments other than Montevideo none is more than about one-seventeenth as large as the great metropolis. For that reason, if for no other, local government is necessarily organized on a simple basis.

The disproportionate position of Montevideo is constitutionally recognized by making its departmental council slightly more than twice as large as that of each of the other departments. Local councils may be established in towns outside the departmental capitals. They, like the departmental councils, are organized with proportional representation of the parties. The members of both serve without pay which, though the members themselves would doubtless often deny it, is one of the best features of the system because a crying need in most Latin American countries is the instilling of a sense of civic responsibility unrewarded by any consideration of monetary gain. The basic law makes provision for popular appeal, on constitutional grounds, from the decisions of local officials and, further, it provides for referendum elections. These evidences of a willingness to decentralize the democratic process are but little built upon: the first referendum election ever held in Montevideo— on the subject of whether bus and tram fares should be increased—occurred in 1951, seventeen years after such elections were first authorized; a disappointingly small fraction of the possible vote (only about a quarter) took part in the election. The initiative, also constitutionally set up, has remained even further from fruition.

It would be easy and gracious to conclude simply that government is good in Uruguay, that all is political sweetness and light. But some qualifications are in order. Government is very much with the Uruguayan. It tells the Montevideanos that they need pay no more than twenty-six centésimos a liter for milk (that would be about ten cents a quart) or fourteen centésimos for a like amount of kerosene, or this or that price for butter, a kilo of rice, a loaf of bread, and various other staples. Most of these are thus sold below production cost and the government makes up the difference by subsidies. The lowered cost of living is, at least in part, offset by higher taxes. Government tells the *pensión* or hotel keeper that he may charge only a fixed scale of prices and that during the tourist season he must rebate tò "tourists" 45 per cent of the rate; government makes it good to the owner and charges it off to advertising. Government tells even the transient house tenant or *inquilino* that he must pay several pesos a month for school taxes, taxes for pensioning the aged, and other forms of payment. On the other hand, government collects garbage and trash daily. It will send a repairman within minutes to remedy a temporarily defective lighting system. It operates an ambulance service available at all hours. It provides a fantastically accommodating telephone service.

A qualification needs to be made with regard to the number of government employees. They are many.[4] The legend of the railroader who took an assistant along to help him listen as he tapped with his hammer to locate defective parts might almost be duplicated in real life in the Uruguayan public service. In some agencies the government has found ways of making two inspectors, two supervisors, two repairmen grow where only one grew before. A foreigner of long residence in Montevideo met an old friend, the head of one of the large public-service corporations, whom he had not seen for a long time. "How is your work going?" he asked. "When I was in closer touch with your agency several years ago it had a great reputation for efficiency." "Oh, *así así* (so-so)," was the reply, "but we could

[4] The whole number of government employees in Uruguay, including the thousands in the service of the autonomous entities, was reported in December, 1953, to be 145,691. This is approximately 5.82 per cent of the population of the country. The number of such employees in the United States in Oct., 1953, was 7,094,000 (federal civilian, 2,384,000: state, 1,126,-000; county, 561,000; city, 1,379,000; other, 1,644,000). The percentage in the United States was thus about 4.41. It is estimated that about half a million Uruguayans (families included)—about a fifth of the population of the country—depend for their living on government funds.

get along better if I had a thousand employees instead of the seven thousand they have given me." Even allowing for a bit of natural exaggeration, the comment has a moral. The law fully protects the civil servant, perhaps even more than is desirable—it is difficult to discharge inefficient ones.

The proliferating bureaucracy inevitably breeds conditions in which clerks and others get under foot. The result is delay— in capitals, italicized, exclamation pointed. The *aduana* or customs house is the example par excellence of delay and inefficiency. (Some of it may be explained, of course, on the basis that its operations affect in considerable measure the outlander rather than the national.)

The critic terms this state of affairs creeping Socialism, but the proponent, on the other hand, calls it an enlightened governmental conscience. It is certain, at any rate, that Uruguay has set the Latin American pace in social legislation, in a widened horizon of governmental responsibility and activity. Businessmen, those ruggedest of rugged individualists, might be expected to be the first to view with alarm. Many of them in Uruguay seem, however, if not to take it in their stride, at least to view it with a not too shoulder-shrugging resignation. Bankers, for example, do not seem too concerned by the fact that twenty-eight or thirty private banks share about one-third of the country's commercial banking business while the gargantuan Bank of the Republic takes the other two-thirds; nor do they seem to feel themselves mistreated. In other areas in which the government's commercial and industrial activity treads on the toes of private enterprise, a species of accommodation seems to have been reached which involves a good deal of mutual toleration and respect.

Uruguayans take a sturdy attitude toward their government. They are stockholders in the corporation and they know it. They don't, on the other hand, like to be pushed around by anyone in government. The corner traffic cop in Montevideo would never begin to adopt an "Oh, yeah!" attitude toward pedestrians or motorists as a policeman in Kokomo or Keokuk or Kalamazoo might do. On the other hand, the average Uruguayan is quick to take an understandable pride in his government. He has voted it in, he believes in it, he resents unfair or unthinking criticism of it.

As Latin American governments go, Uruguay's seems to be a superdemocracy. And, indeed, it is one that can hold up its head in any company. It is a democracy that works. Which, after all, probably entitles us to say Q. E. D.

*¡Viva la democracia uruguaya!*

# 12

## Government with a Conscience

Latin America, says Charles Morrow Wilson in a study of American tropical medicine, is a subworld of sick people—"Sick of everything from sprue to leprosy. Sick of almost all the diseases that we in the United States encounter in our own lives, and of a multitude of savage and highly fatal diseases about which we know almost nothing. A figure of fifty million sick men, women, and children . . . is reasonably close to the truth." [1] Luis Quintanilla in his notable book *A Latin American Speaks* writes that "The naked truth is that of the one hundred twenty-six million Latin Americans, certainly *no fewer than eighty-five million are actually starving*." [2] And, finally, Francis Violich has stated that "Bad conditions of health and sanitation are the factors which lead to the filth of forgotten corners of some of the Latin American cities. These always exist in [inverse] proportion to the economic well-being of the particular country." [3]

These men write truly, but they are not writing of Uruguay. Fever-ridden swamps, t.b.-devastated slums, dank, miasmic pestholes, leprosy and yaws and yellowjack—all these may form part of a sometimes overdone stereotype of disease con-

[1] *Ambassadors in White* (New York, 1942), p. 1.

[2] *A Latin American Speaks* (New York, 1943), p. 81; italics in the original.

[3] *Cities of Latin America* (New York, 1944), p. 47.

ditions in Latin America, but they do not help paint the picture of Uruguay. In discussing that country one writes primarily not of disease but of health, not of death rates but of hospitals, not of famine but of plenty. Hygeia goes to the head of the class and Lethe gets pushed virtually out of the room with distinctly unUruguayan inhospitality.

Getting a comparative picture of the health of various countries of the hemisphere or the world is an exceedingly difficult undertaking because of the lack of reliable statistical and other raw material with which to work. The Uruguayan government's officially reported figures for 1951 showed a total of 19,190 deaths for the entire country. Twenty-three preceding years, going as far back as 1916, had actually exceeded that total of annual deaths though the country's population was increasing all the time.[4] The deaths for 1951 gave the phenomenally low rate of 7.8 per 1,000 of population, one of the lowest rates of any country in the world.

A comparative study made about a decade ago by the United States Bureau of the Census showed Uruguay with the then lowest rate, 9.3 per 1,000 population, not only of all countries in the hemisphere (including the United States and Canada) but actually of all the thirty-seven countries surveyed. Uruguay consequently stands regularly at or close to the bottom, which is to say the best, in terms of world death rates.[5]

With regard to infant mortality—the number of deaths under one year of age per 1,000 live births—Uruguay did not fare so well as of the time the Census Bureau made its survey. Her infant mortality rate was eighty-three per 1,000, and four countries in the hemisphere (Argentina, Canada, Paraguay, and the United States) had better rates. On the other hand, two countries of the hemisphere had infant mortality rates more than twice as high as Uruguay's. A later figure showed Uruguay's infant mortality rate to have been reduced to 64.2.

[4] The population, now estimated at 2,500,000, has at times shown the most rapid proportionate increase of that of any Latin American country. Between 1800 and 1900 the percentage increase was 2,990; the percentage increase between 1800 and 1944 was 6,900!

[5] It should be stressed that in the interpretation, and even in the recording, of vital statistics one is on exceedingly risky ground. The causes of death may be so intricately interrelated that it often is arbitrary to assign the death to one cause rather than another.

What kills Uruguayans? It is known that during the colonial period and at various times in the nineteenth century, serious epidemics, especially of smallpox, cholera, scarlet fever, and yellow fever, occurred. The lack of systematic vital statistics from those periods prevents us from knowing just how serious they were.[6] Epidemics are now far more rare, and vital statistics are better. For example, of the total of 19,190 deaths (exclusive of stillbirths) reported by the government in 1951 the dozen most frequent causes of deaths were: cancer, 3,380; apoplexy and related diseases, 1,810; "other heart diseases," 1,382; tuberculosis, 1,299; diarrhea and enteritis, 756; bronchopneumonia, 730; accidents, 680; myocardial heart diseases, 631; high blood pressure, 606; chronic nephritis, 465; diabetes, 342; premature birth, 341. These twelve causes accounted for more than three out of five Uruguayan deaths that year. The most serious venereal disease is syphilis which in 1951 took 280 lives. A total of 276 persons took their own lives in that same year.

Charles M. Wilson several years ago included among the principal causes of death for all of Latin America malaria, diphtheria, infantile paralysis, and meningitis, but those four diseases together accounted, according to government reports, for only nineteen deaths in all of Uruguay in 1951. Wilson's conclusion about Latin America's health as a whole was that pathogenic, or disease-causing, organisms were by far the greatest killers in that area but that the United States had largely conquered such organisms and hence the worst causes of fatality in this country were degenerative breakdowns of the human mechanism such as certain heart diseases, cancer, cerebral hemorrhage, and diabetes.

The Uruguayan pattern of causes of death shows an interesting and significant evolution from that which prevails generally in Latin America toward that which is characteristic of the United States. Relatively many more Uruguayan than other Latin American deaths are caused by degenerative dis-

---

[6] In general, health conditions during the colonial period were allegedly good. One Ramírez, a Spanish explorer, wrote in 1529, only a few years after Uruguay's discovery, that it was a very healthful land and no one fell sick there! Another Spaniard wrote somewhat later that the Charrúa Indians seemed to live longer than the Spaniards, their hair often not turning gray until they were eighty or older.

eases. Germs are being conquered in Uruguay as in the United States. And yet, the picture in Uruguay shows important differences from that in the United States. The Census Bureau's survey some years ago showed that the death rate from heart diseases in the United States was more than twice as high as that in Uruguay—perhaps a striking commentary on the tempo of life in the two countries though some medical authorities would ascribe it, at least in part, to dietary differences. On the other hand, Uruguay's tuberculosis death rate was more than twice and her diarrhea-enteritis rate more than five times as high as those of the United States. The latter country's rates for nephritis and accidental deaths more than doubled those of Uruguay. The detailed differences footnote the danger in making broad comparisons.

As is true of virtually all highly civilized countries, Uruguay's birth and death rates both declined over a considerable period of years, the former much more rapidly than the latter. The birth rate dropped from 33.4 per 1,000 population in 1900 to 18.5 in 1950; the death rate in the same period dropped from 14.1 to 7.9. Thus, while the number of annual births has generally shown a steady increase to supplement the population increases by immigration, the proportionate increase has declined.

The mortality-natality picture is, then, a generally good one. Uruguayan life expectancy was estimated in 1944 at 39.2 years. It depends on several factors: the food the people eat, the medical services they get, the hospital facilities available, the state of sanitation and hygiene, and the measures taken to relieve social as well as physical ills.

Governmental concern for public health in Uruguay has gone through several stages since the first half of the nineteenth century. A contemporary account written of conditions in Montevideo in 1834 painted a dismal picture. From the "quagmires" in the plaza fronting the cathedral in the Old City more than 1,000 wagonloads of mud and debris were removed in a single month. At first, then, the protection of the collective health and the defense of the individual against disease was supported by engineering plans and projects. Some of the earliest steps dated back as far as 1838. An early law required the annual paving of a minimum of some 15,000 square yards of streets, half to be charged to the adjacent property owners and half to the public treasury. Another early action was the establishment of a large market in Montevideo to improve the highly unsanitary conditions under which meat and other foods had been sold.

Political instability interfered with the early impetus and little could be accomplished until the end of the Great War in 1851. In 1852, however, the Old City took steps to extend its still rudimentary sewer system. Montevideo became the first city in all of Latin America to have a complete sewerage system. Action to provide running water was begun in 1866.

The legislature in 1847 passed an ordinance providing for vaccination against smallpox. Vaccination, which had begun for school children as early as 1829, was made compulsory for infants in 1850. The 1850's saw the first systematic and extensive steps taken to provide quarantine and disinfection services. Montevideo established a "House of Disinfection" in 1883 and four years later a lazaret, considered a model of its kind, was set up on the Isla de Flores.

Perhaps as great a contributor to nineteenth-century medical development as any was Dr. Teodoro Vilardebó (1803–57). He studied and practiced medicine in Barcelona and Paris. As a young man he served on international medical commissions in Europe and was honored by the French government. Later he organized the first systematic work in public hygiene in Uruguay, was responsible for the introduction of hospital medicine, encouraged medical treatment for the poor, and aided in still other ways. He lost his life in combating a yellow fever epidemic in Montevideo.

A second stage in Uruguayan health development, closely following standards evolved in world progress along such lines, placed greater emphasis on preventive medicine and a more effective alliance between medicine and biology. A third stage (at present) employs a sociological approach, involves the more systematic collection of statistics, and stresses health education.

Great medical leaders have followed Vilardebó of the nineteenth century. Francisco Soca (1862–1922) was the first physician from any Latin American country to be made an associate member of the Academy of Medicine of Paris. Luis

Morquio (1867–1935) has been characterized as "the greatest of Latin American pediatricians." [7]

With the general level and wide diffusion of Uruguayan prosperity it follows logically that the people would eat well. They do. The average per capita daily calorie intake was estimated in 1950–51 at 2,650, a figure which compares very favorably with any corresponding one in Latin America. Uruguay being, as it is, a land of millions of cattle, the nation's inhabitants are great meat eaters. Beef is normally one of the cheapest staple foods and Uruguayan per capita consumption is perhaps double that in the United States. Montevideanos have been said to average more than a pound per person per day and many *estancia* workers eat considerably larger quantities of mutton.

Uruguay, like its larger neighbor across the Plata, produces considerable quantities of wheat. Per capita consumption of that cereal is much higher in Uruguay than in the United States; the use of corn, on the other hand, is markedly lower in Uruguay. Widespread drinking of milk is limited to the cities, especially Montevideo. Consumption of milk products in the capital has increased greatly in recent years, reflecting primarily, it has been held, larger use by workers' families.

Uruguayan per capita consumption of fresh fruits and of fats and oils is about the same as that in the United States, but the use of fresh vegetables, eggs, and sugar is lower. The overuse of starchy foods and the relative lack of protective foods makes for some degree of nutritional imbalance. The situation in Montevideo is not really bad, however. In the interior the diet of the vast majority of rural workers is characterized by its monotonous lack of variety. Mutton, mutton, and more mutton is virtually the beginning and the end of the meals of countless *estancia* hands.

The training of doctors began early in Uruguay, but not nearly so early as in some Spanish New World possessions, because there was no university in colonial Uruguay to include a medical school as one of its parts. Indeed, Montevideo was reported in 1761 to have but one surgeon; twenty years later it had one physician and three surgeons. During the pre-medi-

[7] Arístides A. Moll, *Aesculapius in Latin America* (Philadelphia, 1944), p. 331.

cal-school period many of those who posed as doctors were in reality nothing more than charlatans. But a Faculty of Medicine dates from 1849 and the first medical society was organized in 1853. The medical school has since been built up as one of the major branches of the University of the Republic and, indeed, as one of the largest medical schools in the world. Its enrollment in 1946 was 1,837; it regularly draws students from several of the neighboring Latin American countries.

Medical education was at first influenced primarily by French standards and practices. Later, and up to World War I, German medical training exerted an influence over that in Uruguay. After World War I, English methods came to the fore and still later United States developments were influential in shaping Uruguayan medical training.

The number of Uruguayan physicians in 1952 was 2,231 and that of dentists 1,221. This figures out to one doctor for every 1,121 and one dentist for every 2,044 Uruguayans. The ratios are better than those for all but two or three Latin American countries.

A small, early nursing school was established in 1910 by Dr. Carlos Nery. A school of nursing, as part of the national university, was organized in 1950. Assuredly the school was needed—the number of graduate nurses available at that time for all of Uruguay's hospitals was under 200.

Health education, as distinguished from medical training, is more an adjunct of the public-school system. Since 1944 it has been under the direction of a permanent commission which meets twice a year to discuss and approve plans for courses in health education in schools of all levels. Every effort is made through the co-operation of teachers to effect the approved plans, which are either incorporated as regular subjects in the curriculum or else are set up as special courses. The commission also gives advice on the importance of preventive medicine and environmental hygiene. Its work is widely publicized through the press, by organized programs in social clubs and public libraries, by moving pictures, slides, and radio chats, by conferences, slogans, and exhibits. It is one of the effective and significant tools in the whole public-health picture in Uruguay.

The organization of the Ministry of Public Health is most

elaborate. Immediately subordinate to the Minister and a handful of high-level assistants are seventeen offices, secretariats, departments, sections, and other agencies. Then come the five big operative divisions: hygiene, technical matters, assistance, pharmacy, and administration. These are elaborately subdivided into clinics, laboratories, hospitals, institutes, offices, and services. The Ministry operates seventeen departmental centers, twenty-seven auxiliary centers, and 133 rural polyclinics.

The Ministry's yardstick is its Office of Statistics, operating highly efficiently for some years past under the able direction of Dr. Adolfo Morales. It has developed into an agency whose statistical finger on the pulse of Uruguayan health has a perhaps more accurate touch than is to be found anywhere else in Latin America. Systematic collection of vital statistics began about 1940 (although the first halting steps had been taken as early as 1837) and led to the publication in 1942 of Uruguay's first manual on vital statistics.

Uruguay's first real hospital, the Charity Hospital, was established at Montevideo in the early 1830's.[8] Its early annual cost was the not inconsiderable sum of 36,000 pesos, raised partly by a lottery and partly by a one-half per cent import duty. By the middle 1850's the Charity Hospital had expanded its organization and services to the point where it had six divisions or *salas* with a total of 179 beds. In addition it had a section for orphans and one for the insane. In the latter 1850's steps were taken to establish on the outskirts of Montevideo an institution for the insane and to include in it, with the aim of reducing street begging, a section for mendicants.

The contemporary picture of hospital service in Uruguay is really a by-product of the impetus given by President Batlle. Along with the idea of free medical care for the poor he propounded and popularized the concept that it was a responsibility of the state to provide adequate hospital facilities for the country's inhabitants. At present Uruguay has eighty-four hospitals of all types with a total of about 16,000 beds occupied annually by more than 100,000 patients. The disparity between Montevideo and the rest of the country is illustrated

---

[8] There had been an institution which posed as a hospital set up at Montevideo in 1787, a sick ward in a Montevideo convent in 1743, and a so-called hospital at Colonia in 1732.

by the fact that more than two-thirds of the hospital beds are in the capital. The available hospital beds in Uruguay figure out to 6.4 per thousand of population, a higher ratio than is found in any other Latin American country.

The Italian, British, and North American communities have all established their own hospitals which, of course, are not limited to the respective nationalities. Various other hospitals are either almost ready to open, are under construction, or are projected. The most spectacular of all these structures is the enormous Hospital de Clínicas near Batlle Park in Montevideo. Towering twenty-two stories high and with an ultimate capacity of more than 3,000 beds, it is designed as one of the most modern and complete hospitals in all Latin America. The structure was virtually complete by the end of the 1940's but was long delayed in opening because of incomplete equipment and a jurisdictional dispute over its control.

Even though a disproportionate share of the hospital facilities of Uruguay are located in its capital, other parts of the country are conscious of the need. When a town or city in the interior becomes actively conscious of health problems, the first objective of aroused local public opinion is usually a hospital. The inhabitants of the locality may themselves subscribe thousands of pesos toward its construction. Usually financial assistance from the government is forthcoming. In this manner the pattern of hospital facilities is being more equitably extended to even the remoter parts of Uruguay.

The concept of governmental responsibility in the public-health problem, beginning in reality with the Batlle administration, has come to its fullest fruition in the past decade. Probably the foremost evidence and symbol of it is Scisp. This strange word—foreign to Spanish as well as English—is but the telescoped common manner of reference to the Servicio Cooperativo Interamericano de Salud Pública. This joint Uruguayan-United States venture in practical good neighborliness stemmed from an agreement concluded on November 18, 1943, between a representative of the United States government's Institute of Inter-American Affairs and the Uruguayan Minister of Public Health. The Uruguayan congress approved the convention on September 15, 1945, and it has already been renewed by mutual agreement for successive periods.

*The gaucho, with his passionate love of freedom, is part of the epic legend of Uruguay.*

*Batlle Park, Montevideo. The 3,000-bed Hospital de las Clínicas is one of the most modern in Latin America. At right, a glimpse of José Belloni's famous bronze depicting the colonial covered wagon with yoked oxen and a mounted gaucho guide.*

*Fishing for merluce (hake) in Uruguayan coastal waters.*

The early work of Scisp centered in four areas spaced throughout the republic: Treinta y Tres, a town of about 14,-000 in the northeast; Melo, a town of some 18,000 people in the eastern part of Uruguay; Fray Bentos, with about 10,000 inhabitants, on the Uruguay River; and the working-class section of Montevideo known as Cerrito de la Victoria. In each location a specially designed health center and clinic was built. Though these four health centers were most accessible to the people of the towns themselves their services were also available to and urged on the surrounding rural populations. Hence, the total population served is more than 112,000. In the year 1950–51, the four centers were responsible for almost 42,000 immunizations, almost 40,000 clinical consultations, more than 7,000 laboratory examinations, more than 36,000 public health nursing visits, and more than 3,000 sanitary inspections.

An important part of the work of the health centers is performed by the auxiliary nurses or *visitadoras* who have carried the gospel of sanitation and elementary health precautions into many rural areas. The rural work is aided by the operation, since 1948, of a mobile sanitary unit in the form of a modern omnibus equipped for X-ray examinations, vaccinations, and general immunizations as well as motion-picture demonstrations and other exhibits. The objective set by the Uruguayan government is the opening of at least one health center, of the sort already established, in each of the nineteen departments of the republic.

Another important aspect of the work of Scisp is that aimed at improving the care of maternity cases. It has been notably successful. The infant mortality rate at Treinta y Tres, for example, declined from 155 per thousand live births in 1943 to less than fifty in 1949. The goal of each new health center has been to build up its maternity service to the point where at least half of the births of the town occur among women who have attended a prenatal clinic. These clinics have been pointed at general treatment, if necessary, of all expectant mothers (fathers, too, whenever possible) with especial reference to venereal diseases and tuberculosis.

The well-organized and extensive campaign against tuberculosis enlists the co-operation of Scisp but involves other agencies as well. The machinery of the Ministry itself is strongly arrayed against the disease. Another agency of great importance is the Honorary Commission for the Struggle Against Tuberculosis. It is supported by government funds and wages vigorous, widespread, and intelligent war against t.b.

Not strictly medical but none the less important is the work of Scisp along lines of sanitary engineering and health education. The former involves problems of urban water supply, household sanitation, and town sewer systems. In propagandizing for prevention of disease the agency in its first four years alone published almost a million copies of bulletins, pamphlets, books, leaflets, posters, etc. Perhaps the outstanding feature of this work is the bulletin *Salud*, now published in monthly quantities of 6,000. In its first four years, Scisp also gave 800 motion-picture programs to more than 287,000 people, almost 800 radio broadcasts, and more than 900 articles to the press. Such work has since been continued on an even larger scale.

The guiding genius of Scisp was for some years a friendly North American medico, Dr. H. Jackson Davis. Seemingly casual and carefree, he proved a dynamo of energy and endurance and an unending source of inspiration and encouragement to Uruguay's Ministers of Public Health and other officials. Given to tweeds, pipe smoking (many Uruguayans called him *"el hombre de la pipa"*), and informality, he proved himself *simpático* as few other foreigners have. His emphasis was constantly on preventive medicine and on encouragement of a sense of community responsibility. Stress upon the latter has at least partially reversed what could have become a harmful trend: the attachment of more and more physicians to the medical services of the government with the resultant atrophy of a feeling of community responsibility. Though he has now returned to the United States, Dr. Davis long will be remembered in Uruguay not only as a great colleague but also as a great friend.

Total cost of Scisp activities to the middle of 1951 was $1,403,048.42. When the agency first got under way, the United States government paid about five dollars to one expended by Uruguay. That ratio has now more than been reversed and Uruguay is assuming greater and greater responsibility, not only for financing but also for personnel. The whole program has been one of the most systematic, constructive, and intelligent ever devised and applied in the health work of any Latin American country.

An interesting and significant part of the health picture in Uruguay is the numerous beneficent or mutual-aid societies. The Uruguayans refer to them generically as *mutualistas*. They are now about a hundred in number and have from 130,000 to 140,000 members. The oldest, but not the largest, is the Española, established in 1853; it now has about 16,000 members. The Fraternidad has some 54,000 members. The other two organizations in the "Big Four" are the Mutualista Nacional and the Círculo Católico, each with about 12,000 members. The societies are found in all parts of the country, but naturally those other than the four mentioned are far smaller in membership. Their respective economic resources, and hence the services they can offer, are in direct proportion to the numbers of their members. They usually provide some combination of medical and dental services, surgery, drugs, hospitalization, X-rays, baths and massages, other therapeutic services, and nursing for maternity cases; only the Fraternidad furnishes all of those services.

The *mutualistas* provide a bridge between activity strictly concerned with health and that which is more in the nature of social welfare. Ill or disabled members of some of the societies receive subsidies of up to 100 pesos monthly during incapacitation. Some of the organizations pay small pensions, others pay the burial expenses of their members. All in all, the *mutualistas* are an accepted and important part of the socio-medical picture in Uruguay. Their operation not only provides low-cost medical and other services for thousands of middle-class people who are less able to benefit from government programs oriented more toward the poor but it also affects the pattern of strictly private medical practice.

It is probably for her recognition of and action on the problem that man can become socially as well as bodily ill that Uruguay has gained her greatest fame in the near and far corners of the earth. "Social laboratory," "advanced labor legislation," "economic experimentation," and "governmental conscience" are among the phrases which are meant to imply that Uruguay is in the van among all the nations of the world in her cognizance of social problems and the government's partial responsibility for solving them. Again, as at so many points, the major credit must go to Batlle. Although the first law on such matters antedated Batlle's first presidency by almost two-thirds of a century it was Batlle who gave the great impulse which still moves government, parties, and people.

It, is only a fine line at best, and sometimes a fictitious one, which can be drawn between the categories of "social legislation" and "labor legislation." Viewing the matter broadly, because the two classifications are often intricately interrelated, Uruguay now has a record of more than eighty statutes on such matters as hours of labor, a weekly rest, paid annual vacations, minimum wages, domestic labor, compensation for dismissal, unemployment compensation, labor accidents and occupational diseases, family allowances, the labor of women and children, maternity insurance, the intellectual and moral protection of children, night work in bakeries, rural labor centers, unemployment and labor exchanges, economical housing, and old-age pensions.

Ardent batllistas have demanded much additional social legislation, chiefly in the direction of strengthening and extending principles already established, but covering also such matters as rural workers' diet, trade-union organization and regulation, employment contracts, profit-sharing for employees of government-operated enterprises, and the social orientation of taxation.

It was in 1838, when the republic was only ten years old, that a law required the deduction of one day's pay per month from the salaries of public employees in order that civil pensions and retirement allowances might be serviced. Pensions were to run from 25 per cent to full salary, depending on the length of the employee's service. The disorders of the nineteenth century made it impossible to apply the legislation effectively and it was supplanted by a new and more detailed law in 1904. In the meantime a teachers' pension and retirement fund had been established in 1896.

The flood tide of Uruguayan social legislation began during the first decade and a half of the twentieth century. That period was essentially the years of Batlle. A law passed in July, 1914, dealt with labor accidents and occupational diseases. Perhaps the most famous and certainly the most controversial of all pieces of Uruguayan social legislation was the law passed November 17, 1915, which established the eight-hour day. It was this law for which Batlle and his colleagues had fought eight years! Then the new constitution drafted in 1917 to replace the original one of 1830 contained a number of fundamental references to social welfare. The social philosophy of the new basic law was neither as pervasive nor as apparent as that in the Mexican constitution, drafted the same year, but it laid a constitutional flooring under the many laws later adopted.

One broad category of social welfare legislation has dealt in general with conditions of work. In addition to the pioneer law on hours of work adopted in 1915, a law of 1931 decreed a weekly rest of thirty-six hours for employees of commercial establishments. This had the effect of instituting a Saturday half-holiday (the "*sábado inglés*," as people of the Plata region often call it). Further laws in 1943 and 1944 regulated hours of work for banking employees and made more detailed the governing of commercial employees' working hours.

The original requirement of one day's weekly rest was applied by law in November, 1920, to domestic workers and drivers of privately owned vehicles. The following month the principle was extended to all employment except for workers in agriculture and stock raising. Subsequent legislation has made the principle of the weekly rest day flexible in order to fit the needs of various sorts of establishments but at the same time to protect the interest of the worker.

A law of 1918, re-enforced and supplemented by later legislation, forbade night work in bakeries, candy-making establishments, and similar enterprises; such laws also provided for sanitary inspections, selection of workers with reference to their health, etc.

The first legislation requiring annual paid vacations was enacted in 1933 but the basic, general law on the subject had to wait until 1945. The required two weeks of vacation may be divided into two periods and it has become customary for many commercial houses to close during carnival week and Holy Week (which the government propagandistically but ineffectively tries to rename Tourist Week) and thus give their employees the vacation at times when trade would be slack.

Industrial safety and hygiene are the subjects of various

laws. In one of the earliest laws (1914), industrial employers, including those in state and municipal establishments, were required to install safety devices to prevent accidents in the use of machinery. Occupational diseases were brought under the incidental cognizance of the government by a law of 1934 which dealt primarily with the reorganization of the pension fund for industry, commerce, and the public service. Several of the provisions of international labor conventions dealing with industrial hygiene and safety have been incorporated in Uruguayan legislation.

Industrial accident and disease compensation was originally the subject of legislation in 1920. It was expanded and made more generous in 1941. The new law extended to broad categories of employees, including rural and domestic workers, and based compensation on more satisfactory concepts. Government enterprises employing manual workers were equally subject to the requirements of the act along with private employers and were additionally required to insure such workers with the State Insurance Bank. The law also contained detailed provisions, aimed at protection of both the employer and the worker, with regard to occupational diseases.

Uruguay's first law for the protection of employed women and children, adopted in 1918, required the provision of seats for such workers. Legislation of 1934 provided for a month's maternity leave before and another month's leave after childbirth and contained other provisions for protection of working mothers. Protection of various sorts is provided to minors either by Uruguayan direct legislation or by the government's ratification of different international labor conventions.

The basic source of protection of the welfare of minors is to be found in the famous Children's Code of 1934. This comprehensive legislation was drafted by a special commission of Uruguayans appointed by President Gabriel Terra to study the problem. The code contemplates a large degree of state responsibility for the intellectual and social protection of children from the time of birth (or, indeed, of conception) to that of their majority. The protection and care of pregnant women is involved, considerable detail is devoted to the mother and the infant child, and special care is prescribed for abnormal and sick children. The education of minor children and youth of all ages is regulated. The code deals with the sale to minors of alcoholic beverages, tobacco, and books deemed inappropriate. Begging by children is prohibited. The social problems of illegitimacy are dealt with. Administration of the code is placed in the hands of a specially created and partially autonomous Children's Council. The conception and operation of the Children's Code constitutes a milestone justly noted far beyond the borders of Uruguay.

The government in 1934 began, as a depression measure, a program of establishing low-cost restaurants where well-balanced meals could be served to workers at minimum prices. As early as 1937–38 such restaurants served within a single year more than 1,500,000 meals in Montevideo and more than 2,000,000 in other parts of Uruguay.

Paid industrial work done in homes was carefully regulated and restricted by laws of 1934 and 1940. Regulations of conditions of rural work were only tardily tackled. A law of 1940 fixed minimum standards for work on rice plantations. By an act of 1944, certain other kinds of rural workers were extended benefits previously granted urban employees. An Agricultural Workers' Code was enacted in October, 1946, to provide general coverage to rural workers on such matters as wages, housing, weekly rest and annual holidays, unfair dismissal, etc.

Minimum-wage legislation dates back to 1926, but a more basic law on that subject was adopted in November, 1943. The latter law set up wage councils (with workers', employers', and government representatives) which are authorized to fix hourly, daily, weekly, monthly, or piece-rate wages in detailed classifications of employment. Wages are determined in accordance with local economic conditions, the purchasing power of the peso, the worker's capacity, the risks involved, and other factors. The law also provided for an obligatory system of equalization funds for payment of family allowances to wage and salary earners based on the number of children, both legitimate and illegitimate. The allowance is limited to an amount such that it, plus the worker's and his wife's earnings, will not exceed 200 pesos monthly. The act of 1943 is complex and has not been easily or entirely satisfactorily administered.

Systematic legislation dealing with compensation for dismissal was first adopted in 1944. Several later acts have been concerned with the same subject. The principle is now extended to broad categories of workers.

Pensions and social insurance have been treated in a number of laws. Uruguay's pension systems for old age and sickness are considered by many to be the world's most liberal. Virtually the entire working population is covered by one or another retirement or pension fund. Payment of unemployment compensation to shipwrecked sailors was required by law in 1939; the principle was later extended to other groups. As of the end of 1953 some 60,000 former commercial and industrial employees and about 16,000 former civil servants were drawing old-age pensions. General unemployment insurance, however, has not yet been legislated.

Very few, indeed, of these several score pieces of social legislation were enacted without prolonged political controversy, both in the congress and the press.[9] It was reassuring, however, that they were adopted in practically all cases by democratic process after full and free discussion and not by dictatorial ukase aimed at currying proletarian favor.

Sometimes one or another act was adopted with a too naive reliance on the law to solve the social ill attacked. The insurance and pension plans in particular have been subjected to a good deal of criticism. Insurance legislation has not always been conceived or administered on a basis of sound actuarial practice. Taxes levied to support pension funds have not always had productivity geared to need. Funds have at times accumulated large deficits. Criticism is heard in Montevideo that when a person retires from a job because of old age he must sometimes wait five years before his pension papers are processed and he begins drawing his allowance. It is also charged that the liberality of the legislation encourages too early retirement and hence unduly interferes with Uruguayan productivity.

Nonetheless, shortcomings granted, it is doubtless true that both the bodily and the social ills of Uruguayans are responsibilities weighing more heavily on the public conscience than can be said of any other Latin American country.

[9] Cf. Simon G. Hanson, *Utopia in Uruguay* (New York, 1938), pp. 122–83.

# 13

# The Fourth Estate

One of the great social and political forces in Latin America is the press. In an area that in some respects, economically, psychologically, perhaps intellectually, is still partially colonial, the press serves almost more than any other element to catapult one section (or country) or another into the middle of the twentieth century. The history and the social impact of the newspapers of Latin America have been too little studied. Uruguay's press affords a partially representative and certainly a significant case study.

Uruguay is a literate nation. It is a nation of newspaper readers. The newspapers make an impact on public life. They deserve more consideration than they have received.

In surveying the Uruguayan press one might almost as well start *and* stop with Montevideo. Little harm would be done to the picture by omitting the rest of the country outside of the capital because, in terms of journalism as in so many other ways, it is a case of Uruguay belonging to Montevideo rather than the reverse. In all of Uruguay outside of the capital city there are but five newspapers with a circulation of 1,000 or more each; one of those is published only three times weekly; the largest has a circulation of only 8,000.

In no other country of South America does such a degree of imbalance exist in the organization and significance of the

press. Argentina and other Latin American states have disproportionately large capitals, but in none of the other states is
the press outside of the capital so sterile and juvenile in appearance as is the case in Uruguay. The reasons are not hard
to find. They are products of the country's geography, topography, and transportation, of its history, politics, and economics.

Uruguay's small size and relatively mountainless land make
transportation little of a problem, at least so far as distribution of newspapers is concerned. Hence, it is not at all difficult
for Montevideo papers to be sent to all parts of the country.
They can and do go by plane to the more distant parts of Uruguay; by truck, using the better roads found in the southern
part of the country, they circulate widely within the more immediate neighborhood of the metropolis. There is virtually no
place in Uruguay where Montevideo morning newspapers cannot be read the same day.

The whole historical emphasis on Montevideo at the expense of other cities in the country discourages any effort to
set up independent and vigorous papers in the interior. A centralized form of government means that political news and inspiration emanate largely from the capital; the press of the
*campo* reflects the lack of that source of journalistic nourish-
ment. The contrast in circulation and advertising potentials
between Montevideo and other cities of the country is obvious
and no less apparent is the fact that the financial resources to
maintain even a "political" paper, which does not depend primarily on either advertising or circulation, are not so easily
found outside of the capital.

A statistical summary of the Montevideo press reveals, as
of recent date (the situation is, as they say in the army, fluid),
ten daily and three weekly papers, two weekly, one bimonthly,
and one monthly review, all in Spanish; and in foreign languages an English daily, an English weekly, a German daily,
and some others of little consequence. Circulation of the daily
and weekly Spanish-language newspapers (excluding reviews)
is approximately 413,500. If each paper has from two and a
half to three readers this means a Montevideo newspaper-read-
ing public of from some 1,030,000 to 1,240,000. That figure is,
of course, larger than the whole population of Montevideo, but

avid newspaper followers will often read two, three, or more papers daily. The number of newspaper readers for the whole of Uruguay is estimated at 1,500,000. The circulation field in Montevideo is rather well monopolized by eight of the daily papers.

Montevideo's newspapers are, almost without exception, political. That is to say, they consciously, strongly, and professionally reflect a partisan point of view. They have not, as have so many large-city papers in the United States under pressure of the business office, become politically colorless and neutral. Uruguayans take their politics seriously and enthusiastically and they like their papers to express a vigorous partisanship. A family that has inherited a batllista affiliation will "just naturally" subscribe to *El Día;* a strongly Catholic family will just as naturally read *El Bien Público* from one generation to another.

That some of the Montevideo papers are also quite profitable enterprises is almost incidental. In all cases it is reasonably safe to say that they are political papers first and commercial ventures only second. Some of the smaller papers obviously can make no pretense of being other than wholly political. The amount of advertising they carry is insignificant and their mailing lists are anemic. Party funds or partisan contributions are their life's blood and they are political sheets (sometimes only tattered rags) and nothing more. The strong party inclination of virtually all of the papers of at least Montevideo is doubtless the reason for the considerable degree of slanting of news stories which prevails widely. In local news stories the slanting is accomplished in the writing itself. The same end is achieved in wire stories by selection or editing. But the fact remains that straight and unbiased news coverage is far from a universal characteristic of Montevideo's newspapers.

In addition to a common denominator of political-mindedness, the majority of the Montevideo papers share certain other characteristics. They are, with few exceptions, for example, democratic (and hence antifranquista and antiperonista), internationally conscious, pro-United States, and sports-minded—very sports-minded.

With the long-standing and deep-rooted democratic tradition prevailing in Uruguay, it would indeed be unusual were the leading papers not to reflect such an orientation. Uruguay's democracy is not a garment worn lightly but a deep and abiding conviction. The majority of the newspapers, consequently, are staunchly and toughly democratic in their point of view. This makes for an entirely logical position in opposition to the regimes of Franco in Spain and Perón in Argentina. If papers are to be democratic why, they reason, should there be any truckling to dictatorship, whether it be Spanish or Argentine. There is particular reason for losing no love on the peronista regime in Argentina. It has been too critical of, too threatening toward, the Uruguayan state to allow a patriotic Uruguayan press to take other than a skeptical and generally unfavorable attitude toward it.

The international awareness of the Uruguayan press is a product of circumstances. The country is small and, perforce, outward looking. It is sandwiched in between the most powerful two states of the continent. Its main trade is foreign rather than domestic. Though politics in Uruguay, or at least in Montevideo, is perennially lively and newsworthy, the interior of the country is peculiarly and persistently unproductive of important news.

It is true that Montevideo's newspapers lack the reputation for an international orientation and coverage that *La Nación* and the earlier *La Prensa* of Buenos Aires long enjoyed. However, the Montevideo papers show a degree of sophistication and world-mindedness that many newspapers in cities of similar size in the United States cannot match. An example of that world-mindedness was Montevideo's hosting in October, 1951, of the Inter-American Press Conference. Despite the petty flurry caused by the walkout of the governmentally chosen Argentine delegates the conference developed smoothly and constructively. Uruguayans did themselves proud in entertaining the meeting and delegates from other countries carried away a profoundly favorable impression of the country.

A well-qualified observer who was very familiar with the Uruguayan press, as well as that of other Latin American countries, once remarked that in Uruguay, to a greater degree than in any of its nineteen sister states, the press sympathized with and supported the United States. The attitude is basically predicated on the assumption that the United States is the world's great champion of the democratic way and that a small democracy has that deep faith in common with a large one. Then, too, Uruguayans in general like *norteamericanos* in general and the papers probably simply reflect that attitude. On two matters the Uruguayan press is apt to be rather consistently critical of the United States: the northern republic's recent rapprochement with the Franco government in Spain and, in the second place, the status of Puerto Rico. The explanation of military expediency in justification of the first of those points just does not seem valid or sufficient to Montevideo papers; Franco is a dictator: ergo, democracies should have none of him. With regard to Puerto Rico some of the Montevideo papers feel that it is truly Latin American territory and hence should constitute an independent state. The economic illogic of this is overlooked.

To speak of "the sports page" of a Montevideo paper is rhetorical—usually it is two sports pages and sometimes three or four. That in most cases they come at the back of the paper is of no moment. It is as easy for a Montevideano to gravitate to that part of the paper as for his sports-minded cousin in the north to turn automatically to determine the current standing of Yanks or Dodgers. The big attraction on the Montevideo sports pages is, of course, *fútbol* (or soccer). Other sports are fully covered, however, and it is a reasonably safe conclusion that, with the possible exception of the Buenos Aires papers, the press of Montevideo gives more attention to athletics in all forms than is done anywhere else in Latin America.

Other newspaper features are much as we would find in Stateside metropolitan papers. The same comic strips (in Spanish, of course) seem to have as big a following in Montevideo as in Hoboken or Hamtramck or Hot Springs. Sometimes the names must be changed: "Mary Worth" becomes "María de Oro," "Blondie" is converted into "Vida Conyugal," and "Henry" into "Cero Pelo," but Mrs. Worth still has a heart of gold, Blondie is just as naive, Henry as wordlessly disconcerting as in the States. Official advertising and vital statistics, market reports and "want ads," letters to the editor and ship sailings—all might be found in any metropolitan paper anywhere. Some aspects are different: front-page advertising appears strange to most readers in the United States; the frequent official lists of lottery winners would, of course, be illegal in papers in the States; the pages and pages of classified advertising in issues that seldom run more than sixteen or twenty pages seem out of proportion.

Advertising rates have, incidentally, considerably increased in the past year or so, due primarily to the difficulty and expense of getting newsprint. The problem has not been so acute as for Argentine papers but still is a serious one.

The personnel of Montevideo papers is rather sharply divided between the managerial and editorial executives on the one hand and the mechanical staff, compositors, and pressmen on the other. The latter category are poorly paid in general but are well organized and have at times successfully struck to obtain better wages and working conditions. Reporters have a loose inter-paper organization, the Círculo de la Prensa, and while they have not struck to obtain higher pay scales, those who know the press situation best believe they might have the collective strength to win a strike.

Local news reporting is not especially notable in Montevideo; many reporters are said to go about their work in a quite casual fashion. Foreign news is provided primarily by the Associated Press and the United Press, but one or more papers also receive service from the *Chicago Daily News* syndicate, France Presse; the *New York Times* syndicate, the International News Service, and the National Catholic Welfare Service.

In terms of editorial personnel, Montevideo papers have no such giants of the press as Eduardo Santos, Alfonso López, or Laureano Gómez of Bogotá (national presidents, all of them, and largely because of journalistic influence), or Alberto Gainza Paz of Buenos Aires, proprietor of *La Prensa* until the peronista government confiscated it as a political reprisal. It is, consequently not too surprising that Uruguayan newspapermen have only infrequently won any of the Maria Moors Cabot awards for journalistic pre-eminence granted annually by Columbia University to outstanding editors of the Americas. The explanation may lie in the fact that in Bogotá, for example, newspapermen seem to dominate their parties and can be independent of them, but those in Montevideo are controlled by their respective parties. The differences are relative at most, and subtle, but they apparently operate to prevent as great a monopoly of politics by newspapermen in Uruguay as exists in Colombia. Such a man as Eduardo Rodríguez Larreta, director of *El País*, has been, and may again be, the Uruguayan foreign minister, but it is rather because he is an influential party figure than a prominent journalist.

The Montevideo papers individually deserve a word of mention. Probably the foremost of them, though not in terms of either age or circulation, is *El Día*. It can be called pre-eminent very likely for the reason that it represents political, social, and economic gospel to the dominant wing of the long dominant Colorado party. *El Día* is a living monument to José Batlle y Ordóñez, who founded it as a young man of thirty on June 16, 1886. From then on until his death, forty-three years later, it served as his highly effective mouthpiece and was the channel through which he publicized and popularized many of the reforms for which he is famous. Most notable of these, of course, was the extremely controversial *colegiado* or collegiate form of national executive which has already been discussed. Had it not been for the continuous forum provided Batlle by *El Día*, it is doubtful whether the collegiate executive could have been written into the new constitution of 1917 in even the compromised form it was. *El Día* is now closely controlled by the three sons and two daughters of José Batlle and is a profitable property for them. Its tone has been antitotalitarian in general and especially antagonistic toward Communism. There is also a long tradition of anti-Catholicism. *El Día's* circulation is about 60,-000 daily and 75,000 Sunday.[1]

*El Diario* claims a circulation of 130,000, which would make it easily the largest paper in the entire country. Its political persuasion is Colorado but of the blancoacevedista or in-

---

[1] Statistics of Uruguayan newspaper circulations have been obtained from reliable sources in Montevideo which made a careful personal investigation. They differ in several instances from figures published in two reference works in the United States. *Editor and Publisher Year Book Number*, 1953 and *The Political Handbook of the World*, 1951, respectively, gives circulation figures as follows: *El Día:* 65,000 and 60,000; *El Diario:* 102,190 and 100,000; *La Mañana:* 53,000 and 15,000; *Acción:* 10,000 (*Political Handbook*); *La Tribuna Popular:* 18,000 to 30,000 and 25,000; *El Debate:* 38,000 and 25,000; *El País:* 50,000 and 50,000; *El Plata:* 90,000 and 45,000; *El Bien Público:* 25,000 and 5,000; *El Diario Español:* 15,000 (*Editor and Publisher*); *Marcha:* 10,000 (*Political Handbook*).

dependent wing of the party. Still earlier, *El Diario*, which was founded in 1917, reflected the position of the so-called riverista wing of the party, a schismatic fraction which opposed the Batlle-sponsored collegiate executive. Though it sees eye to eye with *El Día* in many respects, *El Diario* takes a more conservative position on economic issues. Prior to World War II, some people found in *El Diario* a tendency to lean Fascist, but at any rate a staunch pro-Allied position had been assumed before Pearl Harbor. *El Diario*, too, is a profitable paper.

*La Mañana* is the morning journalistic companion of *El Diario* and also dates from 1917. It, too, is blancoacevedista and economically conservative in tone. It carries considerable economic and financial news and its clientele is relatively more among businessmen. Its circulation is only some 34,000, however.

Still another fraction of the batllista wing of the Colorado party is journalistically represented by *Acción*. It is one of the newest of Montevideo's papers, dating only from October 22, 1948. The chief owner is Luis Batlle Berres, former president, nephew of José Batlle and, of course, cousin of the brothers Batlle Pacheco. That close relationship does not prevent *Acción* from being a rival of *El Día*, however, even though both papers continue to speak for batllismo. As of 1951, *Acción* enjoyed a stance somewhat closer to the government than did *El Día* for the reason that in the election of 1950 *Acción* and its owner, the retiring President Batlle Berres, supported Andrés Martínez Trueba, the leading Colorado candidate (who therefore won the presidency), while *El Día* backed another Colorado contestant. *Acción's* circulation has grown to about 15,000.

Relatively midway in position stands *La Tribuna Popular*, a late-morning newspaper, which can be characterized, not essentially inaccurately, as opportunistic and at times editorially inconsistent. It sometimes supports Blanco candidates and issues and at other times throws its influence to the antibatllista Colorados. Though some of its inclination is toward the Blancos, it has not reflected the anti-United States tone often sounded by that party. It is not taken too seriously by the better-educated classes and finds its chief following among the middle and lower-middle classes. *La Tribuna* gains a certain clientele because of its tendency toward sensationalism in local news coverage and because of its emphasis on sporting news. It is the earliest founded of the major Montevideo papers (December 1, 1879) but has a current circulation of only about 25,000.

The Nationalist or Blanco organ is *El Debate*. It represents the regular or herrerista type of *nacionalismo* in contradistinction to the Partido Nacionalista Independiente, which has its own papers. *El Debate*, founded in 1931, goes down the line in reflecting the point of view of Luis Alberto de Herrera, the virtual dictator of the party whose unofficial name is derived from his own. In economic matters *El Debate* is ultraconservative; in the international scene it is pro-Franco and pro-Perón. Almost by the same token it usually has taken a reserved, skeptical, or even hostile attitude toward the United States. Despite its representation of one of the large political parties of the country, its circulation is only about 20,000.

The Independent Nationalists, a distinct party, have two companion newspapers, *El País*, a morning daily with a circulation of about 60,000, and *El Plata*, with an evening circulation of some 42,000. They are essentially twin enterprises, like *La Mañana* and *El Diario*, and share the same presses and to some extent the same personnel. The dominant figure on both is Eduardo Rodríguez Larreta, which is sufficient explanation for the papers' advocacy of collective international intervention when necessary. It was Rodríguez Larreta who, as foreign minister soon after World War II, advanced the challenging doctrine of collective intervention which sometimes is given his name. Interestingly, the two papers failed to see eye to eye on the important constitutional issue of the adoption of a collegiate executive in 1951. The economic position of *El País* and *El Plata* is intermediate between those of *El Día* and *La Mañana*, *i.e.*, moderately conservative. The two papers were founded in 1918 and 1914 respectively.

The oldest of Montevideo's newspapers but still one of the most restricted in appeal and smallest in circulation is *El Bien Público*. It was founded as a Catholic paper on November 1, 1878, and continues to speak for Uruguayan Catholics, to whom its circulation of about 5,000 is almost entirely limited. More strictly speaking, it reflects the position of the Unión Cívica, the Catholic political party of Uruguay. It is published each morning except Mondays and probably is not financially self-sustaining. Its position has been democratic and sympathetic to the United States, and, of course, consistently and strongly anti-Communist.

The only other Spanish-language daily in Montevideo is *El Diario Español*, founded in 1905 but even now having a circulation of only some 1,500. It caters especially to the Spanish colony in Montevideo. Its political orientation has been franquista and with the recent engagement (not yet a marriage!) of expediency between the United States and Spain its tone has become more friendly to the northern republic. It has little importance in the general picture of the Montevideo press.

The largest of Montevideo's weekly papers is *Marcha*, with a circulation of about 15,000. It is distinctly the reflection of its highly individualistic owner, Carlos Quijano. The position of the paper is nominally independent but it often reflects a near-Communist tone. It is usually critical of the United States and professionally bemoans *norteamericano* cultural and economic penetration of Uruguay. It was founded in 1939.

*El Sol*, the Socialist weekly, has a circulation of some 3,000 and is primarily the work of Uruguay's veteran Socialist leader, Dr. Emilio Frugoni. The point of view is conventionally Socialist. The Communist weekly, *Justicia*, has about the same circulation as *El Sol* and is a typically Moscow-inspired Communist voice. Both of these papers are necessarily supported by party funds and in the case of *Justicia* it is said that some labor-union money goes to its support, possibly without the knowledge of rank-and-file union members themselves.

The two English-language papers, the daily *Sun* and the weekly *Montevidean* are both insignificant. The Jewish-community daily, *Unzer Fraint*, with a circulation of about 3,000 has alleged Communist leanings.

The various reviews, the weekly *Mundo Uruguayo*, the bimonthly *Mundial*, the monthly *Uruguay y la URSS*, and the weekly *URSS*, as well as the Sunday supplements of such papers as *El Día* and *La Mañana*, are all to be considered more as cultural than as news publications. It is not seemly, however, to employ too careful a definition of the adjective "cultural"; the two Soviet organs are patently propagandistic.

The only newspapers in the interior circulating more than

a thousand copies each are *El Telégrafo* of Paysandú, *La Tribuna Salteña* of Salto, *El Heraldo* of Florida, *La Opinión* of Mercedes, and *El Ideal* of Colonia, which have, respectively, circulation figures of about 10,000, 5,000, 4,850, 3,000, and 1,000. Some of them run no editorials, but all, and other and smaller papers, have considerable amounts of local advertising. The appearance of most of the interior papers is crude and amateurish. Many look as if they had been hand-set; typography and makeup are unattractive. Uruguay's nonMontevideo press is definitely nothing of which the country may be proud.

If by the term "fourth estate" we mean all those elements which have a hand in distributing the news—which was probably the way Burke would have meant it had he been coining the phrase now instead of a century and a half ago—then some consideration must be given Uruguay's radio stations. They are numerous, influential, and, in most cases, prosperous. As of 1952, the country had forty-five of them, twenty-four in Montevideo and three fewer than that in the rest of Uruguay.

The political, economic, and social impact of the radio in Latin America has not yet been sufficiently studied. It is certainly of tremendous significance, and not necessarily in the same ways or the same degree as in the United States. For one thing, the radio in Latin America provides a means of access for countless thousands and even millions of persons who, by reason of inability to read, would be removed from the reach of newspapers. The argument that economic inability to afford a radio would vitiate such reasoning is of less validity than would otherwise be the case because of the common habit of group listening to the radio in bars and other places of congregating. Of course, a contrary element which must admittedly be given weight is Uruguay's much higher than average literacy rate, which makes the country to a greater degree a nation of potential newspaper readers. The whole problem obviously needs more analysis than it has yet received.

Suffice it to say that the radio has become an important factor in the distribution of news and the formation of public opinion in Uruguay. The number of receiving sets in the country has been estimated at 300,000. Each of these will be heard, at a conservative calculation. by four or five people. The advertising value of the radio has hence become obvious and some of the broadcasting stations have developed into financially profitable enterprises. Some have paid dividends of 10 per cent or more a year.

Several of Montevideo's radio stations are owned by or affiliated with newspapers; one is operated by the government, but it, too, broadcasts news summaries and commentaries as well as entertainment. Stations in the interior are regarded as considerably more influential than local newspapers in shaping the form of public opinion. Radio news broadcasts and commentary, whether in the capital or the *campo*, offer much opportunity, naturally, for news slanting.

Circulation of newspapers in an unfriendly foreign country can be readily prohibited by that country's government but the air waves offer a more fluid medium and are less subject to control from abroad. Three of Montevideo's broadcasting stations, Radio Carve, Radio Espectador, and Radio Ariel, have complained to the Uruguayan government of jamming from Argentina. The first two of these stations operated on international clear channels, which presumably were free from any interference for many hundreds of miles around. They claimed, nevertheless, that broadcasts emanating from Argentina on the same supposedly monopolized wave lengths were sufficiently strong to jam their own. Radio Ariel, which possessed no international clear channel, faced the competition of a much more powerful Argentine station broadcasting on the same wave length and allegedly interfering with Ariel's news broadcasts. The additional comment that all radio broadcasting in Argentina is closely controlled by the government of that country makes the drawing of conclusions superfluous.

The place of television in the whole picture of the fourth estate in Uruguay is as yet undetermined. The simple answer is that Uruguay has no TV, but that is not a sufficient answer. Televising of both entertainment and news programs made an impressive debut in Buenos Aires late in 1951. It is said that special equipment was able to receive some of the programs in Montevideo. Uruguayan authorities have given study to the problem of working out a technical relationship by which Argentine programs could be relayed to Uruguay, but the problem is by no means solved. Indeed, the solution of the scientific and technical aspects of a one-way transmission system might easily raise just as baffling and awkward political and psychological questions. If Argentine TV programs were regularly received in Uruguay, they easily could—and inevitably would—be converted into a more fearsome and effective propaganda tool than is afforded by the Argentine radio. It is conceivable that the international balance currently prevailing in the Plata region might be importantly modified by the development of that tool of communication.

The control and dissemination of news in Uruguay assumes an importance it could not begin to have in a country like nearby Paraguay or Bolivia. It is not only that Uruguay is far more literate. That country's general political and international awareness, its peculiarly delicate relationship to its national neighbors, its democratic way of life, and its personality and dignity all make for a great opportunity for the press and allied mediums. That opportunity has been largely but not in all respects perfectly realized. Certainly the fourth estate must be assigned great significance in the Uruguayan scene.

〰〰〰〰
〰〰〰〰

# 14

# Education: A Monument to Varela

Uruguay had a citizen in the third quarter of the nineteenth century named José Pedro Varela (or, as his baptismal certificate read, Pedro José Varela). He was born March 19, 1845. Dying October 24, 1879, his life spanned only thirty-four years, seven months, and five days—just over a short third of a century. The significant part of that prematurely closed life lasted but eleven years, one month, and six days—only a few months more than a brief decade.

Yet, miraculously, Varela still lives. He lives in the progress made, at any given contemporary moment, by more than a quarter of a million students, over a tenth of the population of the whole country. He lives in the brick and wood and stone and stucco of some 1,700 primary-school buildings and scores on scores of secondary-school, university, and other structures. He lives in what is probably the second highest national literacy rate in all of Latin America. He lives in an educational and cultural impulse that, as much as perhaps any other single factor, has made his country one of the advanced nations of all the earth.

In all likelihood José Pedro Varela, second only to José Batlle y Ordóñez, has left a permanent mark on Uruguay. That his impress was almost wholly in the field of education, and in considerable measure only in primary education, does not invalidate its significance. Before his time systematic educational effort, while by no means nonexistent, had been, in general, in a sorry state. After his decade of endeavor Uruguay could fairly launch itself upon that generation of educational gestation which in the twentieth century would reach remarkable flowering and maturity.

For the very reason that colonial Uruguay—the Banda Oriental—was a forgotten corner of the Spanish domain, a territorial stepchild, so to speak, formal educational development languished, as did other formal development. The education of the gaucho was in the saddle. His textbooks were the *boleadoras* and the branding iron, his laboratory the campfire. There are fragmentary references to the introduction of formal schooling —in Montevideo, of course—just before the middle of the eighteenth century, but the schooling was obviously as fragmentary as the references. Inevitably, such as did exist was clerically conducted and conditioned. It was the Jesuits who were Uruguay's first schoolteachers. Years later, following the suppression of the Jesuit order in 1773, the Franciscans immediately volunteered to and did take over the responsibility. Thus it was during the stormy days of Artigas and the Thirty-three when Uruguay was fighting for life and recognition. Education was but an incident, a dispensable luxury.

Nevertheless, it was in 1826, two years before independence was assured, that Uruguay's first school law was passed. Primary schools, the law ambitiously provided, were to be established in all the towns of the land. England's Lancasterian system was adopted as the basis for school organization and operation. The first budget for public instruction involved the munificent sum of 10,800 pesos. The first normal school, for the better preparation of teachers, was envisioned. The means, even the will, to execute these plans were lacking, but the vision was there.

By mid-century the picture was still dismal. The meager evidence we have is conflicting in detail, but it is all depressing. Varela himself estimated in 1876 that a quarter century earlier Montevideo had had only 1,600 children attending school, and the rest of the country, 1,400; that made, assuming a current national population of 150,000, a ratio of one to fifty. A report of 1855 revealed only thirty schools in all Uruguay, an attendance of but 899. Assuming a national population of 129,000 (as did the report), that meant only seven pupils per thousand inhabitants.

The higher strata of the educational pyramid were similarly shabby. Secondary education cannot be said to have begun, even on a paper basis, before 1830; no substantial development at that level occurred until 1848 and but little between then and 1885. University instruction was similarly tardy in getting under way. The first such effort was in 1810 when Fray José Benito Lamas began teaching a course in philosophy in a Montevideo convent. A project for a national university was approved in 1833. The resulting "House of General Studies" had as its academic furniture chairs of Latin, philosophy, jurisprudence, and mathematics. President Manuel Oribe in 1838 decreed the establishment of the Greater University of the Republic, but nothing substantial was done for some years, the chief deterrent being the Great War in the 1840's. On forming organizations in 1847 and 1848 to develop and control primary and secondary education, respectively, the government concomitantly recognized its responsibility for higher education as well.

The result of that acknowledgment was the establishment, at long last, of the University of Montevideo (officially the University of the Republic) on July 18, 1849, the nineteenth anniversary of the promulgation of Uruguay's first constitution. Montevideo was still under siege at that time. At least eighteen Latin American universities antedated that at Montevideo, the oldest ones dating back three hundred years. Beginnings in Uruguay were modest: the original faculty included two professors of medicine, two of religion, and one each of Latin, philosophy, mathematics, and political economy.

The deadly years of disorder continued through the 1850's and 1860's—and, indeed, through much of the rest of the century.

But then came Varela.

The hero of the saga of educational development came of good stock. His father in 1846 had translated from the French the first book on pedagogy to be published in the Plata region. Young José Pedro was destined for business but had no liking for it. He read widely; French and English he mastered, and some German and Italian. In 1867 he departed for Europe and the United States on what was ostensibly a business trip. The high point of the European phase of the trip was an interview with Victor Hugo on the Isle of Guernsey. In the United States the germination of the real and permanent Varela began. He met Domingo Faustino Sarmiento, the great Argentine statesman-educator, who was then his country's minister to the United States. The young man of twenty-three sat at the feet of the statesman of fifty-seven, but he was friend as well as disciple. Varela also came to know the work of Horace Mann and others who were making pedagogical history. In the United States, too, the young Uruguayan wrote poetry (what Latin American doesn't!) which was later published as *Ecos Perdidos* (*Lost Echoes*). Then, too, he wrote letters back to Montevideo newspapers giving an impressionistic and sympathetic account of the land where he was absorbing so much.

In the summer of 1868, Sarmiento returned to his own land to assume its presidency and to give it the great educational impulse which has made his name permanently famous. Varela accompanied his mentor, arriving in Montevideo on August 28. Twenty-one days later, on September 18, 1868, Varela's career began. On that night he addressed a public meeting in Montevideo on what he had seen and thought and felt of the educational system in the United States. It was a diffident but yet a dedicated young man who addressed his first public audience. Contemporary accounts report his hearers as deeply impressed, even moved, by his words. A tangible fruit of his address was the organization the same evening of the Society of the Friends of Popular Education. Varela became an initial secretary and the following year, on the death of the original president, the young Varela was elected to succeed him. In that same year, 1869, the Friends of Popular Education established an experimental school where in years following many of the innovations were attempted which became the heart of the Varelian reform.

In 1874 Varela published his book, *La Educación del Pueblo*, a profoundly significant theoretical discussion of pedagogy. Two years later, in his *De la Legislación Escolar*, he made the other of his great contributions in book form to the cause of educational reform. This treatise was a concrete proposal for a new school law. The following year Dictator Lorenzo Latorre erected a legislative milestone by decreeing, on August 24, 1877, the Law of Common Education, based almost verbatim on Varela's recommendations of 1876. Varela, who in 1876 had been named director of primary instruction for the department of Montevideo, was now appointed national inspector of the General Administration [*Dirección*] of Primary Instruction, with far broader supervisory powers than any school officials had before possessed.

His career now seemed fairly launched—but its course was almost run. He began a strenuous life of inspections, organization of pedagogical congresses, inauguration of the periodical *Enciclopedia de Educación* (for which he wrote and translated much), drafting of voluminous reports. Never robust, his unrelenting regimen contributed to the undermining of his health and he died in October, 1879. Uruguay's tragic loss was immediately recognized and within two years Varela was being apotheosized as a "Great Citizen."

Varela's reforms were not without opposition, both during his lifetime and afterward. Some persons opposed the new scheme of things simply because it was dictatorially decreed instead of democratically legislated. A more tangible and realistic opposition came from the local politicians scattered over Uruguay because some degree of patronage was removed from their control and the supervision of teaching was centralized and made uniform. Some Catholic opposition was generated because of the liberal spirit of Varela's reforms and because he favored secular control of education. Extremely conservative newspapers viewed with professional alarm.

The original details of the Varelian reform are less important—because some of them were later changed—than the broad, basic principles which their author laid down and which have become the warp and woof of the Uruguayan educational system. Among the most important tenets of the Varelian philosophy were the principles that education must be free, obligatory, secularly controlled, and coeducational.

The first of these principles has been carried out more faithfully and literally in Uruguay than perhaps anywhere else in the world. Schooling, from the *jardín de infantes* (or kindergarten) to the university, carries with it no direct cost to the pupil or student, be he Uruguayan or foreigner. He or his family must provide his own subsistence, but of tuition, fees, assessments, or charges for books there are none. The second of the fundamentals has been less successfully executed. A compulsory attendance law has been on the statute books in Uruguay since 1934, but it has frequently not been possible to enforce it rigidly. Nonetheless, the ratio of school attendance to total population is a more favorable one in Uruguay than in almost any other Latin American country. Many children, especially in the rural areas, leave school before completing the primary grades, but "continuation schools" have been a partial solution of that problem.

The principle of laic or secular control of education gained strength as the Batlle-inspired general skepticism of the Church progressed. The main objective was achieved by a law of 1909 which prohibited the teaching of religion in the public schools. Political sentiment later went beyond that point and now teachers must, by strongly entrenched tradition as well as governmental fiat, refrain from any suggestion of ecclesiastical or religious motivation or influence. Coeducation is now an accepted part of the pattern of Uruguayan school organization and instruction.

Other values and bases of Uruguay's educational system are inherited from Varela. It is to him more than to anyone else that a revision of teaching methods has been due. Prior to his time instruction had been by routine and rote, verbatim answers to catachetical questions were given, individual initiative was looked at askance if not actually penalized. After Varela, the techniques of teaching took on more flexibility, sloughed off much—though not all—of the classical emphasis which had earlier characterized them. Material and curricula were more consciously geared to the needs of the students. More could still be done, especially in the interior, by way of stressing critical thinking on the students' part, though the change from pre-Varelian days is notable.

Again, we may credit largely to Varela an increase in the dignity and status of the teaching profession. The pre-Varelian norm was for teachers to be appointed as part of a petty political patronage which gave chief consideration to the friends of the local *jefe.* In later years the occupation more truly became a profession, training was improved, *esprit de corps* heightened. Possibly the most important of the by-products of Varela's work, even if a largely intangible one, was the much greater public consciousness of and concern for education. A literate and informed people became something to be proud of, the physical school came to be regarded pridefully not only as a utilitarian tool but also as a symbol of national growth and progress. In recent years one of the chief channels of expression of the public interest has been the local Committee of Development (*Comisión de Fomento*), a type of organization which has grown rapidly. It is in some ways a rough equivalent of the Parent-Teachers Association, though doubtless not so much of a political tool.

The whole control over the educational system has changed greatly since Varela's time. His philosophy of education pointed to the desirability of centralized control and that objective has been quite effectively realized. It is reflected, for example, in the uniform choice of textbooks, the identical examinations given (which, incidentally, carry more weight in promotions than do teachers' grades), and in other ways.

The nominally highest agency of control is the ministry of public instruction and social welfare which, under its present title, dates from 1935.[1] However, the existence of independent agencies of more direct control, the autonomous councils, makes the function of the ministry primarily bureaucratic insofar as its responsibility for educational administration is concerned; it deals more directly with the social-welfare portion of its dichotomized assignment.

The four councils which in reality control the educational structure of the country are parts of the famous Uruguayan pattern of autonomous entities. They are constitutionally recognized and have a high degree of independent authority. To a certain degree the coexistence of these separate councils negates the principle of a centralized control over education, but to a

---

[1] Various instances of reshuffling had previously occurred. The first ministerial-level cognizance of the problem came only a few years after Varela's death when the ministry of justice, worship, and public instruction was established. In 1891 "public instruction" became part of a ministry of development. A reorganization in 1907 established a ministry of industries, development, and public instruction. This was changed in 1911 to the ministry of justice and public instruction.

certain extent, also, the councils are interlocking and, furthermore, all operate on a national basis. A defect in the system is
that changes of membership of the councils sometimes result in
unfortunate changes of policy though the personnel of the administrative and instructional staffs is not thereby affected.

The National Council of Primary and Normal Instruction
(*Enseñanza*) dates from 1918, and successive constitutional
revisions, the latest in 1951, have continued it on a firmly autonomous basis. The council includes a president (who serves as
director general), a vice president, and three other members. A
secretary general, an assistant secretary, and numerous other
officials complete the administrative personnel of the council. A
corps of inspectors, organized partially on a regional and departmental (territorial) basis and partially on one of subject-
matter areas, forms an important element in the work of the
council.

The National Council of Secondary Instruction operates
with perhaps less basic freedom than that of primary instruction, due in part to its composition and in part to the philosophy and tradition which have circumscribed the general role
of secondary education in Uruguay. The council is composed
of a paid director general (who exercises the council's presidency) and six honorary members. Three of the latter are
elected by the active teaching personnel of the secondary
schools, one by the Central University Council, one by the
Council of Primary Instruction, and the sixth by the Council
of the Labor University. This secondary council, too, has its
staff of administrative personnel and of well-trained technical
inspectors and subject specialists. The Pedagogical Library
and Museum is a government agency serving principally the
secondary-education level of schools.

The Labor University dates as such only from 1942, but its
antecedents go back much further. The problem of the many
"incorrigible vagabonds" (as a government publication describes them) resulted in the second half of the nineteenth century in the establishment of an institution to bring about reform by the channel of manual labor. The motivation for many
years was corrective and disciplinary, but the vocational pos-
sibilities of such instruction were obvious. Industrial instruction for its own sake came more into the center of the picture

in the second, third, and fourth decades of the present century, with the culmination coming in the creation of the one large organizational tent in 1942. Administration rests in the hands of a paid director general and a Directive Council of honorary members designated by the Central University Council, the National Council of Primary and Normal Instruction, the National Commission of Fine Arts, the Chamber of Industries, the Rural Federation, the Rural Association of Uruguay, the instructional staff of the component schools, and the executive branch of the national government.

The Labor University is the central directive agency for the more than forty agricultural and industrial schools operated under government auspices in various parts of the country. These include schools devoted to forestry, citriculture, milk production, mechanics, construction, electrotechnics, graphic and plastic arts, and shipbuilding. The university also promotes all technical instruction and attempts to improve existing industrial practices and techniques. The political and ideological overtones characterizing the similarly named organization in Mexico have never developed in Uruguay's Labor University, and it has been universally recognized as filling an important and constructive role in vocational education.

Higher education in Uruguay is centered in the University of the Republic, or, as it is very commonly known, the University of Montevideo. (All higher education is, for that matter, concentrated in the capital city.) Each of the ten faculties ("colleges" to *norteamericanos*) which currently compose the university has its own governing council and dean. These deans, together with student and other faculty representatives, comprise the Central University Council which is the supreme administrative and co-ordinating agency of the university. The rector (president) of the university is nominated by the council and appointed by the executive branch of the national government for a four-year term.

The original plan of organization of the university, slightly more than a century ago, provided for faculties of Natural Sciences; Medicine, Surgery, and Pharmacy; Theology; and Jurisprudence. University reforms and reorganizations came in 1862, 1885, 1908, and 1931. Theology was early subtracted from the organization, but the other faculties have multiplied by divisions and additions (which takes care of all the basic mathematical processes!) until they now include: Law and Social Science, Medicine, Economic Sciences and Administration, Dentistry, Chemistry and Pharmacy, Veterinary Medicine, Agriculture, Engineering, Architecture, and Humanities and Sciences. The university has for decades proudly defended its autonomy; an important student strike in 1951 was motivated by a congressional threat to that autonomy as part of extensive constitutional changes which were under consideration.

A privately supported Institute of Higher Studies, enjoying autonomy under Uruguayan law, engages in scientific investigation and research, gives public lectures, and publishes bulletins, but is not authorized to grant degrees. Research activities are also carried on by a number of institutes attached to one or another faculty of the national university.

Public primary schools in Uruguay are basically of three types. The first, traditionally found for the most part in semi-urban areas, has a four-year curriculum which, for many students, is terminal. The second type has a six-year curriculum, and is designed to meet the requirements for admission to the secondary schools. The third operates an eight-year course but is limited to Montevideo and is used chiefly by girls not planning to go on to secondary schools. Some rural primary schools have only a three-year course.

Rural schools in general were in a deplorable condition until the middle 1920's. Many children in them dropped out after the first grade. Beginning with the third decade of the century, a considerable improvement was introduced within a few years: better buildings and equipment were obtained, steps were taken toward consolidation, etc. By mid-century many very attractive rural school buildings dotted the countryside throughout Uruguay. Urban schools, especially those of Montevideo, have traditionally been much more favored, physically and otherwise. Of 1,078 rural schools in 1946, for example, 706 had only one teacher apiece; the typical urban school, on the other hand, had one teacher per class. It is still not easy to obtain teachers for rural schools whenever and wherever needed. Most schools, rural or urban, have until relatively recently lacked adequate playground space. However, a National Commission of Physical Education has existed since 1911 as a dependency of the ministry. Lack of discipline remains an obvious problem in many primary schools and, to a lesser extent, in some at the secondary level.

Many Montevideo schools are named after foreign countries and in numerous cases establish a sort of symbolic rapprochement with the particular foreign state. The Escuela Estados Unidos, for example, displays the United States flag, commemorates the Fourth of July, and is addressed on occasion by the United States ambassador.

Several special kinds of schools and classes are operated. They include ones for the blind, for the deaf and dumb, for retarded and for gifted children, open-air schools, and experimental schools.

An important educational impulse came to fruition in 1933 when a special commission including teachers, physicians, judges, lawyers, and others, made a study of six months which resulted in the promulgation of Uruguay's famous Children's Code (*Código del Niño*). This social milestone created a Children's Council (*Consejo del Niño*) which is charged with concerning itself with everything relating to the child "from his gestation to his majority," as a government publication describes it. A salaried president and six honorary members comprise the council, and it is organized in a number of technical divisions: prenatal, lower infancy (up to the age of three), higher infancy (to fourteen), adolescent and vocational (to twenty-one), hygiene, education, social service, and juridical.

Perhaps the chief problem at the secondary-school level has been one of educational philosophy and tradition: were those schools to be regarded primarily as preparation for the university or were they to be considered as an end in themselves? The first of those points of view formerly prevailed, even to the extent of placing the secondary schools under the supervision of the university administration. It is only in recent decades that the latter school of thought has made many converts.

The Uruguayan secondary school is the *liceo*. The nineteen departments have eighty-one *liceos* of which forty are in the capital and forty-one in the interior. Of the four score schools at this level, thirty-two are privately operated, most of them by religious organizations, but licensed and inspected by the government. Middle-class families often prefer to send their children to private *liceos*, many of which maintain excellent standards. Entrance to the *liceo* is generally at the age of twelve after completing six years of primary schooling and the passing of an examination. The work is organized in two levels, the first of a general nature, involving four years, and the second a more specifically pre-professional two-year course. Graduation from the *liceo* carries with it the bachelor's degree (*bachillerato*) and represents a level in some ways rather more advanced than does a high-school education in the United States.

The emphasis in Uruguayan secondary education is on the classical humanities and history rather than science. Hence, the facilities for the sciences are not so good as for other subjects. This means that but little student laboratory work, which many teachers would like to see, can be done. There is a growing tendency to include in the curriculum more of modern literature, a more practical training in civics, and similar innovations. Teachers often seem to be more fluent in the mechanics of their subjects than is true in the United States.

The professional training of teachers for the primary schools has made great strides in recent decades; the training of secondary teachers has been less systematic, however. Teacher training is given in normal institutes, and some schools have provision for student observation and practice teaching. Almost all teachers are chosen by competitive examination and are advanced by merit. All teachers except those in private schools are licensed by the national government and all are eligible for pensions. The basic point of retirement on pensions is reached when the years of service plus the years of age equal ninety. Secondary teachers are normally appointed for an initial five-year term and after successful completion of a second five-year term receive permanent status or tenure. Salaries paid are not large, but regular increments are provided for and the considerable degree of financial stability and certainty has aided greatly in giving the teaching profession a spirit it does not have in many other Latin American countries. The heightened morale is reflected by the existence of an important and professionalized organization, the Uruguayan Federation of Teachers (*Federación Uruguaya del Magisterio*).

Uruguay's national university represents an educational capstone of which the country may well be proud. With an enrollment of more than 8,000, it is one of Latin America's largest universities and certainly, by qualitiative measurement, it is one of the best. The university, unlike those of Mexico, Colombia, and a few other Latin American countries, has no central campus or "university city"; the several faculties occupy buildings in widely separated parts of Montevideo, as we have already noted.

Except in the Faculty of Humanities and Sciences (the newest of the ten), all courses are required; that faculty offers a considerable number of elective courses. In all except the Faculty of Law and Social Sciences, the courses given are strictly and exclusively professional. The other faculties operate on the assumption that the *liceos* can and do provide all the necessary cultural education. Though this sort of curricular philosophy inevitably narrows the training, it does, by the same token, permit a greater specialization and intensive education, so that the typical four-year course, regardless of the faculty involved, usually represents a greater educational achievement than graduation from the average college in the United States.

The various faculties have their own libraries which, in total, include more than 200,000 volumes. In addition, the National Library is easily accessible to law students inasmuch as it is housed, pending completion of its own structure, in the building occupied by the Faculty of Law.

The University of Montevideo has more than 500 members on its instructional staff, but only about a tenth of them are full-time. The others, as is typical in Latin American universities, represent practicing lawyers, physicians, engineers, architects, and other professional men who teach part-time both for the prestige it confers and because of a deeply rooted sense of social and educational responsibility. Students, as elsewhere in Latin America, are politically minded and frequently register disapproval of policy and practice by going on strike. Their collective attitudes are usually implemented through the various student organizations, the largest of which is the Federation of Students of Uruguay. Each of the faculties has its own student organization as well.

The scattered location of the several faculties militates

against the existence of much student spirit in the sense that United States universities know it. This situation is enhanced by the absence of dormitories and most of the multiform extra-curricular activities in which United States college and university students engage. Nor is there systematic provision for Uruguayan student participation in physical education or athletics, though many students belong to one or more of the 500-odd Montevideo sports clubs.

The typical Uruguayan university student is an indefatigable note taker, a process encouraged by the prospect of the difficult examinations which face him at the end of the year at the hands of boards of three to five members. Most instruction is by the time-honored lecture method; laboratory work is increasing in science courses although insufficient equipment frequently puts the emphasis on demonstrations by the professor. Many classes are regularly scheduled in the late afternoon or night. When the academic year, running from March to December, is over, it is over! Students at once make for Montevideo's magnificent beaches and could not conceivably be corraled in any form of summer session.

Many of the students who go through this rigorous educational process are women. Coeducation is taken for granted, at that level as at lower ones, and women avail themselves widely of it. As they gather between lectures, for example, on the steps of the Law building on Avenida 18 de Julio they chat freely with their male student friends. The groups are not composed, exactly, of Joe and Josephine College, but their members reflect a sex equality and a social maturity which are both gratifying and decidedly atypical as far as other Latin American universities are concerned.

Uruguay supports its educational structure generously. The national budget of 1951 contained total estimated expenditures of 332,096,967.71 pesos. Expenditures for all forms of education were 63,521,657.68 pesos, which formed 19.13 per cent of all expenditures. That category of expenditures consequently formed the largest single item in the budget. The next largest item, for debt servicing (61,948,000.85 pesos), formed 18.65 per cent of the budget. The allocation of the education expenditures was: ministry, 12,182,495.83 pesos; primary instruction 25,954,649.24; secondary instruction, 11,874,842.67;

university (including the Labor University), 13,509,669.94.
Uruguay has no huge military establishment on which to lavish
funds. The schools benefit correspondingly.

As one sees the schools of Montevideo, Salto, Paysandú, or
other cities, or those of the rural districts, his impression is of
groups of healthy, animal-spirited young Uruguayans in whose
hands the future of the country seems safe. They have deeply,
though perhaps too theoretically, implanted in them a knowledge of national history and institutions.

They are clad in uniforms—usually white smocks, though
the uniform differs from one private school to another—as a
reflection of the equalitarian philosophy which permeates Uruguayan education. They are as vivacious and noisy as their opposite numbers in the United States. Some few of their parents
doubtless view such manifestations lugubriously and wonder,
as has been done before, what the younger generation is coming to. The great majority of their parents, however, and their
parents' friends, and Uruguayans in general, point with pride
and take vast satisfaction in an educational system which for
freedom, democracy, intelligence, and maturity has few if any
equals elsewhere in Latin America.

Could Varela but return now, three-quarters of a century
after his death, he would take an understandable satisfaction
in his country's schools. He builded well. Uruguayans see his
monument by looking about them.

# 15

## The Arts Belong to the People

The cultural expression of a people usually stems from deep wellsprings of rich native experience. If the springs be not deep, or if they dry, then the expression—whether it be in literature or painting or music or architecture—will likely be correspondingly sterile. Borrowed experience scarcely serves: the expression is then apt to seem parroted or pale. There is little so pathetic as the counterfeit coin of a cultural expression which has no basic reserves to give it substance; it almost invariably has the dull tone and lacklustrous color of lead.

The wonder, then, is that Uruguay measures up as well as it does—that it has produced a Rodó or a Blanes or a Fabini. For Uruguay's fountains of experience are not so rich and deep and full as those of Mexico or Peru or even Brazil. Uruguay had no great pre-Spanish civilization. It had no long and colorful colonial life. True, the picturesque gauchos ranged the Banda for many decades, but more picturesque ones roamed the pampas across the river—and Argentina has been able to exploit them in song and story as Uruguay has not. Uruguay had few if any epic figures in the nineteenth century who made the history from which sagas are written and ballads sung. Conquests there were, but they were the more prosaic conquests over ignorance and pestilence and poverty. In considerable measure, then, the foundation of Uruguay's cultural expression is, like its population, European.

José Enrique Rodó (1872–1917) was the giant of Uruguayan literature. He was, for that matter, a shining star in the whole Latin American firmament. He was, so Professor Torres-Ríoseco writes, "the *modernista* who ranks second only to Darío," [1] and a Spanish literary critic, Andrés González-Blanco, goes much further: he is "the magician of Spanish prose, the publicist who writes the best Spanish in all the globe, he who has best known [how] to play the instrument of our language in all its mastery. . . ." Rubén Darío himself called Rodó "the Latin Emerson," though some scholars in the United States doubt the validity of the comparison.

Rodó was perhaps the first great literary apostle of Americanism. By the term he meant, of course, the Americanism of the hemisphere, not that of the United States. Men should think of themselves, he wrote, not as Brazilians, or Chileans, or Mexicans, but as Americans. In reality, Rodó's tocsin was directed to Latin American youth against the United States. It is sounded most forcefully in his little essay *Ariel*, published at the turn of the century and written in the form of a teacher's farewell to his students.

The essay had a tremendous effect in underlining a spiritual unity for the countries of Latin America in the face of the devouring materialism that Rodó saw in the United States. The larger country to the north was Caliban to Latin America's Ariel. The United States could become dangerous, Rodó maintained, if it stimulated, as was so likely, materialism and mediocrity. There were values to be found in the United States, he admitted—religious liberty, widespread education, the dignity of labor—but utilitarianism had translated virtually everything into materialistic terms. Spanish Americans must ever cleave to the goals of idealism, delicacy, good taste, nobility; an intellectual aristocracy would lead America—the broader America of Rodó's definition—to a more serene and satisfying experience because its personality would be better realized.

If *Ariel* is Rodó's first and greatest literary monument, it is by no means his only one. In his *Motivos de Proteo* (*The Motives of Proteus;* 1909), he embodied his ideas on a variety of moral and ethical problems. Many of the ideas were fragmen-

[1] Arturo Torres-Ríoseco, *The Epic of Latin American Literature* (New York, 1942), p. 116.

tarily expressed but his writing, as in his *Ariel* and other books, was highly polished, so much so that it became the admiration and the envy of later Spanish American writers. Rodó gave almost his whole time during his relatively short life to his work. Part of that work was editorial: he helped found and direct *La Revista Nacional de Literatura y Ciencias Sociales*. Part of his work was devoted to excursions into politics. His home in the old part of the city became an intellectual center for the whole continent. With his striking height (more than six feet) among the shorter than average Latinos, his aquiline nose, his habit of waving his arms vigorously as he walked, it is little wonder that some who saw him were reminded of the condor which soared so high in the heavens, just as Rodó would have the spirit of man rise.

Rodó lived and wrote at a time when he could well be excused for taking a dim view of the United States. The first decade and a half of the twentieth century was a time of brashness and not a little ostentation on the part of the northern republic. It was the time of Theodore Roosevelt's Big Stick policy, of one after another Middle American protectorate, of Dollar Diplomacy. Rodó, like Argentina's Manuel Ugarte, Nicaragua's Rubén Darío, and Peru's José Santos Chocano, mistrusted a United States of America which he feared—and perhaps did not fully understand. Uruguayans admire him and revere his memory (they have named one of their capital's loveliest parks for him), but he is not now the intellectual guide of the country. Nevertheless, he is undoubtedly a literary figure of the first magnitude. His name and fame are as great as those of any littérateur Argentina has produced; he is therefore an unchallengeable answer the smaller country can and does give if its neighbor across the river becomes a bit literarily patronizing.

Rodó had many literate compatriots. The first of them in point of time were two who were born in the eighteenth century, Francisco Acuña de Figueroa (1790–1862) and Bartolomé Hidalgo (1788–1822). The first of them began a literary career as a monarchist, a position which led to temporary exile, but after his return to Uruguay he became the principal author of his country's national anthem. His writing was almost entirely poetry and much of it a very biting and satiric poetry.

Hidalgo, a man of humble Montevidean ancestry, who tended bar as a youth, is remembered as the first of the "gaucho poets." Later Argentine writers more fully developed and exploited the gaucho theme, however.

The early nineteenth century found Uruguay with its quota of romanticists. The earliest of them, the short-lived Adolfo Berro (1819–41), based his principal work on an old Charrúa legend; Indian nobility and Spanish treachery were the essence of it. The same theme and treatment were used by Pedro P. Bermúdez (1816–60). The foremost romantic lyricist was Juan Carlos Gómez (1820–84), who was in and out of Uruguay depending on the turns of his wheel of political fortune; one of his less happy positions was his journalistic advocacy of the annexation of Uruguay to Argentina. But Uruguay appreciates its literary figures, and Gómez' body was returned in 1905 for final interment in his native land; today a downtown street is named for him. Alejandro Magariños Cervantes (1825–93) was another eminent writer of the nineteenth century, though it is impossible to understand how Professor Coester could have called him "undoubtedly the greatest figure in Uruguayan letters." [2] Magariños Cervantes is especially remembered for his novel *Caramurú* and his poetic legend *Celiar*. He was one of the best literary painters of gaucho life. He ably reflected the general literary scene in the middle decades of the nineteenth century.

The most outstanding among the pre-modernist writers of the nineteenth century was Juan Zorrilla de San Martín (1855–1931), who has been called the greatest romantic poet of the continent. His first claim to fame was through his authorship in 1879 of the patriotic ode "La Leyenda Patria," which he many times thereafter recited in public on ceremonial occasions.[3] His chief renown rests, however, on his long poetic legend *Tabaré* (1888), a composition of great beauty, based on a Charrúa theme. Zorrilla de San Martín, after his university education in Chile, founded the Catholic newspaper *El Bien*

[2] Alfred Coester, *The Literary History of Spanish America* (New York, 1928), p. 176.

[3] Indeed, a somewhat acidulous commentator in 1880 described a particular ceremony as unique because "Dr. Zorrilla de San Martín did not recite the Leyenda Patria." Quoted in George Pendle, *Uruguay* (London and New York, 1952), p. 79.

*Público* in Montevideo. As rewards for his *Tabaré* and other literary achievements, he was given successive diplomatic appointments (to the Vatican, France, Spain) and other honors.

If Uruguay did not see the fullest flowering of the gaucho novel, it at least gave the first of the *gauchescos* to Latin American literature. He was Eduardo Acevedo Díaz (1851–1924), sometime soldier, politician, diplomat, and exile. Acevedo Díaz, perhaps the greatest Uruguayan novelist, wrote a historical trilogy, "a hymn of blood," as he called it, covering the whole epoch of the Uruguayan struggle for independence. The three novels were *Ismael, Nativa,* and *Grito de Gloria (Cry of Glory)*. His greatest work, however, was the gaucho novel *Soledad* (1894), "a model work in its type, [with] all the untamed landscape, the rude elemental characters, the epic sweep, the brutality and violence that are so characteristic of the South American scene"—as Torres-Ríoseco describes it.

The gaucho at a later stage of his institutional evolution is depicted by Javier de Viana (1872–1925). As advancing civilization pushed and crowded and wore down the primitive, heroic, romantic gaucho, he became what Viana writes about, a half-degenerate, drink-ridden "pariah of the fields." Much of Viana's work, especially in his full-length novel *Gaucha,* is Zolaesque in genre. *Leña Seca (Dry Wood)* is one of his best volumes of short stories. In Justino Zavala Muniz (1897–    ), the theme of the gaucho has almost run its course. Zavala Muniz (now a government minister) wrote a trilogy of realistic chronicles, half historical, half gauchesque, *Crónica de Muniz, Crónica de un Crimen (Chronicle of a Crime),* and *Crónica de la Reja (Chronicle of the Country Store)*. He is also the author of several works for the theater and, more recently, an important study of José Batlle y Ordóñez.

The rural scene, though not always the gaucho, was the inspiration for Carlos Reyles (1868–1938). In his novel *Beba* he contributed a psychological study of animal and human inbreeding. His best book dealt with the Spanish setting of his Andalusian mother and was entitled *El Embrujo de Sevilla (The Witchery of Seville;* published as *Castanets* in English); it is generally considered to be one of the finest tributes ever paid to that historic Spanish city. A grateful Uruguayan government established a professorship at the University of Montevideo for him after his original large fortune was gone.

Horacio Quiroga (1878–1937) looked even more to nature for his inspiration. Born in Uruguay, he spent many years in the northern Argentine jungles and part of his voluminous writing gives us a sort of South American counterpart of Kipling's *Jungle Book*. Most critics consider Quiroga to be the best short-story writer Latin America has produced. Many, in fact, think his work can be compared favorably to any in the world.

One of the best known of the modernist poets was the sensitive Julio Herrera y Reissig (1875–1910), whose extravagantly written, eccentric, obscurantist, though thematically simple, poetry aroused a storm of literary controversy. Herrera, a lifelong escapist, virtually lived in the attic of his father's home in the Old City, where he was the center of an admiring group of Bohemians. An appreciative government, after his early death, bestowed a pension on his widow and bought a considerable quantity of his books for free distribution abroad. A poetess, María Eugenia Vaz Ferreira (1875–1924) wrote mystical verse of considerable appeal.

Two of the "post-modernist" school of writers are among Uruguay's many women of distinction. Delmira Agustini (1890–1914), born to a wealthy family of Italian and German ancestry, published a first book of verse at sixteen. As in the poetry which followed, her tragically intense melancholy was almost Freudian in character. The tragedy carried over into her own life: after an unhappy marriage, ending in separation, she was killed by her estranged husband. Juana de Ibarbourou (1895–   ) had a fortunately opposite sort of early personal life. Happily married, much of her poetry was characterized by a sensuous and esthetic appreciation of a healthy, pagan Nature. Graceful tribute was paid her in 1929 by the bestowing of a sort of New World laureateship with the sobriquet "Juana de América." More recently she has allegedly been characterized by a sort of sublimated literary narcissism which has interfered with both the quality and the quantity of her writing. Nevertheless, the Union of American Women selected her as the "Woman of the Americas" for 1953.

The Uruguayan drama might well be thought of as an integral part of the literary scene except that dramas were usually written to be acted and seen rather than read. Montevideo's first theater dated from 1793 and the famed Teatro Solís was inaugurated in 1856. The middle and later decades of the nineteenth-century theater were graced with a number of dramatists, some of whose plays were produced with notable success. Among them were Heraclio C. Fajardo (1833–67), Francisco X. de Achá (1828–88), and Samuel Blixen (1869–1909). Greatest of the playwrights was Florencio Sánchez (1875–1910), Uruguayan-born, although his work was done in Buenos Aires. Torres-Ríoseco characterizes him as "the only important dramatist of South America." A dissolute Bohemian who struggled desperately to earn a living, he finally began to produce at the age of twenty-eight and in the next six years wrote twenty plays. His writing was marked by dramatic intensity and stark delineation of characters; the themes were realistically Ibsenesque, though in craftsmanship he fell short of the Norwegian with whom he has sometimes been compared. The Uruguayan government finally granted him a small subsidy which took him to Italy, where he soon died.

The contemporary scene is too close to see in perspective. Such a writer as Alberto Zum Felde has gained a deserved renown as a social historian and literary critic. The veteran political figure, Emilio Frugoni, has contributed notable poetry about his native city of Montevideo. Contemporary and recent short-story writers include Adolfo Montiel Ballesteros, Enrique Amorín, Serafín J. García, Francisco Espínola, and Juan José Morosoli.

Literary outlets are found in part in the various reviews published in Uruguay. They include *Escritura, Devenir, Número, Asir, Mundial*, the *Revista* of the Faculty of Humanities and Sciences, the *Revista Nacional: Literatura, Arte, Ciencia*, and *Clima*. The Montevidean record for book publishing falls far short of that of its large sister city across the Plata. Buenos Aires is one of the great publishing centers of all Latin America, but Montevideo's history in that respect has been unimpressive. Many authors have had to finance their own books (not unusual for Latin America), though the government has sometimes assisted by subsidies and purchases of copies. Nor are Montevideo bookstores numerous or large.

In the world of music, as in that of literature, Uruguay's

original inheritance was not extensive. The Charrúas left no traces of cultural pursuits and, as far as musical inclinations were concerned, they have been described as screaming and shouting tonelessly. Gaucho camps were enlivened by song but the musical instruments for it had to be derived from Europe and it took time to develop a body of gaucho music. As was the case with literature, the fullest development of gaucho music took place in Argentina.

The folk music of the gaucho gave rise to what has become the national dance of Uruguay, the *pericón*, an old round dance in triple time, somewhat resembling the French minuet. This dance, choreographic historians have determined, is distinctively Uruguayan rather than Argentine. An official arrangement of it for military bands was made as long ago as 1887. It was revived in 1889 by a theatrical company and has since gained wide popularity. Uruguay can lay part claim to the tango; the best known song of this type, "La Cumparsita," is the work of a recent Uruguayan popular composer, Gerardo H. Matos Rodríguez. Such folk music forms as the *cifra*, the *vidalita*, the *milonga* and the *estilo* are also shared with Argentina. Some of these forms were developed by an evolutionary combination of creole and Negro folk music on the water front.

Aside from gaucho folk songs, music inevitably became a monopoly of the city, which is to say, for practical purposes, Montevideo. European travelers visiting the capital as early as 1800 were agreeably surprised by the music rendered and the lovely voices heard at the *tertulias* or evening receptions in Montevideo. Yet the first pianos were not imported from Europe until 1824. The pioneer performer of the early nineteenth century, José P. Podestá, is sometimes hailed by Uruguayans as the father of his country's drama, but his and his brothers' work was as much singing and guitar playing as acting. The Italian influence was quickly apparent and as early as 1830 an Italian opera was presented in Montevideo. Italian influence has also been traced in the national anthem dating from 1848.[4] The first serious composers, chiefly of the late nineteeth and early twentieth centuries, were in most cases Italian-trained.

[4] Nicolas Slonimsky, *Music of Latin America* (New York, 1945), p. 283.

Uruguay's best-known composer is Eduardo Fabini (1883–1951), a Belgian-trained composer of symphonic poems whose work is "moved by a sentimental sort of nationalism" [5]; he is not "folkloristic" even though he has become assimilated with the life of Uruguay. An even more ardent musical nationalist is Vicente Ascone (1897–    ), who composed an opera based on a Charrúa theme, a "Suite Uruguaya" for orchestras, and many other works. The young prodigy, Héctor Tosar Errecart (1923–    ), had an imposing list of compositions even by the age of nineteen. Writing originally in a neoclassical vein, he later began to base his work on folk themes; the fiery and talented "Danza Criolla," a piano composition, is a good example. Two of the earliest composers were Carlos Pedrell (1878–1941) and Alfonso Broqua (1876–1946). The former, Spanish- and French-trained, was for the greater part of his life a Parisian expatriate. His compositions were principally impressionistic and stylized adaptations of Spanish melodies and rhythms. Broqua, also a resident of Paris during most of his life, composed a lyric poem, "Tabaré," later operas, ballets, and various pieces of chamber music.

Perhaps the most important contemporary musical figure in Uruguay is Lauro Ayestaran (1913–    ). His musical training was obtained in Montevideo and most of his career has been devoted to the promotion of music in Uruguay's schools and national university. He has, nonetheless, written widely on musical matters. In 1943 he began the task of recording Uruguayan folk music and now has assembled more than 1,500 records made on trips to the interior of the country. He recently represented his country at a Unesco-sponsored congress of music libraries held in Paris.

Francisco Curt Lange (1903–    ) is sometimes called one of the foremost musicologists of all Latin America. Lange was born in Germany and emigrated to Uruguay at the age of twenty. His major work has been the editing and publishing of the six large volumes of the *Boletín Latino-Americano de Música*, an invaluable archive of Latin American musicology. He is the founder and director of the Instituto Americano de Musicología, made official by government decree in 1940, and

[5] Lazare Saminsky, *Living Music of the Americas* (New York, 1949), p. 243.

is also the director of a co-operative music publishing house, the Editorial Cooperativa Interamericana de Compositores. Beyond the field of music he has written books on Nietzsche and Kant!

The forty-five medium-wave radio broadcasting stations in Uruguay (twenty-four in Montevideo, twenty-one in the *campo*) devote themselves partly to music and entertainment, partly to a quasi-journalism, and partly (except for the government station) to the ubiquitous "commercial." Of all of these several dozen stations the most interesting and significant is that operated by the government. The first government station had been operated by the Ministry of War and Marine. Then, by a law of December 18, 1929, the Servicio Oficial de Difusión Radio-Eléctrica—or Sodre, as it is universally known in Uruguay—was created. The following April 1, the official radio station was reorganized and reopened by Sodre and initially began a program of eleven hours daily of broadcast music. At first it was largely recorded music, but gradually lectures and live broadcasts were substituted in considerable measure.

On June 20, 1931, Sodre inaugurated its symphony orchestra. Many of Montevideo's musicians had been thrown out of work by the conjunction of the world-wide economic depression and the advent of sound movies. They welcomed the organization of the new orchestra. From the conductor's standpoint the circumstances permitted the imposition of one of the most rigid regimens of orchestral discipline known anywhere in the world. The regime has paid off in the form of an orchestra of far more than Uruguayan reputation; a distinguished French conductor once favorably compared the Sodre symphony orchestra, now with more than a hundred members, to those of Detroit, Cleveland, Cincinnati, and Minneapolis. The Sodre has at times had transmission connections with Buenos Aires and has broadcast programs from the great Teatro Colón in the Argentine capital.

The government operates a school of popular ballet in Montevideo and also a school of dramatic art. There is no permanent opera, though most of the foreign artists who appear in Buenos Aires' Teatro Colón are also scheduled for Montevideo's Teatro Solís. The Comedia Nacional, housed in the Teatro Solís, presents an annual winter bill of excellently performed semiamateur musical and dramatic productions of both national and foreign authorship. They are usually staged with dramatic simplicity and have proved increasingly popular with Montevideanos.

In the fine arts of design the training and tonal qualities, and in part the inspiration, have likewise been European. Uruguayan art, like that of Argentina, Chile, and Venezuela, says Robert C. Smith, "has remained at heart European, as untouched by the American or African tradition as our own contemporary painting. At present these lands would seem to be the artistic orphans of the New World. Aware of the evils of imitation, technically able, aesthetically sensitive, they have not yet succeeded in directing their own destiny." [6]

Uruguay, furthermore, is almost unique among Latin American countries in having little of architecture and virtually nothing of painting or sculpture from the colonial period. Reasons are not hard to find: Uruguay (or at least Montevideo, which, in this respect, amounts to the same thing) had only a century of colonial history instead of the three hundred years most Spanish colonies had. Hence, there was a lesser period in which to produce works of art. In the second place, the colony was a poor one, much overshadowed by the relatively more dazzling Buenos Aires across the river. Being poor, it simply had not the money that was available in Mexico, Peru, and even Argentina to lavish on artistic expression.

A few architectural examples from the eighteenth century still exist in the interior, but the only noteworthy ones are in Montevideo. Chief among them are the two which adorn the Plaza Constitución in the heart of the Old City. On one side is the cathedral, built from 1790 to 1804. It is of stone and brick construction and has impressive proportions; the design was supposedly drawn by a Portuguese military architect and engineer. Directly opposite the cathedral across the plaza is the *cabildo* or old municipal building, now housing the Ministry of Foreign Relations. It is of early-nineteenth-century construction and presents a somewhat unusual neoclassical façade. The proportions of the building are especially pleasing. The Gen-

[6] Robert C. Smith, "Latin American Painting Comes into Its Own," *Inter-American Quarterly*, vol. 2, no. 3, p. 35 (July, 1940).

eral Artigas fortress, atop the Cerro across the bay from the city, is a colonial fortification now preserved as a military museum. A few colonial-period private homes remain intact, perhaps the most interesting being the Montevideo residence of General Lavelleja, of the Thirty-three, now appropriately maintained as the National Historical Museum under the devoted and intelligent direction of Juan Pivel Devoto. Up toward the Brazilian border are two fortifications now preserved as historical monuments from the colonial period, the Fuerte de San Miguel and the larger and more impressive Fortaleza de Santa Teresa. Both have been restored; the latter, in particular, with its heavy walls and star-shaped bastions, is reminiscent of the work of the French engineer Vauban. Painting and sculpture during the colonial period were accompaniments of church construction and ornamentation and were singularly unattractive.

The development of any significant work in painting had to await independence. A Basque, Juan Manuel Besnes e Irigoyen, and an Italian, Pedro Valenzani, were the first notable painters in Montevideo. Besnes limned the contemporary scene but Valenzani was a portraitist. The first and one of the greatest of native Uruguayan painters was Juan Manuel Blanes (1830–1901), the foremost historical artist the country has produced and one who, Robert Smith says, "for sheer painting had no master in South America." Blanes was Italian trained. His many canvases are notable for their large size, their dramatic and realistic detail, and their skillful use of color. Perhaps the best known of Blanes' paintings is the "Episode of the Yellow Fever," but most of his subjects have military or patriotic themes; among the latter are "The Oath of the Thirty-three," "The Battle of Sarandí," "The Assassination of Florencio Varela," and "Artigas in 1815." Incidentally, perhaps the finest example of the bookmaking art that Uruguay has yet produced is a magnificently illustrated and manufactured volume devoted to Blanes and his work written by Eduardo de Salterain y Herrera. Blanes had two sons, Juan Luis and Nicanor, who followed him in his art, but both died prematurely.

One of the best of an impressionistic school of Uruguayan painters was Pedro Blanes Viale (1879–1926). Blanes Viale was for many years an expatriate in Paris, but the *Libro del Centenario* characterizes him as the leader of the reaction against academic forms in Uruguayan painting.[7] He has two well-known historical scenes displayed in the Palacio Legislativo, but his landscapes in the National Museum of Fine Arts are considered better painting. José Cuneo specializes in moonlit landscapes; he is a great technician and watercolor artist. Among the other eminent Uruguayan painters of this school are Ernesto Laroche, José Luis Zorrilla de San Martín, Guillermo Rodríguez, Milo Beretta, José Pedro Montero Bustamante, and Carmelo de Arzadun. Norberto Berdia, who studied in Mexico and is well known in Uruguay as a muralist, was one of two artists, along with the distinguished Adolfo Halty, to represent Uruguay in an international exhibit in Pittsburgh in 1952.

Possibly the greatest painter in the whole history of Uruguayan art was Pedro Figari (1861–1938). He was a famous lawyer and penologist, but it is for his small, vivid, colorful studies of early-nineteenth-century Montevidean life that he is remembered. He subordinated all other values to color and movement, the *Libro del Centenario* tells us, and his work was favorably received in Europe as well as in Uruguay. Figari has been the subject of a more extensive art literature than any other painter in the last half century of Uruguayan art. Joaquín Torres García (1874–1944) was Uruguay's best-known abstract painter; his inspiration was derived both from Europe and from pre-Columbian Bolivia.

The most familiar pieces of sculpture in Montevideo are the bold gaucho on horseback by José Luis Zorrilla de San Martín, the son of Juan Zorrilla de San Martín, and the *carreta*, or covered wagon, by José Belloni. The Gaucho, defiantly surveying the intersection of the Avenidas 18 de Julio and Constituyente, is a magnificent embodiment in bronze of the deathless plainsman of historic legend; on the pedestal are four excellently done reliefs. One of the principal features of the José Batlle y Ordóñez Park is Belloni's lifelike covered wagon of colonial days with its three pairs of yoked oxen, two free oxen, and a bearded horseman. The piece is wonderfully blended into the landscape above a reflecting pool, and one al-

[7] *El Libro del Centenario del Uruguay* (Montevideo, 1925), p. 604.

most expects to hear the sharp crack of a whip and the hoarse call of the outrider as the wagon, the oxen, and the gaucho pass down through history. Zorrilla de San Martín is also the sculptor of the well-known "Last Charrúa" in the Prado Park. Another work of his is the graceful obelisk at the head of Avenida 18 de Julio, commemorating the signers of Uruguay's first constitution. Virtually every plaza in Uruguay, or so it seems, has its statue of Artigas, but most of them are of little esthetic importance.

One of the most notable aspects of Montevidean architecture—that of other parts of Uruguay offers little of interest —is the way in which the great architectural impulse given by the national university's Faculty of Architecture bids fair to remake the face of the city within a few decades.[8] Much of the result will be apparent in domestic rather than public architecture. The older domestic architecture was typical of much of Latin American house designing and, externally at least, singularly uninspired. The newer houses offer contrasts as great as can be found anywhere in Latin America. Clean-cut, simple, functional, making highly effective use of iron grill work and stone trim, the new exteriors are products any group of architects might be proud of. (Interiors, let us add in humble service to Truth, are not always so well or attractively designed). Part of the face lifting Montevideo is experiencing is due to its rapid growth, which has necessitated a degree of city planning, which in turn has permitted the application of set-back principles, front lawns, verandas, and other features which tend to make the house attractive externally as well as in its interior patio. The influence of Frank Lloyd Wright and some of the more advanced European architects is to be seen in certain of the more radical domestic architecture.

The architecture of Montevideo can consequently doubtless be better discussed half a century hence than now. As of the middle of the twentieth century its chief features are that it tends to climb higher and to turn the streets of the Old City into narrow canyons. Much of the downtown building has been

[8] Uruguay is said to have more architects in proportion to its population than any other country in the world; some of her presidents have been architects or engineers and at one time more than half of her cabinet reportedly were architects.

in a neutral shade of gray; many new outlying residences, on the other hand, are built of stucco made from Uruguay's dazzling white sand, which gives them as clean and fresh a look as anyone could wish.

The outstanding architectural landmark is the huge Palacio Legislativo designed by Cayetano Moretti. Montevideanos are very proud of it but architecturally it leaves something to be desired. Despite its elaborate decoration, the neoclassical design is marred by the poorly proportioned central tower which, as one foreign layman remarked, "sticks up like a sore thumb." Not even the gigantic caryatids ornamenting the tower are excuse for it. The quarters of the Senate, the Chamber of Representatives, and the Legislative Library are, however, most tastefully designed. Montevideo's real architectural monstrosity is the Palacio Salvo, a downtown apartment and office building and formerly South America's tallest structure. Its extravagant design and bulging tower leave much, very much, to be desired. Its twenty-seven stories allegedly give it even yet, however, the palm for being the tallest poured-concrete structure in the world.

The relatively new, monumentally designed building occupied by the Bank of the Republic is much more pleasingly done although it unfortunately lacks the space necessary to set it off properly. Some of the new apartment and business buildings show modern architectural design at its restrained best. The architecture is not so dramatic as some one finds in Rio de Janeiro or São Paulo, but it is pleasing and definitely mid-twentieth-century. One of the newest and best-designed public buildings is that occupied by the Faculty of Engineering of the University of Montevideo. Among the leaders of Montevideo's architectural fraternity at present are Mauricio Gravotto of the Montevideo municipal government, Julio Vilamajó, who collaborated in the design of the United Nations building in New York, and Román Fresnedo Ciri, designer of the building occupied by the Faculty of Architecture in Montevideo.

The Muses find still other ways of becoming vocal in Montevideo. For one thing, they speak through the medium of the city's museums. Aside from those already mentioned, there is the Museum of Natural History in a wing of the Teatro Solís, whose ten display rooms emphasize Uruguayan materials. The National Museum of Fine Arts in Rodó Park houses works of a number of Old Masters as well as modern sculpture and painting. The Juan Manuel Blanes Museum in the Prado Park contains a notable collection of that artist's work. The Prado is also the location of the Municipal Historical Museum. The Pedagogical Museum and Library are located on the Plaza Libertad in central Montevideo. The Zorrilla de San Martín Museum, opened in 1943, houses in his former home the personal effects and books of the national poet. The government also operates an Oceanographic Museum on the shore of the Plata.

Libraries, too, form part of the cultural expression of the country. The National Library, dating back to 1816, is the country's largest and has a collection of more than 200,000 volumes and in addition a considerable archive of historical and literary manuscripts. The Legislative Library contains more than 100,000 volumes. The combined libraries of the several university faculties total more than 200,000 volumes. The International American Institute for the Protection of Children, headquartered in Montevideo, has a specialized library of some 15,000 volumes, notable as one of the best such collections in the world.

Uruguay's bilateral cultural institutes—British, Italian, French, Brazilian, United States—occupy an important niche in the country's cultural activity. Their purpose is in part, frankly, to "sell" their several countries, partially by means of language classes, motion pictures, displays, exhibits, etc. Perhaps most outstanding among such activities is the operation of the Artigas-Wáshington Library under the auspices of the United States Information and Education program. The library, opened in 1943, now houses a collection of more than 17,000 books and is patronized by more than 100,000 borrowers annually. It has a large phonograph-record collection and circulates some 2,000 records monthly.

One of the significant cultural facets of Montevideo is the Ateneo, or Athenaeum, dating back to 1880. It "is, above all," so Historian Zum Felde describes it, "a center of civic life [where], during the raw years of military despotism, were gathered all those whom Montevideo counted as most illustrious and hereditarily acceptable [*gentilicio*]." [9] The Ateneo is an officially recognized institution with a dignified old home on the Plaza Libertad. It is a free organization, with recitals, conferences, and lectures open to the public. Uruguayans rightly prize it.

The Ministry of Public Instruction and Social Welfare in 1943 sponsored the official creation of the National Academy of Letters "to exercise the direction [so the law read] of the literary culture of the country, as well in regard to its spiritual and social sense as in its instrumentality of expression through the language, the purity and preservation of which it is necessary to safeguard." Two years later the law created a Commission of Literary Investigations, under control of the same ministry, to examine manuscripts of Uruguayan writers to see which should be made a part of the national archives.

Uruguay has no genuine motion picture industry. Two agencies produce newsreels and the photocinematographic division of the Ministry of Public Instruction makes a few documentaries, but that is as far as the work goes. Uruguay was making plans in 1951, however, to build South America's first planetarium and was looking forward to television broadcasting. Plans for both are well advanced.

Uruguay's cultural expression is rich and well rounded but not spectacular. It cannot lay claim to the world's—or the hemisphere's—greatest painters, sculptors, architects, or musicians, though in the field of letters Rodó has a stature far transcending the bounds of his native country. Perhaps the most significant thing that can be said of Uruguay's cultural life is that it belongs to the people. It is not the toy of an elite class or of dilettantes playing idly at what they assume to be fashionably correct. Rather, it is a democratic and vigorously exercised possession of the whole people. That is what makes it vital.

[9] Alberto Zum Felde, *Evolución Histórica del Uruguay* (Montevideo, 1945), p. 275.

# 16

# Uruguay Worships

It is an easy and not an essentially inaccurate generalization to say that Latin America is a Catholic world. If we begin to apply the generalization more narrowly, caution and reservations become increasingly necessary. In parts of Haiti, for example, the Catholic veneer is thin. A useful book about Mexico published some years ago carried the intriguing title *Idols Behind Altars*. Its author did not mean the connotation exactly as it sounds, but she might well have so meant it. In large parts of Indo-America, especially in those areas such as the Andean highlands and parts of Central America and southern Mexico where the pre-Columbian Indian cultures were best developed and most tenacious, Catholicism had to make a degree of accommodation which adopted and adapted various pagan practices. The same process had occurred about a millennium earlier when Christianity moved into pagan Germany.

In Uruguay, too, qualifications and reservations need to be made and caution used, but for different reasons. No early Indian culture or pantheism lived or lasted in Uruguay. There may have been idols but the Charrúas, Chanás, and other aborigines were in no position to put them into competition with altars. And yet Uruguay is probably less strongly Catholic than any other country in Latin America. That broad and possibly gratuitous generalization even includes Mexico, where the bitterest friction ever to characterize the Church-State issue in Latin America flamed and flamed again over long decades.

The explanation of the religious picture in Uruguay is an involved and curious complex of social, intellectual, political, psychological, and perhaps other elements. Three historic or demographic factors contribute to an interpretation or explanation of the weakened Catholic position in Uruguay: effective Spanish colonization did not begin until the eighteenth century, by which time the religious fervor of the earlier generations and centuries had in considerable measure atrophied; during that colonial period Uruguay remained largely an ecclesiastical appendage of Buenos Aires, and its intensity of spiritual development and devotion was correspondingly diminished. The oldest Uruguayan diocese, that of Montevideo, dates only from 1878, more than half a century after Spanish authority was expelled from the country. In the second place, the revolutionary period was characterized by a large influx of foreigners, especially English and French, who were either non-Catholic or only nominally Catholic. Third, the large immigration beginning late in the nineteenth century, while it came in great part from Catholic countries, represented social and economic strata which were often of less than fervent attachment to the Church.

And in considerable degree it is again, as at so many points, the lengthened shadow of a man—that of José Batlle y Ordóñez —which helps account for how Uruguay worships, or fails to worship, today. Batlle early developed a skeptical and questioning attitude toward the Catholic Church. His religio-intellectual development in that wise somewhat resembled that of Benito Juárez in Mexico. The similarity stops at an early point, however, because the Church had been extremely strongly entrenched in Mexico, economically and politically as well as ecclesiastically, while in pastoral, gaucho-inhabited Uruguay its hold had never been as solid. True, the constitution of 1830 (drafted by an assembly including five clerics) had firmly and formally established an orthodox relationship of Church and State. It had said that "The religion of the State is the Roman Catholic Apostolic," (although other religions were tolerated). That was about as flat a statement as could be made, but the constitution also began its preamble, "In the name of God, the All Powerful, Author, Legislator, and Supreme Conservator of the Universe." Moreover, the president was required to take his inaugural oath "before God, our Lord, and these Holy Evangels."

Even before Batlle's time the Church suffered blows in Uruguay. Franciscan convents were suppressed in 1838. The Jesuits were expelled in 1859 (but allowed to return in 1865). A law of 1880 deprived the Church of its previously almost exclusive control over cemeteries and over the registration of vital statistics and the solemnization of marriage, though some latitude for the marriage of non-Catholics had previously existed.

A tenet of Batlle's program in the late nineteenth and early twentieth centuries came to be that the two institutions, one ecclesiastical and spiritual, the other political and governmental, must be separate. So confirmed did he become in that conviction, so far did he go in translating it into reality, that many persons aver that Batlle became an atheist. It is difficult to say. The several lines between atheism, agnosticism, deism, freethinking are hard to draw. Batlle became more interested in positive reform of other sorts, economic, social, political, and once his convictions on religious matters were formed, they remained to color and influence but not to take precedence over his interests in other areas. His magnetism and force of personality were sufficient to transmit the stamp of his ideas on religion to the dominant batllista wing of the Colorado party. It is today a staunch supporter of the principle of separation of Church and State and is, on the whole, unsympathetic toward Catholicism and, in considerable measure, other denominations as well.

Colorados, relatively more than other Uruguayans, have become adherents of Freemasonry, a fraternity which has prospered more in Uruguay than in most Latin American countries. Individual batllistas in some cases retained a sense of religiousness and even Batlle himself was known privately on rare occasions to render aid and comfort to such an organization as the Y.M.C.A., partly, perhaps, because of its concern with physical education. On the whole, however, the great mass of the followers of Batlle were weaned away from an attachment to the Catholic Church without substituting for it any other denominational affiliation.

The result was a large amount of freethinking in Uruguay. The Catholic Church has suffered correspondingly. Some of its priests assert that 85 per cent of Uruguayans are Catholic.[1] That is a figure which cannot be substantiated, of course, for permanent want of any accurate religious census,[2] and which in all probability is based on a large amount of wishful thinking. Ardent batllistas put the percentage of Catholic adherence far lower, but their individual estimates vary so greatly that it is perhaps not practicable or significant to attempt to strike a mean.

The Catholic Church has suffered quantitatively. Both in Montevideo and in the country the number of both churches and priests is considerably smaller than one finds in most Latin American countries. The churches are usually smaller and more modest than in other parts of Catholic America. Even the cathedral in Montevideo is much less impressive than those in various other Latin American cities of comparable size and importance. In Bogotá or Quito or Lima the clerical black is in constant evidence—but not in Montevideo or in the smaller interior cities. The Catholic clerical personnel includes one archbishop, two bishops, and some 250 secular priests. This figures out to a clientele of about 10,000 Uruguayans per priest; in Spain, on the other hand, the ratio is about twelve times as favorable for the Church. As is common in most Latin American countries, men have fallen further away from the Church than women. Children? Well, it depends to a large de-

---

[1] But a strongly Catholic layman, a franquista Spanish diplomat in Uruguay, wrote a few years ago that "Catholic Uruguayans do not appear to form a majority among its citizens." Ernesto La Orden, *Uruguay, el Benjamín de España* (Madrid, 1949), p. 296. Not only would it seem that Catholics represent a minority but there is evidence that they are at least relatively declining in numbers.

[2] The national census of 1908 (the latest taken in Uruguay) included certain data on religious affiliations. The total population of 1,042,686 was classified as follows: Catholic, 637,681 (61.16 per cent); Protestant, 16,498 (1.58 per cent); freethinkers, 150,669 (14.45 per cent); unspecified or "without religion," 237,838 (22.82 per cent). The total number of inhabitants more than fourteen years of age (the usual age of confirmation) was 614,-222. They were classified: Catholics, 430,095 (70.02 per cent); Protestant, 12,232 (1.99 per cent); freethinkers, 126,425 (30.59 per cent); unspecified or "without religion," 45,470 (7.40 per cent).

gree on the family. In the strongly Catholic families the children are likely to receive a strict indoctrination in Catholic practices and principles; in other families, as the twig is bent—

Not only has there been a decrease in numbers of Catholic adherents, but also a weakening of religious feeling has often taken place among many of those nominally professing Catholicism. When a bus or streetcar passes a Catholic church, virtually none of the men doff their hats and only a fraction of the women are to be seen crossing themselves.[3] Jewelry stores display relatively few crosses or other religious insignia for sale. Vested Catholic clergy do not accompany funeral processions to the cemeteries. In municipal cemeteries Catholic crosses are to be found over graves, it is true, but, Consul La Orden observed, they are intermingled with "pagan and Masonic symbols, obelisks, triangles, Jewish stars, profane sculptures, and irreligious inscriptions." Weekday attendance at Catholic churches is small. Increasing numbers of Uruguayan women enter those churches with heads bared.

Perhaps less superficial than such evidences is the great decrease in religious processions. This decrease is due in some part to an official governmental frown several years ago. The explanation was that religious processions caused an undue distraction in children's schooling. No famous Catholic sanctuary exists in all of Uruguay nor does the country have any universally recognized patron saint. The pilgrimage to the statue of the Miraculous Virgin atop the Cerro de Verdún near the city of Minas is too recent a development to have become invested with much of an institutional air of sanctity.

The official separation of Church and State in Uruguay was made by the constitution of 1917. It provided that all religious cults were to be free; the State supported no religion; it recognized the ownership by the Catholic Church of all temples constructed wholly or partially with national funds except those small churches intended for service as "asylums, hospitals, jails, or other public establishments"; it declared tax exempt all temples intended for worship by any religious faith. The constitution further omitted any reference to deity

---

[3] Some persons account for this on the basis of the degree of sophistication of the Uruguayan population which allegedly leads them to forego formalistic or, some would say, "superstitious" manifestation.

in the presidential oath and entirely discarded a preamble with its invocation of divine aid. A by-product of the disestablishment was the raising of a popular fund of 1,000,000 pesos as an endowment to compensate the Church for its loss of governmental financial support. A further consequence was the termination of diplomatic relations with the Vatican in 1919.

By the time that new basic law had taken effect in 1919, batllismo had had some eight years (counting from the beginning of Batlle's second term as president) in which to consolidate itself. The three decades and more since 1919 have simply served to confirm the government, consistently Colorado through the period, in its anticlerical position. The new constitutions of 1934 and 1951 made no change of importance in the provisions, nor did the dictatorship of Gabriel Terra, from 1933 to 1938, attempt to turn the clock back.

The government's chief avenue of implementation of its policy of separation of Church and State has been through its control of the public-school system. Private schools exist in Uruguay, of course, both those organized on a cultural basis (the French lycée or the British school, for example) and those operated by churches. The latter include both Catholic and Protestant. The government, operating through the autonomous councils which control primary and secondary education, specifies a large core of subject matter which is required of both private and public schools. What the former ones add on top of that can be in the nature of religious instruction if they wish, but there is little time left for work beyond the officially prescribed curriculum.

The public schools, of course, religiously avoid anything savoring of religion. It would be worth a teacher's job were she to read anything from the Bible, make sympathetic comment about things religious, or similarly flout the canons. Uruguay is not a country which, like Colombia, for example, leaves a large part of the operation of the schools to the responsibility of the Church, and hence, because public education looms as large as it does, the government has a potent instrument at hand in forging and applying its policy.

*La Semana Santa* is in almost all parts of Latin America a well-established institution in which the Church simply takes the lead in organizing and directing what is nominally a major religious celebration but in actuality becomes a public, if not a governmental, festival. Not so in Uruguay. For some years past in that country Holy Week has been officially *La Semana de Turismo* and, though it comes at a time when the season is getting on toward winter, the government goes through straight-faced efforts to dedicate the several days to the divine cause of tourism. The people in the street don't take the change of labels too seriously—"Tourist Week" is only an official and not a popular designation—but the renaming is symptomatic. Many business houses are closed during the week, but again caution in interpretation is necessary. The reason is not to any great extent the fact that the proprietors so respect the faith of their fathers that they will not profane the week by the sordid business of selling goods. The paternalistic government specifies two weeks of annual paid vacations for the employees of business firms and it is, then, simply convenient for the owners to make that particular week one of the two. The more so since the favorable exchange rate contributes to what amounts to almost a mass exodus of Montevideanos to Buenos Aires and other vacation spots during the week. Fewer home customers, less need for clerks, Tourist Week (or Holy Week, as you will) observed—the whole thing works itself out in a reasonably neat pattern. Doubtless the ointment's only flies are perceived by the store owners who see all that good trade going across the river to Buenos Aires and by the Catholic Church which deplores this hedonistic "desecration" of Holy Week.

In similar vein, though with less of the economic overtones, Christmas Day is officially The Day of the Family. The new appellation is viewed by the people with still more of a tongue-in-cheek attitude, as if the government must be humored in going to even absurd lengths in grinding a favorite ax, but again the action is symptomatic.

The government has, since 1885, required civil marriage in Uruguay. A church ceremony, Catholic or otherwise, is permissible, but it may not supplant the civil ceremony (which increasingly becomes the only one). The possibility and the increasing practice of divorce also undermine traditional Catholic control over the social structure.

A footnote is added by a curious little journalistic practice. There is obviously a close entente between batllismo and the government. It is difficult to describe or define the party-government connective tissue, but it is clearly apparent—not so close, probably, as in the case of Mexico's dominant Institutional Revolutionary party and not so close, certainly, as in the instances of the former Nazi and Fascist parties in their relationship to the German and Italian governments. But, to cite widely dissimilar examples, as the *Osservatore Romano* can speak unofficially for the Vatican, *Pravda* for the Kremlin, or *Democracia* for the peronista-dominated Casa Rosada in Buenos Aires, so can *El Día* reflect the viewpoint of the Uruguayan government, in many cases without assuming all of the responsibility of an official publication. It is the paper founded in the 1880's by Batlle himself, and it still carries the most authentic banner of batllismo. The tone of *El Día* is often ruggedly anticlerical. Its most obvious red (but certainly not Soviet!) flag is its persistent practice of spelling *"Dios"* with a lower-case *d*.

It is difficult to say, and perhaps the architects of batllismo do not themselves consciously know, to what extent the negative attitude of the man, the party, and the government has been the cause of the advanced and positive position of those in control in Uruguay toward matters and opportunities of social service and social reform. Certainly it seems a tenable argument that the social consciousness of the batllistas may at least have been intensified by the insensible wish to substitute something for the socio-spiritual orientation and expression normally found within the Catholic orbit. If Nature abhors a vacuum, the emptiness of a portion of the batllista horizon may in like manner have been filled in by what at least the party leaders would regard as a sublimated course of action. Such a rationale might not seem so logical in the freer intellectual setting of another area, but to those who are familiar with the subtle and all-pervasive psychological influences of a long-standing Catholic society, the interpretation might appear more valid. At least, it is advanced by some Uruguayans who seek to account for a political trend which in certain respects goes far beyond the experience of most Latin American countries.

Under normal circumstances we might look for some

roughly Newtonian development of a "law of politics" and assume that in the political area, too, we could find, for every action, an equal and opposite reaction. That would mean that, religion-wise, the batllistas being strongly anticlerical, another major party (logically the Blancos) should be as strongly pro-Catholic. But politics cannot be reduced to the formulas and laws of physics. Sometimes a strong political movement will operate to shift the whole center of political gravity rather than just to magnify and continue counterbalancing the extremes. The position of the Uruguayan Blancos or Nationalists vis-à-vis religion, and especially Catholicism, is a case in point.

By analogy to physics the Blancos, a traditionally and strongly conservative party, should be ardent defenders of the Catholic Church. But they are not. The shift in the center of gravity carried the party over into a semblance of official neutrality. Many Blancos were and are professing Catholics, but they regard it as a matter "of private conscience." So disappointing has this attitude been to Catholic spokesmen, especially in view of the professional conservatism of the Nationalist (or Blanco) party, that the Blancos have been referred to as characterized by "agnosticism," "spiritual denaturalization," and "dogmatic debility." Strong words, those.

The Catholic answer to this Colorado hostility and Blanco neutrality in the field of politics was the organization of a professedly Catholic party. The initiative was taken by a bishop in 1872 and resulted in the establishment of the Unión Católica del Uruguay, a name later shortened to the Unión Cívica. This party for many years represented an orthodox Catholic point of view reflected in its quadripartite aims of "Religion, Fatherland, Family, and Property." It usually maintained a small congressional delegation composed of men who, because of personal integrity and dignity, enjoyed a high political reputation. It rejected the concept of statism involved in what it claimed was "Colorado Socialism," although it was willing to accept subsidiary intervention by the State to achieve ends of social justice. The Unión Cívica attacked gambling, divorce, and dueling. More recently, under the liberal leadership of Dr. Dardo Regules, the Unión Cívica has disappointed the most orthodox and conservative spokesmen of Catholicism by veering in part toward the social and political philosophy of Jacques Maritain. The publication of its newspaper *El Bien Público* provides an authentic voice for Uruguayan Catholicism.

The Church in Uruguay has also operated through a number of subordinate agencies, some of which have at times shown more vigor than the formal Church organization itself. The parent of them, so to speak, was the Catholic Club of Montevideo, dating back to 1875. Later organizations included labor groups, a Social Union, a Women's League, an Economic Union, and Catholic Action. Secular clergy have at times been surpassed in their energy by members of the various orders. Those working in Uruguay at different times have included the Jesuits, Mercedarians, Salesians, Capuchins, Maronites, Redemptorists, and others.

Uruguayan Catholicism in recent years has shown some rebirth of activity and vigor. If it has suffered quantitatively, a counterreaction may have brought a qualitative improvement. The flattery of imitation of what some Catholics refer to as the "notorious" Y.M.C.A. has led the Church to establish a similar organization for the *juventud* of Montevideo, although such Catholic activity is not as vigorous in Uruguay as, for example, in Belgium, Canada, or France. Some Catholic priests have demonstrably become characterized by more of a sense of mission. Various Catholic festivals are advertised more widely and openly than was formerly done. The Church, by and large, has experienced a lift, much of it intangible but none the less real.

A case in point illustrating the Catholic Church's new animation (and therefore perhaps deserving of a brief description) is its recent work with laboring groups, urban and rural. Catholic labor unions, as such, date back only to 1947, but they had an institutional ancestor in the earlier *uniones gremiales* or guild unions. They also represented an inherited tradition of Catholic interest in certain aspects of social welfare implemented through the Círculo Católico de Obreros. This organization is not, as its name would suggest, exclusively a workers' group; it includes many employers and conservative professional men whose economic interests are not necessarily parallel to those of labor. The Catholic Workers' Circle was established in Uruguay before 1900, as it was in other countries, and was a direct product of the social philosophy embodied in the famous encyclical *Rerum Novarum* issued by Leo XIII in 1891 (reaffirmed and re-enforced by Pius XI's *Quadragesimo Anno* in 1931).

The Workers' Circle has broader interests than just those of organized labor. It provides its members with a good medical service, operates various dispensaries and a sanatorium, and renders other social services. It controls union activity by means of its social action committee. This committee organizes and benevolently controls a new Catholic union, operating through "men of confidence" in the labor union itself. The whole organization of Christian Syndicalism, as it is called, is not large: there are but five affiliated unions in Montevideo and three in other cities, with a total membership of only about 2,500. One of the most interesting member groups is the Christian Syndicate of Chauffeurs, a sort of guild rather than a true union, for private chauffeurs only, taxi drivers being excluded.

The Catholic labor unions, small though they are, represent an element of stability, but they face a basic dilemma. The Uruguayan worker is less concerned with the "imperialism" of the United States, of which the Communist would persuade him, or the Soviet brand of imperialism, as presented by the Catholic leadership, than he is with the "imperialism" of Uruguayan employers. Are devout Catholic laborers, then, to be workers first and Catholics second, or are they to reverse that allegiance? The two affiliations are at times in at least potential conflict, and as a result the larger movement of Uruguayan organized labor scarcely knows whether to regard the Catholic unions as a part of itself or not.

Rural labor organization affiliated with the Catholic Church presents different problems, objectives, and aspects. As of 1948 the Church claimed an affiliation of some 6,000 rural families (not restricted exclusively to Catholics, as is also true of the membership of some urban unions) in about sixty local unions grouped in three regional confederations. These unions have in general had more influence and impact than their urban counterparts, and they have, on the whole, earned the respect of many segments of Uruguayan society.

The partial religious vacuum left by the decrease of Catholic membership and general influence would seem to have been a situation made to order for the introduction and diffusion of Protestant activity. It is true that Protestant Churches have been more vigorous for a longer time and in more varied ways in Uruguay than in possibly any other Latin American country. But it would be short of the mark to say that they have entirely filled the void caused by the decrease in Catholic operation and membership. Large numbers of Uruguayans have weighed the anchor of any sort of church affiliation, Catholic or Protestant, and seem permanently indifferent to church membership or activity. This is perhaps relatively more true of the professional classes than of others, but it cannot be accurately measured with any social or economic yardstick.

Some of the Catholics, especially the clergy, refer to the Protestant denominations as sects, perhaps thinking that some artful condemnation is thereby implied. Some Protestants speak of their own groups as Evangelical, seeking in that way to avoid the negative connotations of the more widely used term. The Catholic attitude toward the Protestant groups has been, as might be expected, one of complete aloofness. Nonetheless, whether from lack of vigor or for some other reason, the Catholic hierarchy has not at any time attacked the spread or activity of Protestantism by means of a pastoral letter as Catholic officials across the river in Argentina have done. Protestant Churches in several instances have exploited a subtle psychological fact by building edifices more than normally imposing as Protestant practice goes in Latin America. Latinos, especially in the lower economic and social levels, are often struck by display, and the narrowing of the normal gap in impressiveness of church architecture between Catholic and Protestant structures in Latin America thus probably operates in some small degree in favor of certain Protestant churches.

Some, at least, of the Protestant Churches have been much more energetic than the Catholic in carrying their message to the people at large. This has meant a missionary zeal which has likely been a major factor in antagonizing the more conservatively operating Catholics. Indeed, a line is hard to draw for some of the Protestant Churches between what is missionary work and what is activity of a more orthodox nature.

The oldest and largest of the major Protestant denominations working in Uruguay is the Methodist Church. Its Uruguayan operations may be considered as typically reflected, in lesser degree, by several of the other Protestant denominations. The history of Methodist work in Uruguay goes back to the late 1860's and has, quite naturally, been confined principally to Montevideo. Two large (and several small) Methodist churches function in Montevideo, one primarily for members of the foreign community, the other for Uruguayans. More recently, Methodist churches have been established in Salto and Paysandú, the country's next largest cities, and the denomination has taken beginning steps toward branching out in other directions. Some Catholic clergy regard it as "aggressive," but Protestants would doubtless interpret the description as meaning simply that it has made more headway than any other non-Catholic church.

Aside from its more conventional work, the principal "outlets" of the Methodist Church in Uruguay have been education and social work. For many decades past it has operated a school, now one of the largest private schools in the country, with about 1,000 students. It offers both Uruguayan- and American-type curricula and many of its alumni have now taken an established place in Montevidean life. In the Cerro across the bay from Montevideo proper, the Methodist Church undertakes a type of settlement work through a social-service center.

Montevideo's Anglican congregation worships in a church on the river front in the Old City, a symbolic location because it marks the spot where the English forces first breached the walls of the city when they stormed and captured it in 1807. The Anglican group is chiefly High Church, and it engages much less than do most of the Protestant denominations in missionary and related activities. Among others of the older and better-known Protestant denominations the Baptists and German Lutherans both have churches in Montevideo.

Other religious groups working at least in Montevideo, and in some instances in the *campo* as well, include the Russian Orthodox Church, Jews, Waldensians, Seventh-Day Adventists, the Church of God, Christian Scientists, Mormons, Jehovah's Witnesses, Mennonites, and the Salvation Army. In some cases these groups are only late entrants into the Uruguayan scene. Many young Mormon missionaries (some say more than a hundred), working in their familiar pairs, have entered Uruguay since World War II. The Waldensians are the oldest Protestant group in Uruguay and have worked in the vicinity of Colonia Suiza, east of Montevideo, for about a century. Both the Young Men's and Young Women's Christian Associations have long been vigorous in Montevideo and each has established itself in the affections of succeeding generations of Uruguayan youth. Each occupies its own building in central Montevideo.

Protestantism has, on the whole, made only a dent in converting Uruguayans. It seems unlikely that the country will ever become predominantly Protestant, although it is entirely possible that an increasing leaven in the social structure will result from the degree of freedom allowed all faiths, including the Protestant. The social and intellectual impact of Protestantism has undoubtedly been greater than the scanty numbers on its church rolls would indicate.

An underlying, and perhaps most significant, feature of the religious picture in Uruguay is that this little country offers the best example of a Latin American land which can take its Catholicism or leave it, and all in a peaceful fashion. The bitter flowering of anticlericalism in Mexico left an aftermath that still mars the country's social landscape. Chile and other Latin American states have broken the ties that previously connected them formally with the Church, but in those instances the populations have usually remained strongly, if not fanatically, Catholic. France gives us a European example somewhat resembling the Uruguayan experience: a situation where freethinking, agnosticism, religious indifference have affected considerable segments of the population of a previously staunchly Catholic country. The details differ so as between France and Uruguay, however, that it is unsafe to push the comparison too far.

In the case of the South American republic we have an example, almost Latin America's only instance, of a country working out a social and economic program with virtually no impact from the influence of the Roman Catholic Church. It is much more than just a simple severance of formal Church-State relations. Excepting the case of Mexico, where it developed in a sort of pathological fashion, Uruguay's is the first large-scale American experiment in the rejection of the norms and mores of a dominant Church as projected especially into the political realm but felt also in economic, social, and intellectual areas. Whether this emancipation from a conditioning Catholic milieu is a step in the right or the wrong direction is of course a matter of individual and highly personal opinion. But, without doubt, it is a significant step.

# 17

## The Pincers—Argentina and Brazil

If you live in a neat but modest cottage sandwiched in between the great mansion of the somewhat arrogant town millionaire on one side and the vast estate of a rising and expansive industrialist and entrepreneur on the other, your humble abode probably doesn't attract much attention. And you may feel that you have to keep a wary eye on the millionaire lest he cavalierly walk across your lawn, and on the industrialist for fear his gardeners may casually pre-empt a bit of your back yard to add to his already endless acres. But you can be happy in your unpretentious home. And proud—with pride in a sturdily built and well-kept house, pride in the fact that you don't litter the street as you walk down it, pride in your habit of being a good neighbor. And the town knows you as a Solid Citizen, and admires and respects you for what you are, not for those airs that you wisely do not assume or for that frenetic effort to keep up with the Joneses which you so fortunately forego.

Neighbors can cause problems, and Uruguay's are a case in point. It is a grim jest to say that Uruguay is an Argentine province in Brazilian territory, but more than once in the nineteenth century those larger adjoining states seemed determined to make something like that come true. Nor is the pressure—now usually more subtle—even yet removed. Uru-

guay's situation is unique in Latin America. Ecuador is geo-
politically somewhat similarly located, but Peru and Colombia
do not play in the same league with Argentina and Brazil.

It is not sufficient to say that Uruguay was suckled from
her national birth on a bitter tea of foreign brewing. From the
earliest dawn of European acquaintance with her rolling plains
Uruguay was but a pawn in an international political game
for high stakes. Denied a national, or pre-national, individ-
uality, the land which became Uruguay was but a geographical
expression—the "East Bank." No one thought in terms of
conceding a separate colonial role to the east bank of the Uruguay River: it was obviously an appendage of the great focal
point of Buenos Aires across the Plata. Montevideo, the later
capital, was only a military outpost and a young and raw one
at that. Asunción (also a later national capital) and Tucumán,
Córdoba and Mendoza, were other outpost tributaries of Buenos Aires—and more prominent ones.

Asunción and Tucumán, for example, were important way
stations on the overland route from Lima to Buenos Aires. The
Spanish preferred the continent-wide trek from Peru to the
Plata to the vastly simpler Atlantic approach to Buenos Aires.
That was the Hapsburg mind at work! Where did that put
Uruguay? The Banda Oriental became simply that part of the
Platine provinces which lay over toward the sprawling, restless
Portuguese colony of Brazil. Those acres were hence to be
occupied watchfully. It was from that direction that smug-
glers might come like a thief in the night. It was from that
direction that Portuguese forces might march to gratify the
gargantuan Luso-Brazilian appetite for ever more territory.
Make of the Banda, then, a forward defense zone against the
pressure from the north. Fill it with soldiers but not with settlers. So ran the Spanish reasoning.

Brazilians, on their part, considered the Banda as fair
game. With the pace set by the ambitious and restive paulistas,
Brazil had expanded fantastically beyond the Demarcation
Line by which Pope Alexander VI would have divided the un-
known world between the two great Catholic empires. Expanded even far beyond the Tordesillas line of 1494 which,
had it ever been surveyed, would have given all the Banda and
more, to the north and east, to Spain. Imperial rivalries knew

no Queensberry rules. The Banda was not a no man's land but an every man's land. If the Portuguese could win it, they could put a cork in the Plata and effectively bottle up Buenos Aires. By the same token its retention was as important to the Spanish. Colonia, the Portuguese outpost directly across from Buenos Aires, was passed back and forth, depending not so much on the fortunes of war as on those of diplomacy.

The achievement of independence by Uruguay was almost incidental to the operation of a sort of subcontinental *Machtpolitik* in that corner of the world. Artigas—gaucho extraordinary—had the curious notion that the Banda should be independent, or at least autonomous. Later the Thirty-Three echoed and then effected that sentiment. But Argentina and Brazil, now both independent, were the political and territorial heirs of Spain and Portugal, and their inheritance included the rivalry over the Banda. That rivalry was intensified on the small stage of the Banda by the fact that it was now substantially the only stage on which the drama could be played. Back and forth the contending troops marched. From 1825 to 1828, Uruguay was a theater of war between the two giants on either side of her. To Argentina, the land was her "East Bank;" to Brazil, it was her "Cisplatine Province."

This was not to Britain's liking. It would be advantageous to England for the Plata to be flowing between two independent states rather than through one state. With a tremendous foothold in Brazil, the product of long Portuguese obligation to her, Britain had, in addition, successfully undermined the Spanish commercial monopoly over her former colonies and now hoped to capture the bulk of Argentine trade. Trade likes not war. Therefore, Britain's Lord Ponsonby entered from the wings and "persuaded" Brazil, for whom the war had not been going well anyway, to agree to the ending of the conflict on the basis of Uruguayan independence. A buffer state, itself perhaps gratefully obligated to Great Britain, would thenceforth separate the two giants and the trade of all three might flow toward England. But both Argentina and Brazil were given the right of approval over Uruguay's first constitution!

Thus the little state was born, almost accidentally, because two more powerful neighbors were locked in struggle over its possession and because it pleased a still more powerful state that it should be independent. But Uruguay's trials with foreign powers continued: independence only changed their characteristics. During the first half of the nineteenth century, Brazil was sufficiently under British dominance that it perforce had to intervene cautiously in alluring Uruguay to the south. Argentina felt no such restraints. The late 1830's, the '40's, and the early '50's saw the meddling and the invasions of Rosas become almost chronic. A large part of the domestic instability which was such an incubus in nineteenth-century Uruguay can be blamed on the willingness of foreign elements to exploit and even to promote that instability for their own ends.

Nor were Great Britain and France through with Uruguay. Minister Strangford and Lord Ponsonby were followed by Ministers Ouseley and Defaudis, by Consul Hood, by Lord Howden and Count Waleski (with an assist from Commodore Herbert and Captain Le Predour), by Captain Gore and Baron Gros. The unhappy land of Uruguay seemed permanently mortgaged to war, dissension, and intrigue, both internal and foreign.

The end of the Great War in 1851 at least removed the surface excuse for British and French interference. Now, however, ,Brazil, which had become freer of British domination, was enabled at long last to supplant Argentina as the chief neighboring intermeddler in Uruguayan affairs. One of Brazil's first actions was the imposition of the boundary treaty of 1851, by which Uruguay had to renounce her earlier claim to an area in the north almost equal to what was thereafter left to her. Later in the decade Brazilian troops were sent into Uruguay on one or another occasion to "stabilize" the government. Argentina, too, was not above trying to continue her habit of interference in Uruguayan affairs even though the irresponsible years of Rosas were now past. The two big states had agreed in their convention of 1828 that Uruguay be "declared and guaranteed as an absolutely and perpetually neutral state between Brazil and the Argentine Confederation" but "absolute" and "perpetual" turned out to be conveniently relative terms.

For a rare change Uruguay found herself allied with her erstwhile intermeddlers in the tripartite war against the Para-

*Afterwards*

guay of Francisco Solano López from 1865 to 1870.[1] The principal difficulties of the period were internal, however, and the chronic disorders could not but breed financial difficulties. The persistent Latin American specter of foreign debts began to rear its head over Uruguay. One event of the "terrible year" of 1875 was the presentation to the Uruguayan chief of state of a note by the ministers and consuls of Brazil, Argentina, the United States, Spain, Italy, England, France, and Germany protesting debt defaults. By this time the Uruguayan government felt somewhat more capable of standing on its own feet: it replied tartly to the note.

An international collaboration of more pleasant tenor and constructive purpose was the Congress on Private International Law held at Montevideo in 1888–89 at the invitation of the Uruguayan government. Representatives of Argentina, Bolivia, Brazil, Chile, Paraguay, and Peru joined with Uruguay's in negotiating multilateral treaties on procedural law, literary and artistic property, patents, industrial and commercial trademarks, international penal law, civil law, and commercial law, and the liberal professions. It was Uruguay's first experience at hosting an international conference, and she acquitted herself well.

A small tempest which might have become a big one occurred in 1893 as a result of the prolonged rebellion by the state of Rio Grande do Sul against the Brazilian federal government. The unrest in the southernmost Brazilian state was accompanied by frequent rebel escapes into Uruguayan territory and culminated about the middle of 1893 in the assassination of an Uruguayan army officer and a police official in a northern border town. Feeling ran high at Montevideo, and the government, prompted by street demonstrations, protested to Rio that there existed "an atmosphere truly menacing to the preservation of peace." The incident passed from the critical stage, however, when the Brazilian government made handsome apologies, paid indemnities, and took steps to punish the culprits.

---

[1] An Uruguayan-Paraguayan treaty of 1883 fixed at 3,690,000 pesos the sum due Uruguay from the Paraguayan treasury because of the war. Uruguay renounced payment of the sum and, in addition, returned to Paraguay the trophies captured by Uruguayan forces during the war.

The impulse given Uruguay by José Batlle y Ordóñez, was primarily domestic, but it had certain international expressions. Chief of these was Batlle's representation of Uruguay at the second Hague Conference in 1907 during the interval between his two terms in the presidency. We have seen that had the proposals Batlle made in a notable address at the Dutch capital on July 29, 1907, been acted upon, the League of Nations would have been anticipated, at least in a skeletal way, by a dozen years. Batlle based his proposed "alliance" on the compulsory use of international arbitration. The address and the proposals were an earnest of the distinguished role Uruguay was later to play in international affairs.

After the conception of the League of Nations, Mariano Drago, son of an eminent Argentine internationalist and foreign minister, wrote generously on July 9, 1919, in *La Nación* at Buenos Aires, in evaluating the new international order, that "The sentiments of justice and humanity which inspired the appeal of Uruguay to the civilized nations for constitution of an International Tribunal were expressed with insuperable clarity and eloquence in the draft declaration presented to the Conference [by Batlle]. . . . That which was considered a chimera at The Hague has had its full realization at Versailles by virtue of the events which have paralleled [the proposals of] Sr. Batlle y Ordóñez, to whom belongs the honor of the initiation of so memorable a conquest in human progress."

Adulthood may be said to have been reached by Uruguay in 1903. Her debut on a world stage then came with Batlle's role at The Hague. In point of grand design, though not necessarily in detail, the elements of Uruguay's international position were worked out by the time of World War I. That position was determined by her permanent location as a buffer between the two largest and most dynamic of South America's states. Uruguay's policy was shaped, then, more by continental than by world-wide considerations. At the same time, it would be to Uruguay's advantage as a relatively weak unit in the South American area (*a*) to play an active and mature part on the inter-American and world stages and (*b*) to orient her policy toward that of the United States insofar as it was feasible. The traditional Colossus of the North was less to be feared than the closer and more threatening Colossus of the South. As between Argentina and Brazil, other things being equal, the state at Uruguay's front door would logically be more to be watched, and perhaps dreaded, than one across her back fence.

To understand the position of Uruguay between the jaws of the pincers it is necessary to look briefly at the position of each of those jaws. Argentina, though suffering the same sort of dichotomy between capital and *campo* which plagued Uruguay, was superficially unified under the glamorous leadership of Buenos Aires. Among the Latin American states Argentina was first not only alphabetically but also in point of prestige, position, and power. Given to a certain degree of grandiose dreaming, some Argentines thought in terms of a revival of the old colonial viceroyalty of La Plata. That would mean the subjection to colonialism—economic, psychological, and probably cultural, if not political—of Uruguay, Paraguay, and probably Bolivia. A former Argentine foreign minister, Dr. Estanislao Zeballos, advanced the thesis some years ago (even before the advent of Perón) that Argentine sovereignty in the Plata extended clear to the Uruguayan shoreline. Delusions of grandeur were beginning to characterize the Argentine mind, and Uruguay obviously stood in the way. If the fascinating and imperialistic guise of a revivified viceroyalty could not be donned again, perhaps a more prosaic, but still effective, customs union (under Argentine domination, of course) would serve the same purpose.

As for Brazil, at the time of World War I that vast land was still in large measure a slumbering giant. There was as yet little reason for the Argentine fear of Brazil which later became almost an obsession, at least with certain Argentine army officers. Uruguayan relations with Brazil tended to improve. The two states in 1909 negotiated a supplementary boundary treaty by which Brazil made generous concessions regarding Uruguayan use of waters which formed in part their common boundary. Loans which the Brazilian government had made to Uruguay during the latter country's struggle against Rosas and later during the Paraguayan War were adjusted by a convention of 1918 by which Brazil agreed that the 5,000,000-peso debt should be devoted by Uruguay to border works of mutual benefit to Uruguay and Brazil. In consequence, the southern republic constructed as the principal such work the great Mauá international bridge across the Yaguarón River. The Brazilian actions were a reflection of an international policy and a diplomatic personnel probably more consistently outstanding than those of any other Latin American country. They paid dividends from a grateful Uruguay not only in the form of graceful gestures such as the naming of a border town and a Montevideo street for the eminent Brazilian foreign minister, the Baron Rio Branco, another street for Brazil itself, and so on, but also, and more importantly, in a general rapprochement between the foreign policies of the largest and the smallest states of the continent.

Uruguayan interest was actively aroused from the outbreak of World War I. Popular sympathy was undisguisedly turned toward the Allies. The German invasion of Belgium (like Uruguay, a small nation), the long-standing cultural influence of France,[2] the important trade relations with Britain, and the presence of tens of thousands of sons and daughters of Italian ancestry would scarcely have allowed a different reaction. Batlle's second presidency ended with February, 1915, and he had relatively little contact with the war, but Uruguay was fortunate during two periods included within the war years in having as foreign minister an exceptionally able man, Dr. Baltasar Brum. His handling of wartime problems was distinguished.

The government scrupulously observed its obligations as a neutral during the early years of the war. Upon the United States' severance of diplomatic relations with Germany early in 1917, the Uruguayan government recognized "the justice and nobility of the sentiments" which had guided the United States action. During these middle years of the war, Uruguayan opinion, both official and private, slowly evolved the doctrine of inter-American solidarity to which Brum as president a few years later would give more tangible and ambitious form. The government, on June 18, 1917, decreed that "no American country, which in defense of its own rights should find itself in a state of war with nations of other continents, will be treated [by Uruguay] as a belligerent." This reasoned declaration of inter-American idealism was later interpreted by Uruguayan officials themselves as equivalent to an abandon-

[2] Uruguay in 1915 made Bastille Day a national holiday.

ment of neutrality. The policy was a years-long forerunner of the doctrine, hailed at the Lima Conference in 1938 as something new under the inter-American sun, that aggression against any one American republic should be considered as aggression against all of them.

Curiously, Uruguayan diplomatic relations with Germany were not immediately suspended. The latter step was taken on October 7, 1917; external and domestic measures in accord with it rapidly followed. The most important of such measures was the taking over of some 40,000 tons of German shipping which had sought refuge in Montevideo harbor early in the War. In the spring of 1918, after damage caused by the sabotaging of their machinery by the interned crews had been repaired, the ships were leased to the United States.

Uruguay was represented at the Versailles Conference, approved the principle of an international league, ratified the treaty on October 24, 1919, and deposited its ratification on January 10, 1920, thus becoming an original member of the League. Uruguay's role in the League of Nations has been characterized as unusually selfless: it "ever held the view that all matters shall be decided from the point of view of the advantages accruing to the Members as a whole rather than to any individual nation." [3] It was usually Uruguayan ministers to European states who represented her in the sessions of League organs and on the League staff. Chief of them were Alberto Guani, later foreign minister and vice president of Uruguay, Benjamín Fernández y Medina, Juan Carlos Blanco, and J. A. Buero. Uruguay served from 1923 to 1926 as a nonpermanent member of the League Council. The League representatives of Uruguay often took active roles in furthering humanitarian and cultural objectives: protection of children, restriction of narcotics, promotion of education, advancement of arbitration. The first international conference to meet in Latin America under League auspices convened in Montevideo in June, 1927; it was a conference of health experts on infant mortality.

In the meantime Uruguay was pursuing a conscientious and constructive course in the inter-American orbit. In addi-

[3] Warren H. Kelchner, *Latin American Relations with the League of Nations* (Boston, 1930), p. 106.

tion to sponsoring the conference at Montevideo in 1888–89, Uruguay attended all the early conferences in the new "series" beginning at Washington in 1889–90. The exposed position of Uruguay, coupled with her small size and complete contemporary lack of militarism, made it natural, almost inevitable, that she would be basically interested in the development of machinery for the pacific settlement of disputes. For example, the unratified ABC treaty of 1915, which was designed to facilitate the peaceful settlement of disputes among Argentina, Brazil, and Chile, provided that a prospective permanent commission for such a purpose be located at Montevideo.

The administration of President Baltasar Brum (1919–23) saw Uruguay reach imaginative and constructive heights of participation in inter-American affairs certainly not previously and perhaps not since attained. The new president had perhaps caught some of the vision of Woodrow Wilson who had invited him, while he was Uruguay's foreign minister, to visit the United States as a guest of the government. In a notable address at the University of Montevideo on April 21, 1920, on the subject of "American Solidarity" Brum laid down the outlines of an "American league of nations"—"if the powerful nation of the North will lend itself to the fulfillment of a policy of justice and of equality with its sisters of America, it will be our duty to cooperate in its proposals." The basis of the association of nations propounded by Brum in 1920 and elaborated on later occasions was the entire equality of all the states represented, obviously a point of great importance to a small but dignified state such as Uruguay. Brum's proposed league would work in harmony with the League at Geneva and would have authority and responsibility over peculiarly American problems, including defense of the American states against either Old World or New World aggression.

Baltasar Brum's proposals, if realized, would have had the practical effect of converting the Monroe Doctrine into a multilateral Pan-American doctrine. The Uruguayan government in submitting suggestions for the Fifth Inter-American Conference at Santiago in 1923 advocated consideration of what was essentially the Brum plan. The Monroe Doctrine was still being maintained and applied unilaterally, however, and the Uruguayan proposals never came to a vote, "due almost certainly,"

one authority avers, "to the opposition of the United States." [4]
The United States in the following decade would reverse its attitude at a conference held, appropriately, at Montevideo and agree implicitly to the multilateralizing of the Monroe Doctrine. But Brum had by that time died a tragic death some nine months since. He was years ahead of his time. His proposals adumbrated the hemisphere security pact of 1947, the tighter inter-American organization evolved at the Bogotá Conference in 1948, and the relationship between that organization and the United Nations. But as of the 1920's Brum's was but a voice crying in the wilderness.

By the end of the 1920's Uruguay was gradually emerging into a new prominence in inter-American affairs due, in part, to the isolationist policy then being pursued by President Irigoyen of Argentina. In the several years after December, 1928, Uruguay assumed a prominent role in the efforts to bring order into the long-muddied relations between Bolivia and Paraguay, and from 1935 to 1938, Uruguay served as one of the six American republics sponsoring the peace conference at Buenos Aires which ended the Chaco War between the two landlocked republics. In December, 1933, Uruguay played host to the Seventh Inter-American Conference, meeting at Montevideo. A combination of circumstances made the atmosphere as notably clear as that of the Fifth and Sixth Conferences had been cloudy.

At the end of 1935, Uruguay, which had been the second American republic to grant diplomatic recognition to the Soviet Union, broke off relations with the U.S.S.R. [5] The reason was the poorly concealed use of the Soviet legation at Montevideo as a Communist propaganda center for much of southern South America. The following year Russia's Maksim Litvinov tried vitriolically but unsuccessfully to hale Uruguay before the Council of the League of Nations for her action. Poetic justice was served when in 1939 Uruguay was in a position to participate in the expulsion of the Soviet Union from the League of Nations.

As World War II approached, the Nazi menace seemed

[4] Percy A. Martin, *Latin America and the War* (Baltimore, 1925), p. 571.

[5] Under the stress of co-operation in a common cause the two governments re-established diplomatic relations in July, 1943.

greater than the Communist, however. Hugo Fernández Artucio, an Uruguayan professor and publicist, has revealed vividly in his sensational book, *The Nazi Underground in South America* (New York, 1942), how prewar Nazi propaganda, plotting, and espionage were built up in Uruguay, the "key of the Nazi strategy." The post-Weimar German devotion to *Geopolitik* gave Haushofer and his school a full, even an exaggerated, realization of the strategic importance of Uruguay in controlling the whole Plata basin—all of Uruguay and Paraguay and important parts of Argentina, Brazil, and Bolivia. Uruguay must become a *Gau* in the Nazi scheme of things.

With the German invasion of Poland, Uruguay was alerted for co-operative action with the other democracies of the hemisphere. The country little realized that within short weeks it would become the location of the most dramatic single incident of the opening months of the War. On December 12–13, 1939, the German pocket battleship *Graf Spee* engaged in a running fight off the Uruguayan coast with the British cruisers *Ajax*, *Achilles*, and *Exeter*. The German ship gave a good account of herself but the superior fire power and marksmanship of the British flotilla badly damaged her and she put into the harbor of Montevideo for refuge and repairs. The Uruguayan government, in accordance with international law, ordered the *Spee* to leave within three days. After futile protests the ship did leave but forestalled sinking or capture by the waiting British vessels by being exploded and scuttled by her own commander just outside the harbor. It was a historical moment of vast excitement for the Montevideanos. Hamburg shipping firms soon afterward allegedly displayed in their windows photographs of the scuttled and burning German vessel with a picture of Hitler pointing to a legend underneath: "Uruguay will pay for this!"

The prospective exaction of a Nazi toll for Uruguayan forthrightness in the affair of the *Spee* seemed to come within a year. Actually, it was less a levy for the humiliation and damage of that incident than it was part of a long-range Nazi blueprint. At any rate, evidence came to light in 1940 that one Arnulf Fuhrmann, a German "photographer" at the Uruguay River city of Salto (but actually a highly placed Nazi government and party agent), had perfected plans for a coup by which the Uruguayan government would be overthrown and the country made into an agricultural colony of Germany. Not only would the conquest give the Nazis the coveted foothold in South America ("Antarctic Germany!"), it would also serve as a diversion, keeping United States attention focused and troops committed and hence turned away from Europe.

The developments were sensational, but they encountered a curious governmental paralysis. The fault was not entirely that of President Alfredo Baldomir who, as early as February, 1940, had made strenuous efforts to get congressional approval for defense measures. The peculiar constitutional provision then prevailing assigned one-third of the cabinet positions and one-half of the senate seats to the leading minority party. The Blancos, who traditionally occupied that position, were just as traditionally conservative. Their long-dominant leader, Luis Alberto de Herrera, was freely accused of being not only obstructionist but also pro-Nazi, pro-franquista, and pro-Argentine. He maintained a friendly liaison with the more chauvinistic newspapers and leaders in Buenos Aires who were urging on the increasingly reactionary government of Argentina the assertion of a right to supervise any defense measures Uruguay might take.[6]

When the Nazi conspiracy against Uruguay was finally forced fully into the open in 1941, both the Uruguayan public and the general foreign attitudes were immediately apparent. Despite the fact that Herrera and the Blancos stepped up their vicious attacks, especially through their newspaper, *El Debate*, against the United States and the Uruguayan policy of cooperation, the government arrested numerous pro-Nazis.[7] The Brazilian government loaned arms and munitions to Uruguay in 1941. The United States quickly sent two cruisers to Montevideo as an indication of what might be expected if German efforts had gone further toward precipitating a coup in Uruguay.

The Uruguayan government in June, 1941, proclaimed its intention to make its ports available to the naval vessels of any American republic which might become engaged in war with a

[6] The distinctness of position held by the Independent Blancos, a legally separate party, needs to be emphasized; the latter party was uniformly and highly co-operative in regard to international policy.

[7] Fuhrmann and six others were sentenced in February, 1944, to long prison terms.

non-American state. The action represented a milestone in advanced inter-American thinking. A $17,500,000 loan by the United States government, made over Uruguayan Blanco and Argentine protests, enabled the Uruguayan government to begin construction of a large naval air base on the Atlantic coast a short distance below the Brazilian border. Steps were also taken to develop naval facilities at Punta del Este, the resort town at the broad entrance to the Plata River. Her bases, Uruguay maintained, should be open to all the republics of the hemisphere. Baldomir's hand was strengthened by increased public support, and in 1942 he undertook a coup of sorts by which he precipitated constitutional changes to free the government from the strait jacket curiously of overweighted Blanco participation.

Following the Japanese attack on Pearl Harbor, Uruguay promptly declared her solidarity with the Allied powers. President Baldomir and Foreign Minister Guani expressed the intention to give full nonbelligerent rights to any American states at war. Uruguay's natural inclinations coincided with a realization that, facing an increasingly unco-operative and reactionary Argentina, her wisest and safest course lay along the path of systematic collective security. Close to the end of the Third Foreign Ministers' Conference, which met at Rio in the latter half of January, 1942, Uruguay, along with several other South American states, severed diplomatic relations with the Axis powers. Argentina and Chile were left as the lone holdouts in the hemisphere.

The conference at Rio authorized the creation of an Emergency Advisory Committee for Political Defense with its seat at Montevideo. The CPD, as it was commonly called, included representatives of seven of the American republics. It operated under the energetic and imaginative chairmanship of Uruguay's foreign minister, Alberto Guani. The committee, which began functioning on April 15, 1942, did yeoman work in investigating and publicizing subversive activities in the hemisphere during the war years. Guani continued as chairman of the CPD after being elected vice president of Uruguay late in 1942. In December, 1943, the CPD proposed, after a questionable regime had been installed in Bolivia, that the republics of the hemisphere follow a policy of collective recognition of new revolutionary governments. The proposal, which had a brief vogue, became known as the Guani doctrine.[8]

The mounting truculence and bombast of the Perón-dominated Argentine regime drew a continuously watchful, wary eye from Uruguay. It seemed for a moment early in 1944 that the Uruguayan government's refusal, along with that of most other American republics, to grant recognition to the new and more chauvinistic Fárrell government in Argentina might provoke an armed reprisal by the latter country. Blancos under Herrera were rumored to be sympathetic to prospective Argentine intervention. The crisis passed, perhaps in part because a United States air and naval force made a friendly demonstration at Montevideo. Indirect Argentine interference was reflected at a later date in the encouragement given to allegedly Fascist circles in the Argentine army. The Uruguayan government on July 1, 1946, arrested some thirty leaders of the APRE (Asociación Pro-Renovación del Espíritu), a reputedly secret and totalitarian lodge of army officers which had been in contact with kindred officers in Argentina and was supposedly planning a military-political coup against the Uruguayan government.

The first important evidence of Uruguayan concern with postwar planning came in the preference expressed by its government to the United States Department of State in November, 1944, after the Dumbarton Oaks discussion, for reviving the League of Nations if possible rather than creating a new international organization. Another bit of evidence came in the Uruguayan declaration of war against the Axis powers on February 15, 1945, as a prerequisite to admission to the early conference planned to perfect the United Nations organization.[9]

[8] On the CPD *cf.* "Political Defense—American Style," *The Inter-American,* April, 1943, pp. 30–31; Carl B. Spaeth and William Sanders, "Emergency Advisory Committee for Political Defense," *American Journal of International Law,* April, 1944, pp. 218–41.

[9] The sequence of events was confused and the procedure followed by the United States not entirely well mannered at that point. Six of the American republics (in addition to Argentina) had not yet declared war on the Axis states, though several of them had made inquiries as to whether their inter-American obligations required it. The United States government, though previously having answered that it considered a severance of relations with the Axis governments to be sufficient, now virtually forced the hands of the remaining American republics by making a declaration of

The Uruguayan delegation took a prominent part in the Inter-American Conference on Problems of War and Peace meeting at Mexico City in February–March, 1945. Ever mindful of Uruguay's exposed location, the delegation presented one resolution providing for the collective application of force in case of a threat to the territorial integrity or political independence of any American republic. Argentina's umbrageous nationalism had registered in Uruguayan as well as other minds. The Mexico City conference's chief accomplishment, the Act of Chapultepec, a temporary wartime measure aimed at achieving regional security, owed much to the constructive statesmanship of Uruguay's delegates. Uruguay's representatives later took an active, though not a leading, role in the United Nations conference at San Francisco in April–June, 1945. Uruguay ratified the UN charter on December 15, 1945.

The 1945 inter-American conference at Mexico City had planned another meeting later the same year to deal in more permanent fashion than had been possible at Mexico City with problems of hemisphere security. But Acting Secretary of State Acheson announced on October 3, 1945, that the United States would not enter into a hemisphere security pact participated in by the contemporary Argentine government which, he charged, had failed to carry out its anti-Axis commitments. He added that the Brazilian government had been requested to postpone indefinitely the security conference which it would have hosted at Rio and which had been scheduled to open on October 20.

Into this impasse stepped Uruguay's foreign minister, Eduardo Rodríguez Larreta, with one of the most forthright and imaginative proposals made in years. In a long note to Secretary of State Byrnes on November 22, 1945, Rodríguez Larreta proposed that the American republics adopt a policy of collective intervention in case any member state in the inter-American system flagrantly and persistently violated either its international obligations or "the essential rights of man." He maintained that collective intervention would not infringe the earlier inter-American prohibitions on unilateral intervention

---

war the condition of admission to the forthcoming San Francisco Conference. *Cf.* Lawrence Duggan, *The Americas: The Search for Hemisphere Security* (New York, 1949), p. 108.

by one state in the affairs of another. Though the Rodríguez Larreta doctrine, as it promptly came to be called, naturally did not specifically name Argentina, it just as obviously was tailored to fit the situation in that country. The Buenos Aires kept press immediately protested indignantly against it. Secretary Byrnes quickly and unqualifiedly endorsed the principle. The response from the Latin American governments, which had a deeply rooted fear of intervention (which often had been undertaken unilaterally by the United States in Middle America), was varied and generally either lukewarm or negative.

Rodríguez Larreta might have anticipated the net reaction to his bold proposal, but it does not lessen his and Uruguay's bravery in making it. The consistent Uruguayan devotion to collective security and orderly procedures had again been demonstrated. The persistent threat from across the Plata had again been pointed up. In the postwar years it was obvious that the threat might take one or more of three forms: economic reprisals (*e.g.*, a ban on Argentine wheat exports to Uruguay or on the flow of Argentine tourists; both measures have been tried), the undue encouragement of the Blanco opposition (evidence exists that Perón in 1946 proposed in a letter to Luis Alberto de Herrera the erection of a Platine entente under Argentine hegemony),[10] or armed attack. The wartime and postwar flight to Montevideo of Argentine refugees of all political complections has also been a sore point with the peronista government.[11] Uruguay's freedom of the press has repeatedly irritated Argentina.

The concluding of an Uruguayan-Argentine agreement on February 28, 1948, to settle all further disputes between the two countries by arbitration did not more than temporarily lessen the existing tension. As recently as October, 1952, Argentina sent an "energetic and severe" note to Uruguay protesting because the latter state had opened a consulate in and begun operating a flying-boat service to the Falkland Islands, long sporadically claimed by Argentina! That the protested consulate had been in service for more than twenty years was

[10] The Blanco position on international questions in the war and early postwar years is elaborately documented in the party's publication, *El Partido Nacional y la Política Exterior del Uruguay* (Montevideo, 1947).

[11] *Cf.* Vincent de Pascal, "Escape to Montevideo," *The Inter-American,* August, 1945, pp. 15–17, 38–39.

apparently a matter of no moment to the Argentine government: it still was an excuse to harass the democratic government of Uruguay from whose land emanated the irritating flow of anti-peronista propaganda.

The postwar role of Uruguay in the UN has been active and intelligent. The outbreak of the Korean war led to an Uruguayan proposal that the authority of the General Assembly should be strengthened at the expense of that of the Security Council. The Uruguayan delegation also proposed that the definition of international aggression be broadened to include indirect aggression such as the use of subversive agencies by one state to undermine the domestic institutions of another state. The government in October, 1950, announced a 5,000,-000-peso Uruguayan contribution to the civil population of Korea in the form of woolen blankets and other articles of Uruguayan manufacture. Unesco, the United Nations Educational, Scientific, and Cultural Organization, chose Montevideo as the site of its international meeting in 1954.

The jaws of the pincers must indefinitely remain placed as they are. Uruguay must, as best she can, learn to live between them. One jaw has become padded and relaxed. With few exceptions Uruguay's relations with its giant northern neighbor have, for many years, been peaceful, even cordial. The Uruguayan Colorados in the nineteenth century admired the progressive and liberal policies of Dom Pedro II, emperor of Brazil. Relations with the Brazilian republic were usually amicable.

At the same time and largely by the same token, the other jaw of the pincers has developed teeth, even fangs. The wellsprings of Argentina's relationship with her peaceful and inoffensive sister state are to be found in the curious and tortured psychological complex of the Argentine nation. An abnormal sense of mission has brought a recurrent attitude of imperialistic possessiveness toward surrounding areas.[12] Uruguayan independence has been challenged and resented by Argentina. That independence has usually been conditioned in Uruguay by two political considerations, one domestic and one

---

[12] Uruguayan thought was being given more than thirty years ago to the possibility of a war between Argentina and Brazil and its consequences for Uruguay. Cf. Wáshington Paullier, La Defensa Nacional y los Problemas Militares (Montevideo, 1919).

international. If the congressional opposition—Blancos, Communists, and others—which confronts the government is large, then the government must move with corresponding caution vis-à-vis Argentina. Similarly, if presumptive backing by the United States is uncertain—and the policy of the larger northern republic has been disconcertingly inconsistent at times— the Uruguayan government must also walk cautiously with respect to Argentina.

There are few states in the world, however, the purity and maturity of whose motives are less subject to question than those of stout Uruguay. It is at once her misfortune and her challenge to be located geographically as she is.

# 18

*Challenge and Opportunity*

"Uruguay is the Switzerland of America." Sometimes it is made the Denmark, or the Belgium, or even the New Zealand of the New World. But those who are so intent on comparisons all fall short of the mark. Comparisons are dangerous things, anyway, especially when made so gratuitously and broadly as they often are.

Uruguay is Uruguay. Most people probably mean it as a compliment to the South American country to call it the Switzerland—or the Denmark or Belgium or New Zealand—of the Western Hemisphere, but those European and Pacific countries could consider themselves complimented by the comparison. Let us not forget that.

What makes Uruguay what it is today? What may it expect tomorrow?

Spend a little time in Uruguay—it need not be a long while —and you gradually get an impression of national well-being, a sense of maturity, a feeling of adjustment. It is fluid, invisible, and highly subtle. It is not something you can put your finger on; it is simply there in the air you breathe, in the social radiations and emanations from city and countryside. Spend a little time in thinking about the matter, after it gradually obtrudes itself from the subconscious into the conscious, and you almost inevitably come to the conclusion that it is to be explained on the ground that *Uruguay is an integrated country.*

What is integration, personal or national? The dictionary tells us that it is the act or process of making whole or entire, of achieving internal unification. It is surprising, and somewhat appalling, to realize how many Latin American countries have failed to fulfill that seemingly simple specification—failed, in some instances, by pathetically wide margins. Uruguay in most respects has arrived, happily and successfully arrived.

The country is integrated geographically. No other country in Latin America is as much characterized by the absence of barriers to transportation and communication, to full utilization of the soil; in no other Latin American country are all parts of the land so accessible. No "mountain" in Uruguay is too high to be climbed, few are too steep or rugged to be used agriculturally. There is an inescapable sense of geographic oneness about the land. It completely lacks the extremes of Argentina's Patagonia and Chaco, of Chile's far southern rain forests and northern Atacama desert.

Uruguay is integrated ethnically. The Indian population is, for practical purposes, nil, and the Negro population small. Those who have not been in the Andean countries of South America and in their counterparts in the Latin countries of North America find it almost impossible to realize what a tremendous problem is presented by the large Indian fractions of the populations of those countries. It is no reflection on the Indian as such. It is simply that the social, economic, political, and cultural standards of the various countries are those imported and inherited from Europe and that the great masses of Indians follow a way of life that is almost wholly different. The Latin American Indian tenaciously, though seemingly passively, resists assimilation. It is normally only when his bloodstream is diluted by the miscegenation which in the passing generations produces a mestizo race that the cultural barriers with which he surrounds himself can be broken down and he can effectively be brought within the orbit of a white society and economy.

Uruguay escapes all those problems by having an almost wholly European racial stock. It is true that Uruguay has attracted considerable numbers of Italians and other non-Spanish-speaking immigrants. But the figurative wall separating

Italy from Spain is not high or insurmountable and Italian immigrants in Uruguay have proved remarkably assimilable; they have by no means formed an undigested lump in the stomach of the Uruguayan body politic or social. The same observation is in general true of the smaller numbers of other nationals who have migrated to Uruguay, whether at an early or a late date.

The Negro is potentially perhaps more assimilable than the Indian. Brazil has had a remarkable experience in fusing African and European elements. But again Uruguay escapes whatever problems would be presented by the presence of that large, ethnically alien element. The country has very few Negroes, Montevideo almost none. Some Uruguayans will point out, with perhaps a small and unconscious air of superiority, that the United States has much more of a Negro "problem" than has Uruguay. There is some ground for belief that this pattern of reaction may be Communist-inspired, but it is true that no Myrdal could ever find "an Uruguayan dilemma" stemming from the mutual impact of Negro and white on each other in the same society. Racial homogeneity precludes the sharp cultural tensions which exist in many countries of Latin America.

Uruguay is integrated socially—but at this point it would be well to introduce the typical Spanish American qualification, *más o menos*. It is true that Uruguay lacks the extremes of wealth and poverty which are found in so many places in Latin America. There is no powerful elite group, no class-conscious clique of the rich and the well-born in a Hamiltonian sense, nor, at the other end of the social scale, a large mass of cringing underprivileged persons who are professionally servile and who parrot "*a sus órdenes*" to anyone who is better dressed or more self-assured in manner. It is true that Uruguay is one, and probably the foremost, of the two or three Latin American countries which have a real and significant middle class. Significant in the sense of filling in the social vacuum between the economic "haves" and the "have nots." The large and semibureaucratic governmental organization has contributed unconsciously and directly to this development: virtually all of the thousands of civil servants belong to the middle class and add to its solidarity and influence.

But it is also true, unfortunately, that Uruguay is plagued

by a great psychological and social disparity between capital
and *campo*, a disparity which colors almost all phases of Uruguayan life. The problem is similar to that existing in Argentina, but the social distortion is greater in the larger country
due in considerable measure to that very difference in area.
Nevertheless, the inferiority of the Uruguayan rural areas and
the failure adequately to integrate them in the country's national life constitute to date Uruguay's biggest problem. The
relative glitter of Montevideo obscures the monotony of the
*campo*, and hence even many Montevideanos are either only
academically aware of the situation or else, because of the comfort and greater opportunity presented by life in the capital,
choose to ignore the problem and its implications.

Uruguay is integrated socially in another sense: its women,
especially those of Montevideo, have a much better psychological, economic, and legal status than is true of those in almost
any other country in Latin America. In many parts of Latin
America the female of the species is more a piece of psychological property, either for vainglorious display by some posses-
sive male relative or for pursuit and possible conquest, than
she is a human being. The roving and appraising masculine eye
is not nonexistent in Uruguay, but it is much less in evidence
than elsewhere in Latin America. Women have achieved a
highly commendable degree of social emancipation. It is superficially footnoted by their presence at one time or another in
both houses of the congress and in other important governmental positions, by their activity in the professions, by their
right to own property, sue for divorce, etc. It is footnoted less
tangibly but more importantly by the unconscious attitude
toward them, an attitude which tends increasingly to recognize
them as equals, capable of taking an intelligent part in a conversation, a business deal, a governmental enterprise, or a cultural activity.

The deeply rooted Latin practice of limiting many social
gatherings to men only has by no means been abandoned in
Uruguay, but society—in a narrow sense—involves participation of women to a greater degree than is usually true in Latin
America. The Uruguayan woman at a social affair not only
assumes the positive role of an equal participant, she also
abandons the negative role of being a china doll (the compari-

son must seem slightly absurd to many people who know the typically well-nourished Uruguayan woman!) present only for display purposes.

In yet another way, which is difficult to label, one finds Uruguay integrated or at least emancipated. In many Latin American countries the heavy hand of a privileged ecclesiastical organization—in other words, an established church—has, subtly or openly, dominated the intellectual, social, and political, as well as the religious, life of the country. Sometimes it has been a fine Italian hand, seemingly lightly felt but none the less insistent. At other times it has been a mailed fist smashing down all opposition. Uruguay has solved its ecclesiastical problem in a dignified and peaceful way, not with the bitterness and bloodshed Mexico has known, for example. The Catholic Church has been relegated to a position of respect but lack of dominance. In mid-twentieth century the continued ascendancy of any church organization becomes anachronistic. Uruguay, almost alone of the Latin American countries, has achieved a neat balance of values, has turned not to irreligion but to complete ecclesiastical freedom, has lower-cased Religion.

Just as a sense of balance has been attained with respect to ecclesiastical elements so, too, has Uruguay achieved that balance with regard to the military. Armies, like most other institutions in all but a small minority of Latin American states, have been organized and have operated on an authoritarian basis. The phychological role of many a Latin American army establishment has often been more important than its military or even its political function. It has frequently been, in effect, above the law and certainly above civilian control. This often breeds a sort of intoxication from the actual or potential power and irresponsibility which result. The military establishment, like the ecclesiastical, has at times become a kind of state within a state. Uruguay has none of this. Not only is the army small —and the navy practically insignificant—but its psychological position is one of modesty and subordination. Uruguay's one military president in more than half a century was as much architect as general, and it was he who returned the country to democratic processes after an interlude of dictatorship.

Psychological integration is characteristic of Uruguay in other ways. This is especially true with regard to the attitude of very large numbers of the people who, irrespective of whether they individually are Colorados or Blancos, Montevideanos or *campesinos*, loyally Catholic or religiously indifferent, feel they are all Uruguayans—*orientales*, they still often call themselves. In Brazil the average person is probably psychologically a paulista or a mineiro or a sulriograndense,[1] or what have you, rather than a Brazilian. In Colombia he is a bogotano, an antioqueño, or from some other specific section. In Peru he is a Spaniard from Lima or an Andean Indian. In other words, the individual often sets himself in state, region, or ethnic group.

Not so in Uruguay. Allegiance is more to the nation than to the part or fraction. Colorados and Blancos who, during the nineteenth century, would often neither intermarry nor have business dealings with one another nor at times even speak to each other (even when they were not actually fighting), have now come to the place where on occasion they can actually banter each other in typically North American fashion about their political affiliations. For a Latin that is indeed coming a long way. Country has taken precedence over party. The Catholic and the Protestant or the person or family which has drifted away from a church don't joke about the issue of religion, but they do in most instances show a mutual respect and tolerance which are healthy. Allegiance to a common *patria* has come to transcend any ecclesiastical loyalty. The Montevideano and the typical rural residents often do not speak each other's language—other than merely Spanish—and that is *not* healthy. Each, however, would be patriotically unwilling to exclude the other from the whole body of Uruguayans.

The national psychograph is characterized by maturity as well as integration. The average Uruguayan reacts, both individually and nationally, as an adult. The country lives simply and tranquilly and with an inner peace. It approaches life with a zest unmixed with naiveté. Uruguay has clean air and a clear conscience. Across the river is the potentially great nation of Argentina. The respective capitals mirror and focus the ethos of the two countries. Montevideo lacks the high tension and aggressiveness of Buenos Aires, even if it also lacks its glamour. In one curious and trivial fashion Uruguay shows a sort of

[1] Respectively the inhabitant of the state of São Paulo, Minas Geraes, or Rio Grande do Sul.

psychological lag. People still sometimes maintain the colonial manner of reference to themselves as *orientales*, those on the "east bank" of the Uruguay River. No useful purpose would seem to be served by continuing the solely geographical identification of themselves, especially when that form of identification carries with it the colonial implication of inferiority. They are and should call themselves Uruguayans, not *orientales*. Those Argentines who live across the river do not by that token refer to themselves as *occidentales*.

The attitude of Uruguay in international affairs is also remarkably mature and enlightened. Porfirio Díaz is alleged once to have quipped, "Poor Mexico! So far from God, so close to the United States!" Some pseudo-cynic in Uruguay might paraphrase it for his own country by substituting Argentina for the northern colossus. But it is an open question as to whether Uruguay's closeness to her more powerful and erratically intransigent neighbor may not have developed a poise, dignity, and rationality which the larger state has very often lacked.

The role and contribution of Uruguay in defense of democracy are consequently the more magnified. Democracy is essentially the political way of the middle class. Uruguay has developed that middle class further and better than probably any other country in Latin America. Democracy respects and elevates the individual. Uruguay approaches the individual with the same attitude. The Uruguayan citizen obeys the government because the government respects him. Officials are public servants, not masters. It is in such an atmosphere that democracy can best flourish. Granted the underlying circumstances and attitudes, democracy hence becomes almost inevitable. Its projection from the domestic onto the international stage is, then, natural, though none the less commendable. The hemisphere and the world may well thank Uruguay for its pursuit of the middle way. It is fortunate that the country has avoided the desperate sense of mission which has characterized certain other South American countries. It is typical of the important role that the individual plays in national life in Uruguay that a citizen of that country, Joaquín Serratosa Cibils, was chosen president of the world-wide Rotary International in 1953.

The role of government in the Uruguayan scene is a coin with—naturally—two sides. The one side is the government's willingness to take, and its history of taking, a definite and dynamic attitude of leadership in the country's affairs. The Uruguayan tendency to experiment is nowhere more manifest than on the part of the government. It is not simply a care-taker organism; it does not accept the Jeffersonian dictum that that government is best which governs least; it is, and is expected to be, a positive force in Uruguayan life. The government, qua government, tends to become an institution as well as a machine and in the former capacity to be vested with the permanence, ponderosity, and professionality often char-acteristic of institutions. In its institutional character it par-tially supplants the Church and the army as potentially com-peting institutions.

Thus far Uruguay has been made to seem, by and large, a paragon. There are debits to be recorded, however—fortunately neither numerous nor fatal. Already noted is the dislocation of all sorts resulting from the imbalance between capital and *campo*. It is at once the greatest obstacle to integration and also the country's foremost general problem. Until this dis-tortion can be removed or reduced—by a much broader attack than Uruguay has yet attempted—the problem will remain an insidiously plaguing one.

That other side of the governmental coin now needs not-ing. Governments, Uruguay's included, are not impersonal or automatic institutions or machines. They are made up of men of high and low position who, in spite of all wisdom and good intentions, are subject to human frailties. Pressures for office, the vested interest of those who hold office, the creeping tend-ency of a bureaucratic organization to resist subjection to popular control—these and other problems of the administra-tive process are as operative in Uruguay as anywhere else.

The question of governmental policy also needs considera-tion. It has often been noted that the Uruguayan government's consciousness of the plight of the underprivileged is among the most acute to be found anywhere in the world. A recent English writer calls Uruguay "South America's first welfare state." Thus far, the interests of an expansive and aggressive govern-mental policy in economic and social affairs on the one hand,

and, on the other, private enterprise and initiative have been balanced and mutually tolerant. The intervention of the state in the sphere which, according to nineteenth-century liberal tenets, should be left to the action of the individual has been gradual—a writer several years ago entitled successive chapters in a book dealing with the contemporary Latin American scene, "Uruguay in Evolution" and "Mexico in Revolution." But it is difficult for a government which starts on such a road to change either its direction or its pace; difficult for it to relax, much less to relinquish, its activity of an economic sort, either regulatory or productive. Popular pressures from benefited groups are too great to make change easy.

Some of Uruguay's ventures in the economic area, especially its consumer- and producer-subsidy arrangements, appear to have been opportunistic rather than well thought out. Some of the experiments in the field of agriculture seem to be aimed at superficial rather than basic objectives. It would seem the part of wisdom for Uruguay to pause for an inventory. "Planning" has become a devil-word, though any businessman who failed to employ the process would quite quickly go bankrupt. Governmental planning, especially when it involves functions and activities beyond the minimal and orthodox, requires the best sort of brains, vision, and integrity. Uruguayans have all of these. If only they can resist undue or unwise pressures, if only they can properly integrate the activity of the government with the enterprise of the individual, they will have little to fear; but those are big "ifs." The analysis and integration will need to avoid, if possible, certain of the pitfalls which have already occasionally developed.

Montevideo has in recent years had more than its share of strikes. Too many of them can leave social and psychological as well as economic scars which are a long time in healing. In time of economic tightness certain experimentation, which under more normal circumstances may operate reasonably smoothly, may tend to backfire to the embarrassment of the government. Concern has already been expressed in some quarters in Uruguay over the size of the public debt. Although the per capita share of the Uruguayan public debt is only a little more than one-twelfth of that carried by the average United States citizen, prudence should dictate that a debt of more than a billion pesos, a debt which has increased in all but a few years of the past century, should be held fast or preferably reduced.

Most of its problems, specific and general, Uruguay has worked out. As it faces tomorrow it could, with reasonable assurance, plan to carry on in much the same fashion as in the recent past. There is a larger responsibility shaping up, however, which may make still further demands for maturity on Uruguay. It flows from Uruguay's relationship to democracy, already alluded to.

The individual, as an individual, finds his position increasingly precarious in the world of the mid-twentieth century. The current contest between East and West is not simply a struggle between competing forms of government, democracy and dictatorship. It is a phase of the continuing conflict between the individual or, rather, those governments and forms of government which pay a measure of respect to the individual and, on the other hand, authority in one form or another. Whether the authority takes the form of Fascism or Communism is, from one point of view, immaterial. It is still naked authority, apotheosized, and it is inimical to the maintenance of the dignity of the individual.

Despite the historic and basic emphasis put by the Catholic Church on the individual, the whole broad social organization of most parts of Latin America is, for complex reasons, not of the sort to give the individual much advantage in resisting those pressures or forces which would reduce him to social and even psychological subservience. Argentina, in spite of its advances in many directions, fails to provide a social landscape in which the individual, as an individual, is dominant. Most other Latin American countries fall even further short.

Uruguay is almost alone in recognizing and respecting the individual as such. A popular article written about Uruguayans many years ago put that characteristic with homely neatness in its title: "You Can't Kick Me." John Citizen in most Latin American states can be and continuously is kicked around with impunity when and as authority, social, economic, and political, listeth. With the dignity and position of the individual being challenged as they have scarcely been in almost a quarter of a millennium, the role of Uruguay as champion of the individual

becomes more important than ever. The importance is high-
lighted by the presence just across the Plata of a country-
neighbor whose government, more aggressively than any other
in the hemisphere, pursues a policy consciously or unconsciously calculated ultimately to depress the individual to a
mediocrity which he knew in colonial days but from which he
has gropingly been trying to escape. Uruguay must stand out,
then, as the continent's prime leader, as one of the hemisphere's
and the world's great leaders, of the democratic way of life.

More than two-thirds of a century ago W. H. Hudson
made the hero of his *Purple Land* say what lies at the bottom
of the Uruguayan character pointed to meet this need:

> The unwritten constitution, mightier than the written one [he
> wrote] is in the heart of every man to make him still a republi-
> can and free with a freedom it would be hard to match any-
> where else on the globe. The Bedouin himself is not so free,
> since he accords an almost superstitious reverence and implicit
> obedience to his sheikh. Here the lord of many leagues of land
> and of herds unnumbered sits down to talk with the hired
> shepherd, a poor, bare-footed fellow in his smoky rancho, and
> no class or caste difference divides them, no consciousness of
> their widely different positions chills the warm current of sym-
> pathy between two human hearts. How refreshing it is to meet
> with this perfect freedom of intercourse, tempered only by that
> innate courtesy and native grace of manner peculiar to Spanish
> Americans! What a change to a person coming from lands with
> higher and lower classes, each with its innumerable hateful
> subdivisions—to one who aspires not to mingle with the class
> above him, yet who shudders at the slouching carriage and
> abject demeanor of the class beneath him! If this absolute
> equality is inconsistent with perfect political order, I for one
> should grieve to see such order established.

It is Uruguayans, then, who make Uruguay the great country that it is, a true bastion of democracy. It is in the role as a
grand exemplar of democracy that Uruguay's challenge and
her opportunity lie for the second half of the twentieth century
and perhaps for all the decades beyond.

# Bibliography

The literature on Uruguay is unsystematic and, at least compared with that on such countries as Argentina, Brazil, and Mexico, not large in volume. Naturally, that in Spanish is much more ample than that in English. For the reason that Spanish books are generally inaccessible in the United States, however, the number of items in that portion of the bibliography has been severely restricted; it is limited, indeed, to only about a score of the most important works. The number of items in English is larger, but that part, too, is highly selective.

The main canons for inclusion of items have been variety and value. Thus, though the items run the whole gamut from soberly documented and scholarly studies through government reports to popularly, and in a few instances almost frivolously, written articles they all contribute substantially in one way or another to the elaboration of the picture of Uruguay. Those books and articles which in the author's judgment did not so contribute—and they have been numerous—have been omitted.

Other books than those listed below help to give a general picture of Latin America and hence, in part, of Uruguay. Some of these must be used carefully for one reason or another, but among the most useful are the following: Duncan Aikman, *The All-American Front* (New York: Doubleday, Doran, 1941); Germán Arciniegas, *The State of Latin America* (New York: Knopf, 1952); W. Rex Crawford, *A Century of Latin American Thought* (Cambridge: Harvard University Press, 1944); John A. Crow, *The Epic of Latin America* (New York: Doubleday, 1946); Lawrence Duggan, *The Americas: The Search for Hemisphere Security* (New York: Henry Holt, 1949); Edward O. Guerrant, *Roosevelt's Good Neighbor Policy* (Albuquerque: University of New Mexico Press, 1950); Royal Institute of International Affairs, *The Republics of*

*South America* (London and New York: Oxford University Press, 1937); William L. Schurz, *Latin America: A Descriptive Survey* (New York: E. P. Dutton, 2nd edit., 1949); George H. Soule, David Efron, and Norman T. Ness, *Latin America in the Future World* (New York: Farrar and Rinehart, 1945); Francis Violich, *Cities of Latin America: Housing and Planning to the South* (New York: Reinhold, 1944); Arthur P. Whitaker (ed.), *Inter-American Affairs, 1941; . . . 1942; . . . 1943; . . . 1944 . . . 1945* (New York: Columbia University Press, 1942–46).

In addition, certain annual publications have current material on Uruguay along with other countries or topics. Among them may be mentioned: *Britannica Book of the Year, Political Handbook of the World, South American Handbook,* and *Statesman's Yearbook.*

Among the most useful books, chapters in books, and articles dealing specifically with Uruguay are the following:

*In Spanish*

Acevedo, Eduardo. *Manual de Historia Uruguaya: Después de Artigas.* Montevideo: A. Monteverde y Cía., 3rd edit., 1943.

[The third of three volumes on Uruguayan history; this one deals with the independence period, partly chronologically, partly topically.]

Arena, Domingo. *Batlle y los Problemas Sociales del Uruguay.* Montevideo: Claudio García y Cía., 1939.

[A disciple's account of Batlle's position on strikes and other labor problems, divorce, and other matters.]

Blanco Acevedo, Pablo. *Estudios Constitucionales.* Montevideo: Impresora Uruguaya, 1939.

[Excellent essays on the constitutions of 1830, 1917, and 1934, and other topics.]

Chiarino, Juan Vicente and Saralegui, Miguel. *Detrás de la Ciudad: Ensayo de Síntesis de los Olvidados Problemas Campesinos.* Montevideo: Impresora Uruguaya, 1944.

[An excellent and challenging study of Uruguay's greatest problem, that of relations between capital and *campo.*]

*Enciclopedia Universal Ilustrada Europea-Americana.* "Uruguay." Bilbao: Espasa Calpe, 1929.

[The article on Uruguay (vol. 65, pp. 1537–82) is probably the most comprehensive encyclopedia article on that country in any language.]

Giudici, Roberto B. *Batlle y el Batllismo.* Montevideo: Imprenta Nacional Colorada, 1928.

[A monumental, even if laudatory, study (1,200 pp.); includes considerable source material.]

Giuffra, Elzear S. *La República del Uruguay: Explicación Geográfica del Territorio Nacional* [etc.]. Montevideo: A. Monteverde y Cía., 1935.

[A detailed physical geography of Uruguay.]

La Orden Miracle, Ernesto. *Uruguay: el Benjamín de España.* Madrid: Ediciones Cultura Hispánica, 1949.

[La Orden was formerly a Spanish consular and diplomatic official in Uruguay; he writes from a strongly Catholic point of view.]

Lasplaces, Alberto. *Vida Admirable de José Pedro Varela.* Montevideo: Claudio García y Cía., 2nd edit., 1944.

[A laudatory and not too profound biography but in general a satisfactory study of Uruguay's great educational reformer.]

*El Libro del Centenario del Uruguay.* Montevideo: Capurro y Cía., 1925.

[A physically huge book, published under government authorization, at the centennial of independence; it has sections dealing with virtually every aspect of Uruguayan life and activity.]

Martínez Lamas, Julio. *Economía Uruguaya.* Montevideo: Claudio García y Cía., 1943.

[A description of the Uruguayan economy from a very broad point of view, including that of physical geography.]

Martínez Lamas, Julio. *Riqueza y Pobreza del Uruguay: Estudio de las Causas que Retardan el Progreso Nacional.* Montevideo: Tipografía Atlántida, 2nd edit., 1946.

[A comprehensive and profound study of the capital-*campo* problem; the author emphasizes the role of Montevideo as a "suction pump."]

Montañes, María Teresa. *Desarrollo de la Agricultura en el Uruguay.* Montevideo: Tall. Gráficas D. Rural, 1948.

[Presented as a thesis, this study has some of the ponderous earmarks of one but is, withal, a very useful study of various phases of Uruguayan agriculture.]

Pintos, Francisco R. *Batlle y el Proceso Histórico del Uruguay.* Montevideo: Claudio García y Cía., 1938.

[Batlle set in the framework of the historical flux of the period; the author wrote from the standpoint of an adoring lieutenant of Batlle.]

Pivel Devoto, Juan E. and Pivel Devoto, Alcira Ranieri de. *Historia de la República Oriental del Uruguay.* Montevideo: R. Artagaveytia, 1945.

[One of the best one-volume histories of the country.]

Rodríguez Fabregat, Enrique. *Batlle y Ordóñez, el Reformador.* Buenos Aires: Editorial Claridad, 1942.

[Perhaps to be considered as the standard biography of Batlle; a detailed chronology, pp. 550–613.]

Sanguinetti Freire, Alberto. *Legislación Social del Uruguay.* Montevideo: A. Barreiro y Ramos, 2nd edit., 2 vol., 1949.

[A compilation of Uruguayan social legislation; the standard and definitive reference on the subject.]

Zavala Muniz, Justino. *Batlle, Héroe Civil.* Mexico: Fondo de Cultura Económica, 1945.

[One of the better studies of Batlle; particularly good on his early career.]

Zum Felde, Alberto. *Evolución Histórica del Uruguay: Esquema de su Sociología.* Montevideo: Maximino García, 3rd edit., 1945.

[A penetrating historical interpretation, with other chapters on various social, political, and cultural problems; the author is one of Uruguay's foremost intellectuals.]

Zum Felde, Alberto. *Proceso Intelectual del Uruguay y Crítica de su Literatura.* Montevideo: Imprenta Nacional Colorada, 1930.

[An outstanding study by the man who is perhaps the foremost intellectual and social historian in Uruguay.]

*In English*

*The Agricultural Development of Uruguay.* Report of a Mission Sponsored by the International Bank for Reconstruction and Development and the Food and Agricultural Organization of the United Nations. Washington and Rome: International Bank for Reconstruction and Development and Food and Agricultural Organization, 1951.

[The comprehensive technical report of a commission of agricultural experts from Great Britain, the United States, New Zealand, and Switzerland.]

Aguiar, Justo Manuel. "José Enrique Rodó," *Inter-America,* vol. 6. pp. 113–23 (December, 1922).
[A discerning interpretation.]

Albes, Edward. "Montevideo, the City of Roses," *Bulletin of the Pan American Union,* vol. 45, pp. 435–63 (October, 1917).
[Chiefly historical and descriptive; profusely illustrated.]

Beals, Carleton. *Rio Grande to Cape Horn.* Boston: Houghton Mifflin, 1943.
[Ch. 23 (pp. 307–18) is on Uruguay; it is a general, sympathetic survey written by a man who knows Latin America well.]

Bland, John O. P. *Men, Manners and Morals in South America.* New York: Scribners, 1920.
[Written by an Englishman, most of Chs. 9–15 (pp. 172–309) deals with Uruguay; supercilious, flippant, iconoclastic, and dated—but interesting.]

Bracker, Milton. "Gayest Spot South of the Border," *Saturday Evening Post,* vol. 223, Nov. 11, 1950, pp. 30–31+.
[A popularly written, sympathetic article by a *New York Times* correspondent; considerably more substantial than the title suggests.]

Brainerd, Heloise. "Public Instruction in Uruguay," *Bulletin of the Pan American Union,* vol. 62, pp. 1003–13 (October, 1928.)
[A general survey.]

Bryce, James. *South America: Observations and Impressions.* New York: Macmillan, 1914.
[Ch. 10 (pp. 349–65) is devoted to Uruguay; Bryce, despite a lack of background acquaintance with Latin America, was an extremely acute observer and his comments are well worth reading even four decades later.]

Burr, Mildred P. "Uruguay Today," *Foreign Commerce Weekly,* vol. 16, Aug. 26, 1944, pp. 11–13+.
[A factual review of production, trade, etc.]

Cannon, Mary M. *Social and Labor Problems of Peru and Uruguay: A Study in Contrasts.* Washington: Dept. of Labor, 1945.
[A good survey by the chief of the Inter-American Division

of the Women's Bureau, Department of Labor; the section on Uruguay is pp. 13–22.]

Charlone, César. "The Economic and Social Situation of Uruguay," *International Labour Review,* vol. 33, pp. 607–18 (May, 1936).
[A general account by one of the leading public figures in Uruguay.]

Clagett, Helen L. *A Guide to the Law and Legal Literature of Uruguay.* Washington: Library of Congress, 1947.
[A thoroughgoing guide and bibliography (123 pp.) with much complementary information about governmental organization; the author is a foreign law expert in the Law Library of the Library of Congress.]

Coester, Alfred L. *The Literary History of Spanish America.* New York: Macmillan, 1938.
[Ch. 5 (pp. 169–95) gives a good general survey of Uruguayan literary figures and development.]

Collado, E. G. and Hanson, Simon G. "Old-Age Pensions in Uruguay," *Hispanic American Historical Review,* vol. 16, pp. 173–89 (May, 1936).
[A carefully prepared study of one segment of the social security program.]

*Constitution of the Republic of Uruguay.* Washington: Pan American Union, 1952.
[An English translation of the 1951 constitution.]

de Pascal, Vincent. "Escape to Montevideo," *Inter-American,* vol. 4, August, 1945, pp. 15–17+.
[The story of Argentine political exiles and their activity in Montevideo.]

de Pascal, Vincent. "Port of Freedom," *Inter-American,* vol. 3, October, 1944, pp. 14–17+.
[A wartime account of how Montevideo provided a haven for Argentine political refugees.]

de Pascal, Vincent. "Uruguayan Portia," *Américas,* vol. 1, July, 1949, pp. 7–10.
[On Dr. Sofía Alvarez de Demicheli.]

de Pascal, Vincent and Dupont Aguiar, Mario. "Montevideo

Faces Wartime Changes," *Inter-American,* vol. 2, January, 1943, pp. 17–20.

[A vivid account of wartime shortages and other exigencies.]

de Pate, E. M. S. ("Elizabetta"). "Uruguayan Music," *Bulletin of the Pan American Union,* vol. 66, pp. 763–78 (November, 1932).

[A survey of Uruguayan composers.]

Donoso, Armando. "Rodó, an Evocation of the Spirit of Ariel," *Inter-America,* vol. 1, pp. 23–30 (October, 1917).

[An interpretation of Rodó's ideas in the form of a colloquy between "master" and "disciple" on a trip to Santiago, Chile.]

Fernández Artucio, Hugo. *The Nazi Underground in South America.* New York: Farrar and Rinehart, 1942.

[A sensational account by an Uruguayan publicist; Chs. 4 (pp. 41–54) and 7 (pp. 105–21) deal especially with Uruguay.]

Fitzgibbon, Russell H. "Argentina and Uruguay: A Tale of Two Uruguay," *Journal of Politics,* vol. 14, pp. 616–42 (November, 1952).

[An analysis of the changes involved in Uruguay's new constitution in 1951.]

Fitzgibbon, Russell H. "Argentina and Uruguay: A Tale of Two Attitudes," *Pacific Spectator,* vol. 8, pp. 6–20 (Winter, 1954).

[Reasons for the differences in the two peoples' attitudes.]

Fitzgibbon, Russell H., (ed.). *The Constitution of the Americas.* Chicago: University of Chicago Press, 1948.

[The English translation of the 1934 constitution is given, pp. 713–61.]

Forbes, Rosita. *Eight Republics in Search of a Future.* London: Cassell and Co., 1933.

[Two chapters, 12–13 (pp. 77–93), deal with Uruguay; rather better than the average travel book.]

Fournié, Emilio. "Uruguay," *Educational Yearbook of the International Institute of Teachers College, Columbia University, 1937* (I. L. Kandel, ed.), pp. 544–64. New York: Teachers College, Columbia University, 1937.

[One of a series of surveys of educational organization and operation.]

Fournié, Emilio. "Uruguay," *Educational Yearbook of the International Institute of Teachers College, Columbia University,*

*1942* (I. L. Kandel, ed.), pp. 369–88. New York: Teachers College, Columbia University, 1942.

[A factual survey in the country series often presented in this yearbook.]

Franck, Harry A. "Uruguay: A Progressive Republic," *Century Magazine,* vol. 101, pp. 737–44 (April, 1921).

[A sympathetic account.]

Frank, Waldo. *South American Journey.* New York: Duell, Sloan and Pearce, 1943.

[Ch. 31 (pp. 145–61) describes, with insight, an "Uruguayan Interlude"; the author is thoroughly familiar with Latin America.]

*A Guide to the Official Publications of the Other American Republics. XVIII. Uruguay.* Compiled by John de Noia and Glenda Crevenna. Washington: Library of Congress, 1948.

[Chiefly a thoroughly prepared guide, it also includes a small amount of historical information about various ministries and other governmental agencies.]

Gunther, John. *Inside Latin America.* New York: Harper's, 1941.

[Gunther's background on Europe and Asia is far better than on Latin America; his Ch. 22 on Uruguay (pp. 335–49) has much information but some very loose or factually incorrect statements.]

*Handbook of Uruguay.* 52nd Cong., 1st Sess., Sen. Exec. Doc. 149, pt. 10. Washington: Bureau of the American Republics, 1893.

[More than two-thirds of the 347 pp. is taken up with a detailed schedule of import duties but the remainder includes a compendium of useful, though partially outdated, material.]

Hanson, Simon G. *Utopia in Uruguay: Chapters in the Economic History of Uruguay.* New York: Oxford University Press, 1938.

[An outstanding study of public economic policy and its execution in Uruguay; the author is one of the foremost authorities on Latin American economics.]

Harris, C. G. *Uruguay: Economic and Commercial Conditions in Uruguay.* (Overseas Economic Surveys). London: His Majesty's Stationery Office, 1950.

[As is usually true, this issue of the "Overseas Economic Surveys" is factually useful and well organized; the author, First Secretary of the British Embassy at Montevideo, deals with finance, trade, agriculture, industry, transportation, and social questions.]

Hudson, William Henry. *The Purple Land.* Various editions, e.g.: New York: Random House, [1926?].

[A great literary classic; half fiction, half autobiography; Hudson wrote of the Uruguayan *campo* in the 1870's; as William McFee said in his introduction to the Modern Library edition, ". . . the golden age of which Hudson wrote is gone . . . yet it is preserved forever in the crystal clarity of these pages. . . ."]

Inman, Samuel Guy. *Latin America: Its Place in World Life.* New York: Harcourt, Brace, 2nd edit., 1942.

[Inman, a consistent liberal, takes a strongly sympathetic view of Uruguay in his Ch. 15 (pp. 246–56).]

James, Preston E. *Latin America.* New York: Odyssey Press, 2nd edit., 1950.

[Ch. 11 (pp. 340–52) gives a summary geographic treatment.]

Jones, Willis K. "Street-Corner Stages," *Inter-American,* vol. 4, July, 1945, pp. 27–28.

[Montevideo at Carnival time.]

Josephs, Ray. *Latin America: Continent in Crisis.* New York: Random House, 1948.

[A reporter, thoroughly familiar with Latin America, writes penetratingly in his (unnumbered) chapter (pp. 293–330) on Uruguayan political and other matters.]

Kirkpatrick, Malcolm. "A Landscape Architect Looks at Montevideo," *Bulletin of the Pan American Union,* vol. 72, pp. 316–22 (June, 1938).

[A well illustrated article describing parks, boulevards, and other civic improvements.]

Kitchen, James D. "National Personnel Administration in Uruguay." *Inter-American Economic Affairs,* vol. 4, Summer, 1950, pp. 45–58.

[A scholarly article on public personnel administration; it

was condensed from an excellent thesis on the same subject prepared at the University of California at Los Angeles.]

Koebel, William Henry. *Uruguay*. London: T. Fisher Unwin, 1911.

[One of the earliest books on Uruguay; incredibly dull.]

Linington, A. W. "The Republic of Uruguay," *Bulletin of the Pan American Union*, vol. 61, pp. 871–82 (September, 1927).

[Descriptive; illustrated.]

Luisi, Luisa. "The Literature of Uruguay in the Year of Its Constitutional Centenary," *Bulletin of the Pan American Union*, vol. 64, pp. 655–95 (July, 1930).

[A detailed survey of many Uruguayan literary figures.]

Lyford, Katharine Van E. "Uruguay on Stage," *Américas*, vol. 2, March, 1950, pp. 24–27.

[A popular article dealing with recent developments in the theater.]

Maeztu, Ramiro de. "Rodó and the United States," *Inter-America*, vol. 9, pp. 460–64 (June, 1926).

[The author, a Spaniard, expounds what he conceives to be the spirit of the United States, a quite different spirit from that seen by Rodó.]

Manger, William. "Montevideo," *Bulletin of the Pan American Union*, vol. 63, pp. 1220–30 (December, 1929).

[A well-illustrated description of the capital.]

Manini Rios, Pedro. "Uruguay and Her International Relations," *Inter-America*, vol. 9, pp. 141–48 (December, 1925).

[The emphasis is on relations with Brazil, Argentina, and Spain.]

Marden, Luis. "The Purple Land of Uruguay," *National Geographic Magazine*, vol. 94, pp. 623–54 (November, 1948).

[A typically interesting and informative *Geographic* article, profusely illustrated in color and black and white.]

Martin, Percy A. "Artigas, the Founder of Uruguayan Nationality," *Hispanic American Historical Review*, vol. 19, pp. 2–15 (February, 1939).

[An undocumented but carefully prepared article on the national hero; it was originally read as a paper before the American Historical Association.]

Martin, Percy A. "The Career of José Batlle y Ordóñez," *Hispanic American Historical Review,* vol. 10, pp. 413–28 (November, 1930).

[This penetrating and sympathetic account, partly based on personal acquaintance, was published the year after Batlle's death.]

Martin, Percy A. *Latin America and the War.* Baltimore: Johns Hopkins University Press, 1925.

[Ch. 5 (pp. 349–82) of this excellent study is devoted to Uruguay; the book is carefully documented and is easily the best analysis of Uruguayan and other Latin American participation in World War I.]

Martin, Percy F. *Through Five Republics (of South America);* *a Critical Description of Argentina, Brazil, Chile, Uruguay, and Venezuela in 1905.* London: William Heinemann, 1905.

[Pt. IV (pp. 361–417) is devoted to Uruguay; much information unattractively presented.]

Mecham, J. Lloyd. *Church and State in Latin America.* Chapel Hill: University of North Carolina Press, 1934.

[Ch. 11 (pp. 331–39) deals with Church-state relations in Uruguay; the study is thorough-going, a basic analysis for all of Latin America.]

Monteverde, Eduardo. "Uruguay," *Educational Yearbook of the International Institute of Teachers College, Columbia University, 1925* (I. L. Kandel, ed.), pp. 447–66. New York: Macmillan, 1926.

[A factual and well-organized survey as of the end of the first quarter of the century.]

Núñez Rugeiro, Manuel. "Contemporary Uruguayan Literature," *Inter-America,* vol. 3, pp. 306–15 (June, 1920).

[A good interpretation of some of the outstanding literary figures.]

Pendle, George. *Uruguay: South America's First Welfare State.* London and New York: Royal Institute of International Affairs, 1952.

[Notwithstanding its small compass (100 pp.) this is a remarkably meaty book; written by an Englishman formerly resident in Uruguay and Paraguay.]

Piazza, Luis Guillermo. "New Government for Uruguay," *Americas,* vol. 4, January, 1952, pp. 3–5+.

[A popular description of the main provisions of the 1951 constitution.]

Richling, José. " 'With Liberty I neither Fear nor Offend,' " *Bulletin of the Pan American Union,* vol. 59, pp. 881–92 (September, 1925).

[Business and economic development.]

Ross, Gordon. *Argentina and Uruguay.* New York: Macmillan, 1916.

[This English author includes much more on Argentina than Uruguay, but his material on the latter country, though dated and including some curious errors of accenting and overliteral translation, is in general sympathetic and based on a good understanding.]

Salgado, José. "Uruguay and Its Constitutions of 1830 and 1917," *Bulletin of the Pan American Union,* vol. 64, pp. 641–52 (July, 1930).

[A factual analysis of Uruguay's first two constitutions.]

Sanguinetti Freire, Alberto. "Social Legislation in Uruguay," *International Labour Review,* vol. 59, pp. 271–96 (March, 1949).

[A comprehensive topical summary by the man who probably knows more about the subject than anyone else anywhere; he wrote from the vantage point of the deputy directorship of the Uruguayan National Labor Institute.]

Scully, Michael. "That Children Might Live," *Reader's Digest,* vol. 51, August, 1947, pp. 121–24.

[A laudatory article about Dr. Luis Morquio.]

Scully, Michael. "There's Merit in Their Madness," *Reader's Digest,* vol. 52, May, 1948, pp. 90–92.

[A popular description of the "Republic of the *Parvenses*" whose "leading industry is unstuffing shirts."]

Slonimsky, Nicolas. *Music of Latin America.* New York: Crowell, 1945.

[A short (unnumbered) chapter (pp. 282–87) discusses a few of the leading Uruguayan musical figures.]

Smith, Henry L. and Littell, Harold. *Education in Latin America.* New York: American Book Co., 1934.

[Ch. 8 (pp. 163–82) gives a general survey.]

Strode, Hudson. *South by Thunderbird.* New York: Random House, 1937.

[Description by a trained traveler; the section on Uruguay is pp. 255–91.]

Stuntz, A. Edward. *To Make the People Strong.* New York: Macmillan, 1948.

[Ch. 15 (pp. 245–60) gives a chatty view of some of Uruguay's health problems and progress.]

Taylor, Philip B., Jr. *The Executive Power in Uruguay.* Berkeley: (processed), 1951.

[A study, based on field work, prepared as a doctoral dissertation at the University of California at Berkeley; very informative.]

Taylor, Philip B., Jr. "The Uruguayan Coup d'Etat of 1933," *Hispanic American Historical Review,* vol. 32, pp. 301–20 (August, 1952).

[A carefully documented and thorough study of the background, unfolding, and consequences of the Terra coup; the best study of the subject.]

Thomasson, David. "Uruguay's Tribute to the 'Gaucho,'" *Bulletin of the Pan American Union,* vol. 62, pp. 546–54 (June, 1928).

[On the sculptured immortalization of the gaucho; well illustrated.]

Tinker, Edward L. "The Cult of the Gaucho and the Creation of a Literature," *Proceedings* of the American Antiquarian Society, vol. 57, pp. 308–48 (Oct. 15, 1947).

[An excellent account of the development of the gaucho genre in Uruguayan and Argentine literature.]

Tomlinson, Edward. "Utopia in Uruguay," *Collier's,* vol. 90, Sept. 24, 1932, pp. 23+.

[A popular and partially jaundiced but generally favorable article.]

Unsigned. "The National Centenary of Uruguay," *Bulletin of the Pan American Union,* vol. 65, pp. 925–45 (September, 1931).

[The centennial celebration of 1930 described and illustrated.]

Unsigned. "This is Uruguay," *Newsletter* (Health and Sanitation Division, Institute of Inter-American Affairs), No. 135 (March–April, 1950).

[A pamphlet describing the health centers built in Uruguay by the Scisp and the services rendered by them.]

Unsigned. "Uruguay: A Social Laboratory," *Bulletin of the Pan American Union,* vol. 73, pp. 596–608 (October, 1939).

[A popular article describing in general terms the social advances made in the country; well illustrated.]

Unsigned. "Uruguay's Musical Prospector," *Américas,* vol. 1, April, 1949, pp. 25+.

[On Francisco Curt Lange.]

*Uruguay.* (American Nations Series). Washington: Pan American Union, 1949.

[The current edition of a well illustrated descriptive pamphlet forming a part of the Pan American Union's "American Nations Series."]

*Uruguay: Summary of Biostatistics.* Maps and Charts; Population; Natality and Mortality; Statistics. Washington: Bureau of the Census, 1944.

[An excellent and authoritative compilation of statistical information in the form of tables, figures, and maps; unfortunately now some years out of date.]

White, John W. "Uruguay, Bulwark of Pan Americanism," *Inter-American Monthly,* vol. 1, November, 1942, pp. 10–14.

[A popular account of Uruguay's wartime domestic and international democracy; the author was a long-time Latin American correspondent of the *New York Times.*]

Wythe, George. *Industry in Latin America.* New York: Columbia University Press, 2nd edit., 1949.

[The chapter on Uruguay (pp. 128–39) provides an excellent survey.]

Ybarra, Thomas R. "You Can't Kick Me," *Collier's,* vol. 94, Aug. 25, 1934, pp. 13+.

[Superficial but interesting.]

Yriart, Juan Felipe. "Uruguay and the Proposed Basic Agreement for Inter-American Economic Co-operation," *Latin American Studies* (University of Texas, Institute of Latin American Studies), No. 6, pp. 17–30 (1949).

[A thoughtful discussion of Uruguay's relation to various recent international economic problems; given as a paper at a 1948 conference at the University of Texas by the First Secretary of the Uruguayan Embassy at Washington.]

Ysita, Eugene. "National Economy of Uruguay, 1941–1946," *Commercial Pan America,* No. 179 (May, 1948).

[This mimeographed serial publication of the Pan American Union is listed as "Part I" of the study on Uruguay but no further parts were published; it includes, along with several tables, a survey of agriculture, commerce, industry, meat packing, etc.]

Zaldumbide, Gonzalo. "José Enrique Rodó," *Inter-America,* vol. 2, pp. 44–54 (October, 1918).

[An inquiry into the spiritual life of Rodó.]

Zum Felde, Alberto. "Contemporary Uruguayan Poetry," *Inter-America,* vol. 9, pp. 62–84 (October, 1925).

[A very good survey.]

Zum Felde, Alberto. "José Enrique Rodó: His Place among the Thinkers of America," *Inter-America,* vol. 7, pp. 261–74 (April, 1924).

[An excellent interpretation.]

# Index